£65.00

D1438676

LIBRARY
THE NORTH HIGHLAND COLLEGE
ORMLIE ROAD
THURSO
CAITHNESS KW14 7EE

Withdrawn

The
Ethical QALY

Ethical Issues in
Healthcare Resource Allocations

The
Ethical QALY

Ethical Issues in
Healthcare Resource Allocations

LIBRARY
THE NORTH HIGHLAND COLLEGE
ORMLIE ROAD
THURSO
CAITHNESS KW14 7EE

Withdrawn

Andrew Edgar
Centre for Applied Ethics,
University of Wales, Cardiff, UK

Sam Salek
Medicines Research Unit,
Welsh School of Pharmacy
University of Wales,
Cardiff, UK

Darren Shickle
ScHARR, University of Sheffield,
Sheffield, UK

David Cohen
University of Glamorgan Business School,
Pontypridd, UK

Euromed Communications
Haslemere, UK

Euromed Communications Ltd.,
The Old Surgery, Liphook Road, Haslemere,
Surrey GU27 1NL, England

Copyright © 1998 Euromed Communications Ltd.

All rights, including that of translation into other languages, reserved.

ISBN 1 899015 21 3

Printed and bound in Great Britain by Antony Rowe Ltd, Chippenham, Wiltshire

Preface

I am proud to be associated with the research conducted by an international group of academics and health professionals. This work has been funded by the European Commission and co-ordinated by the University of Wales, Cardiff. I feel that this is a natural role for me because of my very long association with the University and also because the work is funded by the European Commission.

The issue of the prioritisation of access to medical treatment, and the allocation of scarce funds to healthcare is of great contemporary importance in Europe as well as the rest of the world. Demand for healthcare appears to be continually increasing and, in addition, the provision of this healthcare requires the use of a great many expensive new medical technologies.

The important issue of how we prioritise is addressed through the 'Quality Adjusted Life Year' (QALY). Development of the QALY can, I have learnt, help us to explore a number of problems associated with healthcare provision today, including how to determine the most efficient and effective treatment that should be funded by healthcare systems and so be made available to patients.

Health economists, doctors, philosophers and, above all, patients are quite rightly given the opportunity to review QALY and to raise issues related to the implications of this approach and also the challenges.

Another very important aspect of this research project relates to the particular issues raised by different attitudes to how we should prioritise in our health systems.

Glenys Kinnock, MEP
Member of the European Parliament
for South Wales East

The Biomedical and Health Research Programme (BIOMED 1) of the European Commission is aiming at improving the efficiency of medical and health research development in the Member States, in particular by achieving a better co-ordination of research efforts.

The work programme of BIOMED 1 includes a research area on Biomedical Ethics and on the legal, ethical and social aspects of Biomedicine.

Research on Biomedical Ethics addresses general standards for the respect of human dignity and the protection of the individual in the context of biomedical research and its clinical applications. It aims at promoting an open dialogue between all involved parties including experts from different disciplines such as medicine, sciences, philosophy, theology, sociology or law as well as patient groups and the general public.

One specific objective of BIOMED 1 is to address the ethical aspects related to the issues of resources allocation and access to healthcare. In this context, the concept of Quality of Life is a key element in the decision making procedures. The research project entitled "The Ethical Quality Adjusted Life Years (QALY): an investigation of the ethical implications of measures of quality of life applicable to a range of diseases and health states for use in the allocation of resources in prevention, diagnosis and treatment" and coordinated by Dr A Edgar, investigated the ethical issues that arose in the definition of QALYs, particularly with regard to potential injustice in the representation of different groups. In addition the project identified the difficulties arising from the application of QALYs in the distribution of healthcare resources and the different approaches to national planning in the participating countries.

The reflections on QALYs carried out by Dr Edgar and the participants in the research project constitute a useful tool for all parties interested in this issue.

Christiane Bardoux
Research on Biomedical Ethics
Medical Research Unit
Life Sciences Directorate
European Commission

Introduction

This book is the final fruition of a research project into the allocation of healthcare resources which was funded by the European Commission between 1993 and 1996, under its BIOMED and PECO programmes. The project, which was originally conceived by Dr Ian Harvey and others working in the Centre for Applied Public Health Medicine at the University of Wales College of Medicine, sought to come to terms with the complex problems of scarce healthcare resources, by examining the role that quality of life measures could play in allocating those resources. From the first, the project was designed to bring together considerations of the technical feasibility of using quality of life measures, with the issue of the justice or moral legitimacy of any such use. The underlying question that the 'Ethical QALY' group debated repeatedly, albeit in different guises and in response to different particular issues, was not simply whether quality of life measures could be used in the planning and reform of a healthcare system, but whether they should be so used.

The objectives of the original project have been reproduced in Chapter 5 of this book, alongside a summary of our response to each problem set. The reader might indeed usefully begin by looking at these objectives. A brief introduction to the general debate over QALYs is not, however, out of place. The concept of the 'Quality Adjusted Life Year' or QALY was developed by health economists to refer to a comparative measure of a person's health, and thus a means to assess the outcome of medical care. (Strictly, the 'QALY' is a specific, and rather unrefined version, of a quality of life measure. However, 'QALY' has taken on the connotations of a generic term, and we use it here in that inclusive sense, to refer to the whole family of quality of life indicators.) A crude measure of the success or outcome of healthcare would be the extra years that a particular medical treatment adds, on average, to the life of the patient. Such measures can be valuable, but are insensitive to the condition of the patient before and after treatment (and are indeed a poor measure of the success of treatments that seek to improve a patient's health, without necessarily thereby extending his or her life). The QALY therefore attempts to take account of the health state of the patient, by adjusting the value of the number of years the patient survives, according to how healthy he or she is before and after treatment. A treatment that takes somebody who is confined to bed, and gives him or her a few years of healthy, active life, might be valued more highly than a treatment that merely extends the life of that person, still confined to bed, for many years, simply because a few years unhampered by illness may be more valuable to the patient than many years spent under the constrictions of severe physical impairment.

Precisely because QALYs are a measure of the output of healthcare, they can be introduced into resource allocation when they are set against the inputs (or costs) of healthcare. Cost-utility measures, using QALYs as the measure of utility, may then be used to determine the efficiency of a particular treatment or medical unit. If resources for healthcare provision are scarce, then this use of QALYs superficially appears to be highly attractive as a way of ensuring that the resources that are available are used efficiently.

The Ethical QALY group was by no means the first to raise ethical reservations about the use of QALYs. The moral debate had a good deal of momentum before our group was formed. It was, rather, in the multi-disciplinary nature of the group that we sought to contribute to the debate. In effect, we aimed to bring about a discussion within a like-minded and mutually sympathetic group, as opposed to an argument between mutually antipathetic factions. The Ethical QALY group therefore brought together public health physicians, health economists, psychometricians, and philosophers. It was through this shared and complementary expertise that we sought to untangle misunderstandings and naive judgements in the moral criticism of QALYs, and so come to a reasoned assessment of the potential that QALYs, if necessary in a more developed form than that presently available, and duly hedged about by moral safeguards, could be used to think about and act upon the pressing problem of scarcity in healthcare provision. (Inevitably, in a group composed of such diverse disciplines and nationalities, individuals would continue to hold different and even opposing views. It should not therefore be assumed that every member of the group, or even every one of the four authors of this book, necessarily agrees with every point made.)

The main body of the book is structured into five chapters. The first sets the context, by discussing the general issue of scarcity, and thus seeks to justify the need for some system of explicit prioritisation of healthcare resources. The second chapter looks at the construction of quality of life measures, their various uses, and briefly reviews some of the many instruments that are in common use. The third chapter, written very much from the perspective of a health economist, accepts as given a number of moral criticisms made against QALYs, but examines ways in which technical adjustments within the design and use of QALYs can be made to avoid those problems. The fourth chapter, written from a philosophical perspective, addresses the validity of the moral arguments made against QALYs, and attempts to develop a moral defence of QALYs, albeit one that challenges the way in which they are usually understood, and thus one that has implications for the design and use of QALYs. The fifth chapter summarises our findings.

Crucially, the Ethical QALY group was international. It was initially composed of representatives from Wales, France, Denmark, the Netherlands, and Greece. This spread brought together a wide range of experiences of different healthcare systems and different European cultures, and served to throw into relief much that we might otherwise have taken for granted about the organisation of healthcare, if we had only our limited, national, experience to guide us. The project was extended, in 1994, into Central Europe, with participants coming from Slovakia, Slovenia and the Czech Republic. The post-communist reform has major implications for the organisation of healthcare provision in these countries, both in the short term, as resources are particularly scarce during the transition period, and in the long term, in consideration of exactly what sort of healthcare system these countries are moving towards.

The authors of this book are based in Wales and England. Because of this, the main body of the book has a more British slant than is perhaps wholly desirable. British illustrations, for example of legal cases concerning access to healthcare, have generally been used in preference to illustrations from mainland Europe. However, the intention of the main body of the book is to raise and debate a series of issues that have wide relevance, throughout Europe and beyond, and British examples illustrated our arguments as well as other examples, and were more easily handled by the authors. The annex to the book seeks to address this bias. The annex is less systematic in its coverage than the rest of the book, but seeks rather to give an impression of what is of importance to five members of the group, representing Northern Europe, the Mediterranean, and Central Europe. These are essays written from the front-line of healthcare organisation, and as such, they seek to provide a snapshot of a uniquely challenging moment in the development of European thinking about healthcare.

Inevitably, in writing this book, and indeed in carrying out the original research upon which it is based, the authors have incurred a series of debts of gratitude. Most importantly, acknowledgement has to be given to the European Commission for its generous financial support of the original project, and particularly to Dr Christiane Bardoux, for support and guidance throughout the project. The members of the Ethical QALY group must be thanked, not just for their ideas, arguments and criticisms, but also for the extremely good company and hospitality they managed to provide at our various meetings. Most importantly, Alan Williams, Rachel Rosser and Vincent Watts very kindly gave their valuable time and energy in order to attend meetings of the group, and contribute to our discussions.

Finally two people gave not just practical and professional help to the Ethical QALY project, but also a great deal of moral and emotional support. Lis Palser was secretary to the project, and worked indefatigably to ensure that meetings went smoothly, that the administration of the project was faultless and that everyone was kept informed and involved. Lis also did her utmost to ensure that the project co-ordinator remained calm and serene under all sorts of pressures. Justine Jenkins was the research assistant to the project, and continued to work on the book. She ensured that the other members of the project had all the textual material they needed, through a continual search of familiar and obscure articles and books, the scouring of libraries, and the maintenance of a constant, critical eye on the ever expanding QALY literature. The bibliography included in this volume is very much her achievement. Above all, her good humour and relentless energy have contributed more than she would ever admit to both the project and to the book.

This report was prepared by a concerted action study group funded by the Commission of the European Communities under Research on Biomedical Ethics.

THE STUDY GROUP

Project Co-ordinator: Dr Andrew Edgar (UK), Centre for Applied Ethics, University of Wales, Cardiff, PO Box 94, Cardiff CF1 3XB.

Administrative Support: Ms Justine Jenkins (UK), Ms Elisabeth Palser (UK).

Other Group Members: Professor Robin Attfield (UK)
Professor David Cohen (UK)
Professor Anne Fagot-Largeault (France)
Ms Susanne Gibson (UK)
Dr Ian Harvey (UK)
Professor Henk ten Have (Netherlands)
Professor Jan Holcik (Czech Republic)
Professor Jørgen Husted (Denmark)
Dr Nicholas Koutouvidis (Greece)
Dr Alain Leplège (France)
Professor Spiros Marketos (Greece)
Ms Janine Hale (UK)
Dr Vlasta Mocnik Drnovsek (Slovenia)
Mr Clive Pritchard (UK)
Dr Martin Rusnak (Slovakia)
Dr Sam Salek (UK)
Dr Darren Shickle (UK)

Acknowledgements: Professor Rachel Rosser (UK)
Mr Vincent Watts (UK)
Professor Alan Williams (UK)

What is a QALY?

The outcomes of healthcare come in many different forms and guises. Pain relief, anxiety reduction, mobility improvement and life extension are all examples of successful outcomes of healthcare. For reasons which will be explained below, what is sought is a measure which can express all these different aspects of achieved health improvement in common units. The QALY is such a measure.

The basic thinking behind the QALY is that health has two main dimensions: length and quality. Effective healthcare must either extend life or improve its quality or preferably both, so in theory all effective healthcare will produce Quality Adjusted Life Years or QALYs, but throughout this book the term 'QALY' is used as a general expression of health achievement.

Contents

1

Choices for healthcare

RATIONING, PRIORITISING AND THE NEED FOR CHOICE

Choices for health care have to be made for a variety of reasons. Clinical choices such as whether an intervention will do an individual more harm than good, or ethical choices such as whether to provide a genetic test which may result in a pregnant woman aborting her fetus, will always have to be faced. Here the concern is solely with choices made on the basis of the relationship between benefits and costs. Introducing cost into the decision making process is inevitably unpleasant but this chapter will argue that it is a necessary part of the pursuit of a health service's broad objectives, that it is ethical, and in any case that it is unavoidable.

QALYs are advocated as an aid to resource allocation decision making on the basis that priority setting and/or rationing are a necessary feature of these types of choices. The term 'priority' has positive connotations with its focus on the extra benefit that will be conferred on some patient group (e.g. the elderly), disease group (e.g. cardiovascular disease), or through the expansion of some related health care activities (e.g. prevention). The term 'rationing' on the other hand has negative connotations with its focus on denial of potentially achievable benefits. Here, we are less concerned with which term is used than with the basic principle that unpleasant choices – that is choices based *inter alia* on cost considerations – cannot be avoided.

In an ideal world of infinite resources neither prioritising nor rationing would be necessary. Sufficient resources would be available to meet all health needs fully and immediately. Unfortunately we do not live in such an ideal world but rather in one where resources for health care are now and always will be scarce. If this statement is accepted then the need to make choices about how to allocate health care resources – to whom, when and in what quantities – is inescapable. Whether resource allocation choices are called 'priority setting' or 'rationing' is largely irrelevant and both terms will be used in this book.

Resource scarcity and the need for choice, however, are by no means universally accepted. The purpose of this chapter therefore is to address this issue and to demonstrate that rationing, prioritising or more simply making choices has always been a feature of health care and cannot be avoided. Subsequent chapters will consider the role of QALYs and other mechanisms to assist resource allocation decision making.

The following sections illustrate how health care expenditure has increased in recent years, explain why health needs are increasing even faster, and address certain 'myths' such as, increased spending can eliminate the need to make resource allocation choices. The chapter presents examples of how the UK courts have dealt with cases where individuals who had been denied health care on grounds of cost have sued the health service. It ends with an introduction to the ethical issues relating to choices for health care.

SPENDING ON HEALTHCARE IS INCREASING

The past few decades have witnessed unprecedented growth in health care expenditure world-wide. It may seem something of a paradox that a growing awareness of resource scarcity relative to needs and an increasing acceptance of the need to formally introduce prioritising/rationing mechanisms into health care policy making and planning is occurring at the same time as expenditure is rising.

An example of the magnitude of this rise in expenditure can be seen in the case of the UK where £3,364 million was spent on health care in 1973: £3,054 million within the NHS (including charges paid by patients), £102 million on private healthcare and £208 million consumer expenditure on pharmaceutical products (including medical dressings and equipment) (OHE, 1995). This was equivalent to £60 per person. By 1995, UK expenditure on healthcare had increased to £47,276 million (£806 per person). When inflation is taken into account, £220 was spent in 1995 on healthcare in the UK for every £100 in 1973. This increase has occurred under both Labour and Conservative governments.

Figure 1.1 (OHE, 1997) shows the relative increase in healthcare expenditure as a percentage of GDP for the UK, USA, Europe and more globally for countries belonging to the Organisation for Economic Co-operation and Development (OECD). All show a major increase in the relative share of total available resources being spent on healthcare.

If expenditure on healthcare has increased at the same time that the problem of resource scarcity has become more acute then healthcare needs must be increasing as well, and at a higher rate.

WHY IS NEED GROWING?

Changes in demography

One reason why need has increased is changes in the population. Improvements in healthcare and general living standards have meant that most Western populations are healthier and living longer. For example, a boy born in the UK during 1948 (the year the NHS was established) could expect to live for 66.4 years. In 1994 life expectancy had increased to 74.3 years. Increases in life expectancy have been seen across the European Union (OECD, 1997) as shown in **Figure 1.2**. Thirty-six out of each 1,000 children born in the UK during 1948 died in the first year of life. The infant mortality rate in 1988 was only 8.9 deaths/1000 live births .

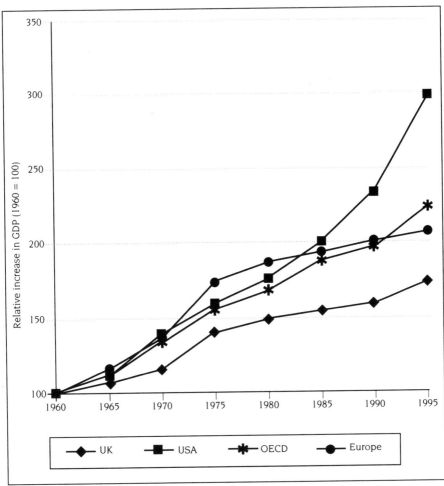

Figure 1.1: Relative increase in total health expenditure as per cent GDP at market prices. (1960=100). (OHE, 1997)

One of the consequences of this success is that healthcare systems have to care for an increasing elderly population, (**Figure 1.3.**) In 1948, 1.7 million people in the UK were over 75 years of age with 200,000 of these people over the age of 85. By 1994, the number over the age of 75 had increased by a factor of 2.4 to 4.1 million while the number over 85 had increased by a factor of 5 to 1 million (OHE, 1995). Projections from the 1991 UK census suggest that the percentage of people aged 75 years or over is likely to almost double by the mid twenty-first century (7.0% in 1992 compared to 13.6% in 2051).

Older people tend to have greater healthcare needs (OPCS, 1995) as shown in **Figure 1.4,** and receive a relatively very large share of overall healthcare resources as shown in **Figure 1.5** (OHE, 1995).

3

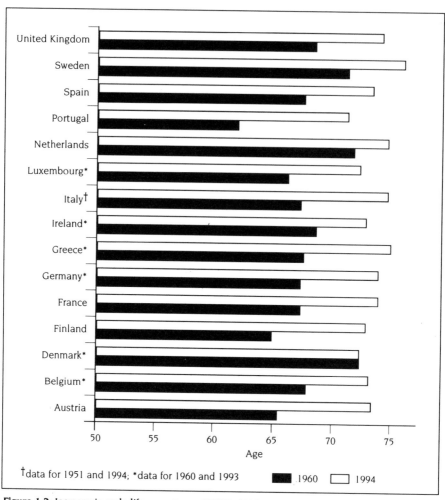

Figure 1.2: Increase in male life expectancy. (OECD, 1997)

The dynamic nature of need

"Need" can be perceived in many ways (Culyer, 1976). Here we regard need as the 'capacity to benefit' i.e. a need only exists if there is something that can be done to alleviate it. Viewed this way, healthcare need increases with every new medical advance. By this way of thinking, very low birthweight babies, short children and infertile couples were not in 'need' until the development of neonatal intensive care, growth hormone therapy and fertility treatment. Similarly, viewing need in this way means that new advances which allow people currently being treated to be treated more effectively, also increase need. Without a commensurate increase in resourcing this will lead to a widening in any existing gap between total need and met need.

While there are numerous examples of new technologies being less costly than

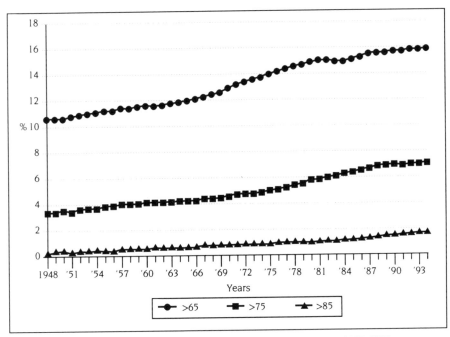

Figure 1.3: Elderly groups as a percentage of the population (1948-1994). (OHE, 1997)

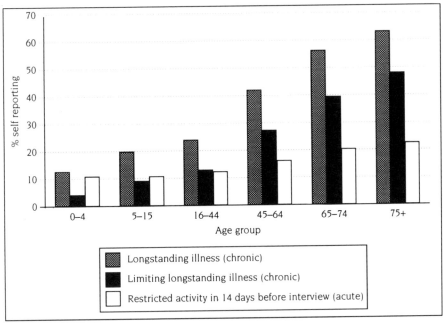

Figure 1.4: Acute and chronic morbidity in different age groups (UK, General Household Survey, 1994). (OPCS, 1995)

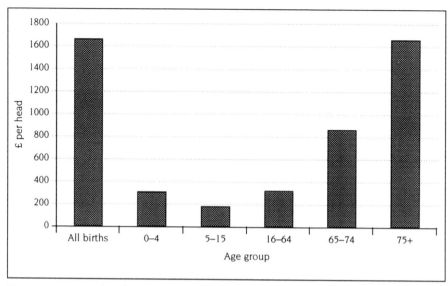

Figure 1.5: Estimated per head NHS spending by age group (1993/94). (OHE, 1995)

those which they replace, for example by allowing procedures formerly requiring inpatient stays to be performed on a day case basis, most new technologies allow people to benefit more but at a positive cost. As the pace of technological advance

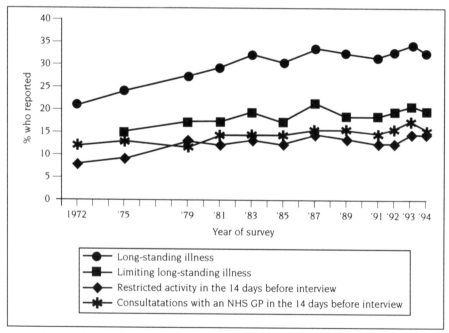

Figure 1.6: Trends in self-reported sickness for all persons in UK General Household Surveys 1972-1994. (OPCS, 1995)

shows no signs of slowing, the ability of any healthcare system to 'meet all need' becomes an increasingly difficult task.

Changes in the perceptions of health

The General Household Survey (OPCS, 1995) in the UK has collected data on self-reported illness over the many years. There has been a gradual increase in the proportion of survey respondents who report having long-standing illness or restricted activity in the 14 days before interview, or who consulted with an NHS general practitioner in the previous two weeks (**Figure 1.6**). These trends could be a result of less healthcare being provided or a decline in the effectiveness of those services that are. UK data suggest that healthcare activity is increasing, and although there have been efforts to make efficiency savings, it is unlikely that these cuts have resulted in significant decreases in effectiveness. It is possible that there have been changes in genetic and/or environmental risk factors which have led to the causation of more disease but it is far more likely that society's expectation of health have changed with time. The quality of life that previous generations considered to be within normal limits may now be considered abnormal, and led to demands for restorative healthcare interventions. This is, in part, a consequence of media coverage of the outcome of medical research, which promise 'exciting' new treatments. On the basis of such reports, the population may expect to live longer, and may become less tolerant of minor physical abnormalities and impairments.

INCREASES IN DEMAND

The above suggests that increase in demand is at least partly due to individuals' changing expectation of what the health service should do for them. This trend is mirrored by the behaviour of health professionals.

In the UK during the early 1980s there were about three quarters of million people waiting for inpatient treatment (in 1981 this was equivalent to 13.3 per 1,000 population). Over the next decade the total number waiting for inpatient healthcare increased to over a million (1,078,000 patients were on the waiting list in March 1992, 18.6 per 1,000 population). Despite a shift towards more day-case care and shorter inpatient length of stays, the number on the waiting lists has continued to grow. In September 1995 there were approximately 666,700 waiting for inpatient treatments and a further 549,800 on the list for day-case surgery. The length of time patients are having to wait has however decreased, following the introduction of the Patient's Charter which set waiting times as important quality outcome measures. For example in 1981 29% of patients on the waiting list in England had been waiting for over one year. In 1986, 1991, and 1995 the percentages waiting for over 12 months in England were only 24%, 9% and 4% respectively.

There is therefore a paradox: the amount spent on healthcare has increased in real terms, resulting in more people being treated. However, the demand for healthcare is increasing (as measured by waiting list rates, although waiting times have decreased), due to changes in demographics and expectations. As a consequence the healthcare systems in most OECD countries are perceived as failing, leading to reviews of government policy and more explicit rationing.

The 'myth' of infinite demand

The basic premise of health economics on which the QALY approach is based is that resources are finite while demand for healthcare is (virtually) infinite (Mooney, 1986). While accepting that demand is increasing, there are many who dispute this, arguing that there is a finite limit on how large demand can grow and therefore there is some level of resourcing which would eliminate the need to make choices in healthcare on the basis of cost.

When the NHS was first established in 1948, it was thought that there would be an initial increase in demand for healthcare, as people with unmet need who could not previously afford treatment came forward for treatment. However, after the backlog was dealt with, it was expected that the population would be healthier, and so the resources required to fund the NHS could be reduced. In practice, demand has increased year-on-year, but to many this does not mean that demand is infinite.

"... is demand for healthcare infinite? After all, many diseases have been eradicated completely, at least in the Western world, and we all have a finite number of limbs and organs to be replaced, removed, or remodelled. Are we really sitting on a complex mass of health problems just waiting to explode as soon as we know that they can be treated? And just because medical science is increasingly capable of prolonging life, will patients necessarily welcome more medical intervention and perhaps more discomfort at the expense of greater quality of life?... Are we sure that demands could not be met completely with a relatively modest increase in resources. If demand were to be met in full, and care was available — unrationed and as soon as it was needed — we could avoid costly and unnecessary problems associated with waiting for treatment" (Hancock, 1993)

CAN INCREASED SPENDING ON HEALTHCARE MEET ALL NEED AND DEMAND?

The above quotation suggests that the problem is not one of infinite demand but of insufficient resources being available to meet finite demand. So why not just spend more? What if the UK spent as great a proportion of its GDP as USA?

There are significant differences in the percentages of GDP which different countries choose to spend on healthcare. In Europe, the percentage of GDP varies from just over 5% in Greece to almost 10% in France (**Figure 1.7**). European Union countries tend to spend less than other OECD countries e.g. Switzerland or USA. On this basis those countries towards the bottom of the spending league tables could spend more, although this would have opportunity costs in terms of foregone

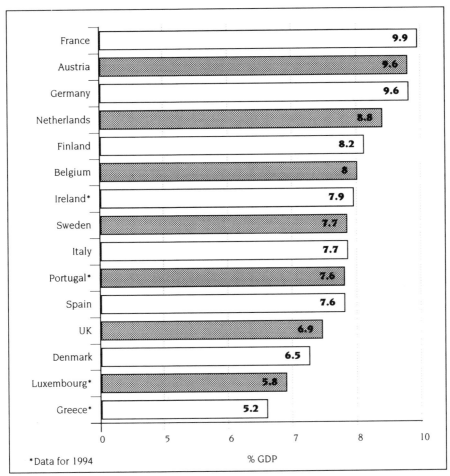

France					9.9
Austria					9.6
Germany					9.6
Netherlands					8.8
Finland				8.2	
Belgium				8	
Ireland*				7.9	
Sweden				7.7	
Italy				7.7	
Portugal*				7.6	
Spain				7.6	
UK			6.9		
Denmark			6.5		
Luxembourg*			5.8		
Greece*		5.2			

0   5   6   7   8   10

*Data for 1994   % GDP

Figure 1.7: Total health expenditure as per cent of GDP in European Union Countries, 1995. (OECD, 1997)

benefits from other areas of economic activity (see **Figure 1.8** [OECD, 1997]).

A decision to increase the proportion of GDP devoted to healthcare cannot, however, be made in isolation, since any such increase means decreasing the proportion devoted to other areas of economic activity. Health creation thus has opportunity costs in that the benefits from alternative uses of these resources are foregone. Attempting to meet more and more health need by increasing the proportion of national expenditure devoted to healthcare will inevitably incur greater and greater marginal opportunity costs as the relative share of expenditure in these other areas decreases. If healthcare is publicly funded, then the opportunity cost will be in the form of foregone benefit from other areas of public activity such as education, defence, transport, social services or protecting environmental quality. These too have moral value, and indeed many of them can also have direct and indirect impacts on health. Society will demand an end to the continued (relative)

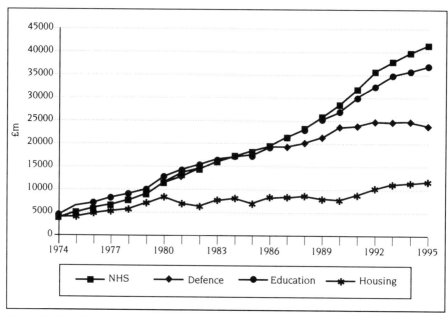

Figure 1.8: Trend in budget for various sectors of public spending (1974-1995). (OECD, 1997)

expansion of healthcare expenditure before every last healthcare need is met.

Over the last decade the proportion of public spending allocated to healthcare in the UK has been increasing, with funding being diverted from among others, housing and defence (OHE, 1995).

DO THE PUBLIC WANT TO SPEND MORE ON HEALTHCARE?

In a survey on attitudes to healthcare rationing among the public, doctors and NHS managers (Heginbotham, 1993), 51% of the public advocated "unlimited funding and said that the extra money should come from higher income tax and national insurance contributions and lower defence spending". A significant minority of doctors (17%) also believed that funding should be unlimited, although virtually all of the managers said that NHS spending should be restricted within budgets, even if that meant that some treatments would have higher priority than others. When asked where the extra money should come from, both the public and doctors said that income tax and national insurance should be increased and spending on defence reduced (**Table 1**).

As part of the 1986 Cardiff Health Survey (Richardson and Charny, 1992), 718 randomly selected residents of Cardiff were asked how they would wish to see available resources allocated to the various areas of public spending. The public's preferences were not dissimilar to the proportion actually spent on each, although not surprisingly they appeared to wish to spend more on healthcare and less on

Table 1: "If additional money is needed, where should the extra money come from?"		
	% of general public n=1018	**% of doctors** n=136
Higher income tax	38	41
Defence	36	47
Higher national insurance	31	36
Transport and roads	10	2
Social security benefits	8	15
State pension	1	2
Education	1	2
Housing	1	2
A combination of these sources	6	9
Other	7	13
Don't know	7	2

defence than was actually being spent (**Table 2**). If these preferences had been translated into actual budget allocation, it would have meant an additional £5 billion available for healthcare. However, care should be taken when extrapolating from this study, since this 4% difference between public preference and actual spending may have occurred by chance. When the opportunity costs are explained to the public, there may not be large increases in resources available. Similarly, a number of opinion surveys have indicated that the public would be willing to pay increased taxes towards the NHS, but they have not demonstrated this at the ballot box (although general elections are fought on many issues other than health).

Table 2: Cardiff Health Survey – Actual and suggested breakdown, in pence, of each £ spent on various services (1986 figures).				
		Allocation of 718 respondents		
	Actual spending (pence in the £)	**Mean**	**Median**	**10th and 90th percentiles**
Social security	28	25.2	28	15,30
Defence	17	10.5	10	5,17
Health and social services	16	19.8	20	16,26
Education	15	16.4	16	12,20
Housing	8	9.3	8	6,15
Environment	6	6.7	6	5,10
Roads and transport	5	5.6	5	4,8
Law and order	5	6.5	5	4,10

INVESTING IN HEALTH OR IN HEALTHCARE?

It could, and perhaps should, be argued that government ought to spend even more on healthcare, using evidence of health need for which there are effective interventions available. However, in the current economic and political climate such debates may distract from the decisions that have to be made. Scarcity of resources for healthcare in the short term (if not the medium or long term too), means that health services are unable to provide treatment for all of their resident population who have identified healthcare needs. In order to adequately fund core services and to allow investment in new developments, disinvestment will be required in areas of healthcare which are demonstrated to be relatively ineffective and result in very little health gain per pound spent.

In a discussion of the proportion of societal resources that should be allocated to healthcare as opposed to other social goods (education, defence, the elimination of poverty, the environment), Flew (1967) argues that "morally, so long as hospitals are needed, hospitals must always have priority over amusement parks". The grounds for this argument are that pain is not symmetrical with pleasure and that the more fundamental duty is to alleviate pain. In response, Childress (1981) felt that:

> "it is not evident (a) that hospitals are primarily to alleviate pain, and (b) that they should always take priority over all other social goods that do not contribute to the aim of hospitals, whether it is the alleviation of pain or some other goal. Health may be a condition for many values for individuals and the community, but it does not have finality or ultimacy. It is not true that when it comes to health, no amount is too much".

While more could be spent on healthcare, a patient who does not receive healthcare may not be able to claim that it is unjust that resources are spent elsewhere, e.g. to give someone else a better standard of education.

Can one complain of injustice if society puts more money into space programmes or defence than healthcare? "Wrong" priorities may not be unjust unless there are certain basic needs or rights that must be satisfied for justice to be realised (Carlson, 1981).

Indeed it may well be that the health of society can be better served by investing in other sectors of public spending other than medical care. Carlson (1981) argued that there were five major influences on health, which he ranked in order of importance as:

- environment
- life-style
- society
- genetics
- medical care

He considered medical care to be the least important determinant of health, giving it a weighting of approximately 6%.

TWO FURTHER ARGUMENTS AGAINST THE NEED FOR EXPLICIT PRIORITISING/RATIONING

There remain two further fundamental arguments that need to be addressed before moving on to issues concerning the conduct of prioritisation.

Firstly, some types of healthcare are necessary to the survival and flourishing of the individual human being: if so, there is a *prima facie* obligation upon a health service to provide at least these necessary healthcare services, and to provide them in preference to the satisfaction of any other service (in healthcare or elsewhere) that are unnecessary (albeit desirable); Secondly, there is the issue of incommensurability: even if it is accepted that resources are scarce, then it is not possible to prioritise because it is not possible to place a value on life or its quality, and hence comparisons cannot be made.

The necessity of healthcare

It may be claimed that the problem of prioritisation can be resolved or eliminated by appealing to the objectivity of clinical need. The claim would have two components. First, it is possible for medical professionals to identify, with minimal ambiguity or dispute, the (most appropriate) assistance that a patient requires in order to regain his or her health, or at least to be restored to a state as close to good health as the patient's conditions and current medical knowledge allow. Second, if unambiguous clinical needs can be established, then the patient has a moral entitlement to the satisfaction of those needs. Thus, if a patient's kidneys fail, then that patient needs either dialysis or (ideally) a successful transplant. The cost of failing to provide for this need is the patient's death. Respect for the patient generates a moral obligation (presumably on the part of the healthcare system) to satisfy that need, and thus facilitate the continued life and flourishing of the patient.

This is an important and potentially persuasive argument (and it will be returned to in Chapter 4 – the "needs" argument). However, a number of reservations may be expressed. Need is actually functioning here as a criterion of prioritisation. One may establish a clear division between the most pressing or urgent needs claims (which is to say those associated with conditions that are life threatening, or likely to result in chronic and distressing disability, if untreated), and non-urgent conditions. From this, one may argue that the health service has an obligation to provide for the satisfaction of the former (for example, in a basic healthcare package that is free to all), although no such obligation is entailed with respect to the treatment of less severe conditions. The way in which such a division is established is itself problematic, not least as needs tend to be responsive to changes in the level of medical technology. (The very availability of dialysis and transplantation creates a medical need, where previously the patient was fated to die.) Conversely, the urgency or severity of need may be understood as a continuum, and those with the most severe needs (for example, those facing imminent death or chronic and distressing disability in the absence of treatment) are to be given the highest priority.

Again, the precise criteria used to judge severity of need are disputable.

As noted above, health economists tend to take the narrow view of need, defining it as the patient's ability to benefit from treatment. For example, it is unclear in what sense a patient who, with treatment, would live only for an additional five days, 'needs' the treatment, or more precisely, how the pressing of such as needs claim would help to allocate scarce healthcare resources fairly. Further, even if clear criteria of the severity of need could be established, possibly making due reference to the ability to benefit from treatment, the mere fact that a particular patient needs medical care is of little relevance if the sum total of needs in the population exceeds the resources available to satisfy them. (Thus, for example, the need for a liver transplant is perhaps of less relevance that the ability to provide a particular patient with a compatible liver within the relatively short period within which he or she would be able to benefit from the treatment.)

Incommensurability

It is possible to accept that healthcare resources are finite and insufficient to meet all demands for healthcare and yet reject any attempt at prioritisation. A number of arguments have been proposed (see for example Griffin, 1977) to support the belief that life is an incommensurable value, and hence it is not possible to trade the life of a patient who potentially could be saved, for any other life or any other outcome associated with utility. For example:

> "In cases of planning, conservation, welfare, and social decisions of all kinds, a set of values which are, at least notionally, quantified in terms of resources, are confronted by values which are not quantifiable in terms of resources: such as the value of preserving an ancient part of a town, or of contriving dignity as well as comfort for patients in a geriatric unit". (Williams, 1972)

Griffin has rejected Williams' arguments:

> "... that some values lend themselves to quantification in terms of resources and others do not shows nothing ... If we are able to enhance the dignity of some geriatric patients by giving them greater privacy or enhance their comfort by giving them better heating, how should we decide which to do? ... If Williams' point is that these two values cannot be got on the same scale, then he is wrong. The patients, when informed, can rank them – and in the strong sense" (Griffin, 1986).

Griffin also quoted an example where quantity and quality of life may be compared:

> "The French government knows that each year several drivers lose their lives because of the beautiful roadside avenues of trees, yet they do not cut them down.

Even aesthetic pleasure is allowed to outrank a certain number of human lives."
(Griffin, 1986)

Economists have used this approach to place various estimates on human life by examining the cost of various public policies where life is at stake (**Tables 3 & 4**) (McGuire et al, 1988; Mooney, 1986).

For example, there may be alternative strengths of barriers that could be placed in the central reservation of motorways to prevent traffic involved in an accident crossing from one carriageway to the other. The stronger barrier costs more (say £1 million more for a stretch of motorway) but it would save more lives (for argument, 10 lives until it has to be replaced). If the motorway planners decide to use the weaker barrier, they are implying that 10 lives are worth less than £1 million, or else they would prefer the utility that could be obtained in using the £1 million for some other purpose. On this calculation, a life is worth less than £100,000. While such calculations may be crude, it demonstrates that some value can be attached to a life. It may not be an accurate value, but it is at least commensurable.

It might be thought that there is something wrong in using money as the common measure for conflicting values:

"[It is not] an accidental feature of the utilitarian outlook that the presumption is in favour of the monetarily quantifiable ... It is not an accident, because (for one thing) utilitarianism is unsurprisingly the value system for society in which economic values are supreme .." (Williams, 1972)

Williams appears to be confusing the use of money as a common measure, with a supreme value. Money is valued because it enables other commodities or services to be purchased from which an individual may derive utility. Money acts as a means rather than an end. There may be misers who apparently love money for its own sake. However, even those prone to avarice may value the security or potential utility that their savings provide.

EXAMPLES OF RATIONING IN THE UK

While many healthcare systems are considering withdrawing funding for specific services very few have implemented such policies. For example, a review in the UK of 1992/3 purchasing plans containing statements of the services that a health authority intends to purchase, found that very few explicitly stated that they would not purchase specific interventions (Klein and Redmayne, 1992). Even such limited disinvestment was controversial, and some health authorities were told by the British Government to reconsider their decision, presumably for political rather than legal reasons.

In a similar analysis of 1993/4 purchasing plans, the authors noted that fewer purchasers than in the previous year were proposing to deny or limit the availability of specific forms of treatment (Redmayne et al, 1993). Surprised at the apparent

Table 3: Estimates of the value of statistical life from revealed preference studies or questionnaire studies.

Data source	Estimated value of statistical life ($US 1983)
Compensating wage differentials for workers in risky occupations (USA)	600,000
Time/safety trade-off in use of pedestrian subways (UK)	520,000
Motorway speed/time/fuel trade-off (UK)	510,000
Compensating wage differentials in industry (UK)	5,990,000
Compensating wage differentials for manual workers (USA)	3,410,000
Time-safety trade-off in use of car seat belts (USA)	560,000
Compensating wage differentials for construction workers (UK)	170,000
Compensating wage differentials for manual and non-manual workers (UK)	2,460,000
Small non-random sample survey [n=93] of willingness to pay for public provision of prevention of death from heart attack (USA)	72,000
Non-random sample survey [n=873] of willingness to pay for domestic fire safety (UK)	330,000
Non-random sample survey [n=873] of willingness to pay for hypothetical safe cigarettes (UK)	170,000
Large random sample survey [n=1,150] of willingness to pay for transport safety (UK)	2,370,000

Table 4: Implied values of life in various healthcare policy areas.

Policy area	Implied value of life ($US 1983)
Pulmonary embolism	19,000
Renovascular disease	25,000
Heart attacks: Ambulance	6,000
Heart attacks: Mobile coronary unit	8,300
Heart attacks: Triage plus ambulance	27,000
Heart attacks: screening	46,000

retreat from explicit rationing, the authors suggested that while purchasers were still deliberately limiting the availability of certain services, they had become more cautious in their tactics, instead preferring to negotiate contracts which restricted access and availability to specific interventions. A subsequent review of 1994/5 purchasing plans indicated a return to explicit purchasing. Eleven out of 66 plans (compared with only 4 in 1993/4) mentioned one or more procedures that would not be purchased and others appeared on the verge of doing so (Redmayne, 1995).

As in previous years, the procedures being rationed tended to be forms of cosmetic surgery, reversal of sterilisation, assisted conception, alternative therapies or other procedures rarely performed and so very few patients would be affected by their withdrawal. As North West Surrey Health Authority (Redmayne, 1995) have argued:

"excluding reversals of sterilisation and vasectomy, or cosmetic varicose vein surgery, can only release marginal amounts of money and that significant savings will depend on reducing more mainstream treatments which prove ineffective, a stage which no purchasers have yet reached".

Exclusions tend to be qualified and individual cases will be considered where there are clinical justifications. There were other health authorities which put the burden of proof for buying certain procedures on GPs and consultants. For example, many procedures would only be purchased in accordance with guidelines. Such guidelines are usually based upon evidence of effectiveness. As a consequence some patient groups will be excluded from treatment. Such an approach is clinician-led, based on clinical criteria and hence will be perceived differently by the public than restrictions imposed by 'men-in-grey-suits' working in health authorities.

CHALLENGES IN THE COURTS

Occasionally, the courts have been asked to adjudicate on the legality of rationing decisions when aggrieved patients or their families have been denied healthcare. Seven examples are given here as illustration.

Regina *v* Secretary of State for Social Services, Ex *parte* Hincks

In 1979 four patients who had spent long periods on the waiting list for a hip replacement took the Secretary of State to court under sections 1 and 3 of the National Health Service Act 1977. It was alleged that their period on the waiting list was longer than was medically advisable and that their wait resulted from a shortage of facilities, caused in part by a decision not to build a new hospital block on the grounds of cost.

Their application was dismissed because the judge did not believe that it was the court's function to direct Parliament what funds to make available to the Health Service and how to allocate them. The duty to provide service 'to such extent as he considers necessary' gave the Minister a discretion as to the disposition of financial resources. The judgement was supported in the Court of Appeal. The phrase "reasonable requirements", in Section 3(1) of the 1977 Act was considered to mean that a failure of duty existed only if the Minister's action was thoroughly unreasonable.

Regina v Central Birmingham Health Authority, Ex parte Walker

In 1987, the parents of a baby requiring surgery for a heart defect sought judicial. review in attempt to force the Central Birmingham Health Authority to provide the operation, which had been postponed on five occasions because of a shortage of skilled nursing staff. The Court refused to order the operation, stating that the parents had no duty to demand immediate treatment for their son. The health authority could only do what was reasonably possible with their restricted resources. The Court of Appeal confirmed the judgement.

Regina v St Mary's Ethical Committee Ex parte Harriott

In another case (1988), a woman had been refused in vitro fertilisation. The local ethics committee supported the decision because the woman had been rejected as a potential adoptive or foster mother and because she had criminal convictions for prostitution offences. The judge held that the grounds for refusing her IVF treatment were lawful. However, he said that refusal to provide treatment on non-medical grounds could be reviewed by a court. It would be unlawful to withhold treatment because of a patient's race, religion or other irrelevant ground.

Regina v North West Thames Regional Health Authority and Others, Ex parte Daniels (Rhys William)

In 1993, a two-year-old boy with Batten's disease was denied an experimental bone marrow transplant when the Unit at Westminster Children's Hospital was closed because the expected workload meant that the Unit was not economical. The child's father claimed that the closure was unlawful because:

1. the District Health Authority had failed to consult the Community Health Council;
2. the decision to close the unit was irrational;
3. the family had a legitimate expectation to be informed of the proposed decision to close the unit and to be given the opportunity to make representations.

Lord Justice Kennedy supported the first submission since the failure to continue the service amounted to a substantial variation in provision of the service and that the duty to consult the Community Health Council regarding any substantial variation was mandatory. However, he disagreed with the submission that the closure was irrational, since on the information available to the court it was difficult to know the basis of the decision. While the Judge agreed that the family had a legitimate expectation to be informed of the proposed decision, this should be as a matter of courtesy rather than from a legal right. Lord Justice Kennedy refused to grant a declaration that the closure of the Unit without providing a service elsewhere in the Authority's area was unlawful, because such a decision would not benefit the child nor would it do any good.

Following media coverage prior to the case, Rhys had been offered treatment at a bone marrow transplant unit in Bristol. Lord Justice Kennedy was sure that the Bristol unit would do all it could without any encouragement from the courts.

Regina *v* Cambridge District Health Authority, Ex *parte* B

In January 1995, Child B, a 10-year-old girl, suffered a relapse of acute myeloid leukaemia. She had previously undergone two courses of chemotherapy and a bone marrow transplant. The doctors who were treating her considered that a third course of chemotherapy and a second transplant would not be in her best interests. Child B's father found a doctor who was willing to offer further chemotherapy and a further transplant if that proved successful, in the private sector. The chances of a complete remission following chemotherapy were put at 10-20%, with a similar chance of survival after a subsequent bone marrow transplant. The cost of the chemotherapy and transplant were £15,000 and £60,000, respectively.

Mr Justice Laws said that it was not the court's function to make medical judgements as not only did it not have the competence to do so but it did not generally re-decide the merits of administrative decisions since to do so would usurp the role of the decision-maker.

The Judge had two questions to decide: whether the respondents [Cambridge DHA] had taken a decision which interfered with Child B's right to life and, if they had, whether they had offered a substantial public interest justification for doing do. The Health Authority claimed that they had done no positive act to violate Child B's right to life, all they had done was to make a decision about the use of public funds. The judge did not believe that there was a difference in principle between an act and an omission and hence the decision had "assaulted her fundamental right to life". Public interest grounds would therefore need to be proven.

The first reason put forward for withholding treatment was that it would not be in the child's best interest because of the suffering involved. In the Judge's view, the expertise of the doctors was rightly deployed in deciding on the effectiveness and disadvantages of treatment. However, there was a third question, which the Judge felt could only be answered by the patient (or her parent in the case of a minor). The Judge decided that the Health Authority had failed to have regard for the family's views.

The second reason given by the Health Authority was that funding the treatment would be an ineffective use of finite resources and that the needs of other present and future patients had to be borne in mind. The Judge said that merely to point to

19

the fact that resources were finite told one nothing about the legality of the decision. However, he accepted that the court should not make orders with consequences for the use of health services funds in ignorance of the knock-on effect on other patients.

Since the Health Authority had not adequately explained their funding priorities which led them to decline funding, the Judge quashed the decision to deny Child B treatment. He also thought that the Health Authority should have only considered the request for £15,000 for the chemotherapy in the first instance. However, if the Health Authority were to carry out their task properly, they were not bound to fund the treatment.

The decision was overturned by the Court of Appeal the same day (*Times,* 15 March 1995). The Master of the Rolls judged that the Health Authority were aware of the patient's wishes as expressed by the family. He also rejected Mr Justice Laws criticism of the Health Authority for not presenting details of their budget, since it was common knowledge that health resources were scarce. He also rejected the suggestion that the Health Authority had wrongly treated the sum required as £75,000 rather than as a two-stage process. The Court of Appeal did not believe that the Health Authority had exceeded its powers or had acted unreasonably.

The child was subsequently admitted to a private hospital after an anonymous donor provided £75,000 for treatment. In September 1995, Cambridge and Huntingdon Health Commission resumed paying for her care. In October 1995, the child's father succeeded in lifting the ban on naming her in order to sell her story to the press. Child B was identified as Jaymee Bowen.

Regina *v* North Derbyshire Health Authority Ex *parte* Fisher

In December 1987, Mr Kenneth Fisher was diagnosed with relapsing and remitting multiple sclerosis. North Derbyshire Health Authority had responsibility for purchasing healthcare services for the area in which Mr Fisher lived. The relevant provider was the Central Sheffield University Hospitals Trust of which the Royal Hallamshire was the provider of neurological services.

On 15 December 1995, the Department of Health issued EL(95)97 asking purchasers and providers to make arrangements for the implementation of a beta-interferon 1B, which was a new drug shown to be of some benefit in the management of relapsing and remitting multiple sclerosis.

On 4 January 1996, Mr Fisher was admitted to the Royal Hallamshire Hospital under the care of Dr Grunewald, who was uncertain as to whether he could prescribe beta-interferon because of the expense of the drug. Following discussion within the Hospital Trust, it was decided that the treatment could not be authorised. Contrary to the Department of Health Circular, no funding had been made available for prescribing beta-interferon. The judge, Mr Justice Dyson, agreed with the Health Authority and the Department of Health, that the Circular should be seen as guidance and not a direction, although this did not mean that the decision was not susceptible to a challenge of reasonableness under the Wednesbury principles.

The Director of Public Health for North Derbyshire was unconvinced as to the effectiveness of the drug, although a Minute of the Health Authority noted that they could not refuse prescription of the drug (because of earlier Government direction that Health Authorities should not 'ban any treatment'). However, the Health Authority believed that while 'blanket bans were not acceptable ... creative constraints could be offered'.

In February 1996, the NHS Executive (NHSE) wrote to all health authorities indicating that they could place restrictions on the prescribing of beta-interferon by only funding it if it was prescribed under the auspices of a clinical trial. However, North Derbyshire Health Authority continued to hope that the use of beta-interferon would be co-ordinated through a national trial. In May 1996, the Health Authority were given explicit instructions by the NHSE to implement the Circular. However, the Authority continued to offer funding (£40,000) for prescribing beta-interferon as part of clinical trials; a policy that was endorsed by the September meeting of the Health Authority.

Various meetings between the Health Authority and NHSE staff were held in October and November, 1996 in order to ensure an acceptable policy was introduced. However, in the Judge's opinion the new policy was not in accordance with the Circular. According to the Judge, the Health Authority had failed to implement the policy because they disagreed with it and hence they could not justify their policy as a rational exception to the Circular and be Wednesbury reasonable. The judge recognised that there is a duty on the Health Authority not to overspend and to make decisions with due regard to resources. However, in the judge's opinion, the necessary resources could have been made available.

Mr Justice Dyson therefore declared that North Derbyshire had acted unlawfully in denying beta-interferon to a patient with multiple sclerosis and directed the Authority to formulate and implement a policy in accordance with EL(95)97 within 14 days. He was not prepared to specifically direct the Authority to reconsider paying for treatment for Mr Fisher, although this would be implied from a new policy which implemented the policy. As in earlier cases relating to rationing, the Health Authority was found at fault for the procedures it had used rather than the specific requirement to provide treatment (although the judge's sympathies could be inferred from the language used in his judgement).

The Health Service Ombudsman

While the courts have indicated a reluctance to become involved in prioritisation decisions, there are other avenues available to aggrieved patients. In February, 1994, the Health Service Ombudsman severely criticised Leeds General Infirmary for discharging a 55-year-old man with a stroke to a nursing home and telling his family that they would have to pay the fees. The Ombudsman ruled that the situation amounted to a "failure in service". The consultant in charge said that they had a duty to provide care but that it "might lead to rationing of other services". Leeds Health Authority were ordered to pay £15,000 compensation and to pay for the man's nursing home costs.

PRIORITISATION AND ETHICS

If the arguments against explicit rationing are rejected, then some systematic mechanism will be required in order to address the resource allocation choices that cannot be avoided i.e. prioritising how resources will be used. The QALY, or more precisely the QALY as a component of cost-utility calculations, has been proposed as one such mechanism. However, the technical issues of how to design, construct and execute such mechanisms cannot be separated from questions of ethics. Any allocation mechanism that is proposed or implemented must be morally defensible. Exactly what this claim entails is more problematic that it may at first appear, and indeed the issue is addressed more fully in Chapter 4. Here, some initial notes upon the nature of ethics and justice may be given in conclusion to the foregoing account of scarcity.

The ancient Greek word for justice was the same as that for equality. Aristotle wanted to make a clear distinction between equality and equity. He rejected claims that justice meant equal shares for all. He describes the nature of what would now be called 'distributive' justice (i.e. the just principle for distributing resources, such as healthcare) as follows:

> Justice is considered to mean equality. It does mean equality – but equality for those who are equal, and not for all. Again, inequality is considered to be just; and indeed it is – but only for those who are unequal, and not for all ... A just distribution is one in which there is a proportion between the things distributed and those to whom they are distributed (Aristotle, 1995).

Aristotle also discussed distributive justice in 'The Nicomachean Ethics':

> If they are not equal, they will not have what is equal, but this is the origin of quarrels and complaints – when either equals have and are awarded unequal shares, or unequals equal shares. Further, this is plain from the fact that awards should be 'according to merit'; for all men agree that what is just in distribution must be according to merit in some sense, though they do not all specify the same sort of merit (Aristotle, 1980).

The principle of justice that is usually attributed to Aristotle is as:

> 'Equals should be treated equally and unequals should be treated unequally in proportion to the relevant inequalities'. This is to argue that a just distribution of healthcare will not make equal resources available to all members of the population, simply because we are not equal in terms of our health, or in terms of our need for healthcare or our ability to benefit from that care. A just allocation must therefore be suitably sensitive to such inequalities. (Gillon, 1986)

As Gillon has pointed out:

> The reason that Aristotle's formal principle remains so widely accepted is, of course, that it has little substantive content. It requires an equality of consideration ...; fairness in the sense that conflicts are to be settled by mutually agreed principles of justice ...; and impartiality in the sense that inequalities of treatment cannot be arbitrary ... but must be justified on the basis of, and in proportion to, relevant inequalities (Gillon, 1986).

If just prioritisation is to be performed, agreement is required on which 'inequalities' are 'relevant'. The various options were described by Raanan Gillon's 8 year old daughter when she was asked how to decide which of three dying patients should have access to the only available lifesaving machine:

> '"Well", she told me, sparing a minute or two from her television programme, "you could give it to the youngest because she'd live longer (welfare maximisation), or you could give it to the illest because she needs it most (medical need), or you could give it to the kindest because kind people deserve to be treated nicely (merit). No, you couldn't give it to the one you liked best (partiality), that wouldn't be fair." Nor, she decided, would "eenie meenie minee mo" (lottery) be fair because the one who needed it most, or the youngest, or the kindest might not get it. Nor did she (much to my surprise) think that the Queen should get it in preference to the poor man (social worth) – "because she's got so much already and the poor man hasn't." Of all the methods, her preferred one was to choose the illest because he needed it most – but not surprisingly, she could not say why that was a better option than the others' (Gillon, 1986).

2

Maximising health gain

It follows that if resources are scarce then resource allocation choices cannot be avoided. Even if promises are made to provide all healthcare that is 'needed', scarcity of resources would mean that no guarantee could be given on when services would be delivered i.e. waiting lists would be established. The nature of waiting lists means that people with chronic conditions often have a lower priority than those with acute or life threatening illnesses. This may be unjust and may not maximise utility if scarce resources are invested in high cost, ineffective interventions. Thus, choices can either be made in advance using defined mechanisms, or a retrospective examination will show what choices were made regardless of whether they were made consciously or by default.

Acknowledging scarcity thus means accepting that prioritising is inevitable. Society must choose which health service to provide, how much of each intervention, and to whom they will be provided. Society may wish to abrogate this responsibility, leaving it to doctors or others, but this does not detract from the fact that the need to choose and the need to prioritise are inescapable.

For prioritisation criteria to be morally acceptable, the rationale which underpins them needs to be explicit. Prioritising on the basis of explicit criteria represents an attempt to impose a greater degree of rationality on the resource allocation process. It is implicit in the QALY approach that more rational prioritising is preferable to less rational prioritising – although it is nowhere claimed that the world is a wholly rational place and that all decisions must always be made solely on a rational basis.

THE IMPORTANCE OF OBJECTIVES

Rational prioritising can only be undertaken if the criteria on which the priorities are to be decided are made explicit. The choice of criteria will depend on the objectives which means that objectives must be stated explicitly, and: the option prioritised should be the one most likely to further the objectives of the organisation. According to Seedhouse:

> "a philosophical review would differ from a conventional health service review by focusing in the first instance upon questions of purpose – what is the basic

rationale of the health service? what is the health service for? — rather than questions of process — how can existing services be delivered effectively? how might the NHS perform its functions at less financial cost?" (Seedhouse 1992)

Seedhouse identified four obstacles to a comprehensive review of the National Health Service in the UK:

- The NHS is extraordinarily large and complex. It is impossible for any group undertaking a review to simultaneously identify and understand all the activities and processes of the NHS;
- partly as a result of this complexity the NHS does not possess an overall plan, and in this sense is not a rational organisation. Much of the services provided by the NHS emerged as the unintended consequence of many disparate plans and processes;
- there are numerous vested interests within the NHS many of which have substantial power to lobby for their point of view; and to resist any changes which might be recommended;
- a vital distinction between the process and the purpose of health services has consistently been overlooked.

Unlike a commercial organisation, a public healthcare system such as in the UK NHS does not have an obviously supreme purpose. The existence of clear objectives would make the process of priority decision making considerably easier. The option to be chosen should be the one that is most likely to further the aims and objectives of the organisation. However, it has never been clear exactly what are the objectives of the NHS.

"There is a widely held assumption that there is a general consensus about the purpose of the NHS. But this supposition is seriously mistaken. Some people share beliefs about the goals of the NHS but there are many incompatible views of purpose abroad in the organisation." (Seedhouse, 1992)

Many people in the UK when asked to state the purpose of healthcare services may refer to the three principles proposed in the Beveridge Report (1942):

- To ensure that everyone in the country "irrespective of means, age, sex or occupation" should have equal opportunities in securing the medical care he/she needed;
- to provide a comprehensive health service of community and hospital care, covering all aspects of preventive and curative medicine;
- to divorce the care of health from questions of personal means and to provide the service free of charge.

These principles were soon eroded with the introduction of charges for prescriptions in 1952, although exemptions do still allow access for those with low incomes. In any case, the apparent consensus on using the Beveridge principles as objectives is illusionary since there is insufficient attention to the meaning of key words such as 'health'.

The 1979 Royal Commission report on the National Health Service (Merrison 1979) noted that the objectives of the NHS were are as laid down in Section 1 of the National Health Service Act 1977 which reiterated the 1946 Act which created the NHS in England and Wales (see annex A). The Royal Commission summarised "the principles and objectives of the NHS" as "the duty laid by Parliament on health ministers to provide a National Health Service".

The Royal Commission recognised that "the absence of detailed and publicly declared principles and objectives for the NHS reflects to some degree the continuing political debate about the service". Although politicians and public alike were agreed on the desirability of a national health service, the Royal Commission were concerned that "agreement often stops there. Instead of principles, there are policies which change according to the priorities of the government of the day and the particular interests of the ministers concerned."

The Royal Commission proposed that the objectives of the NHS should be to:

- encourage and assist individuals to remain healthy
- provide equality of entitlement to health services
- provide a broad range of services of a high standard
- provide equality of access to these services
- provide a service free at time of use
- satisfy the reasonable expectations of its users
- remain a national service responsive to local needs

The Royal Commission was "well aware that some of these objectives lack precision and some are controversial". They were also aware that some were "unattainable", but it was felt that this did "not make them less important as objectives". However, it is more likely that the range of services where some payment is required will be extended rather than reduced.

While the Royal Commission objectives maintain the requirement for equality of entitlement and access that was stated in the Beveridge principles, the commitment to provide a comprehensive service has been replaced by the requirement to provide a "broad range of services". It could therefore be claimed that the NHS is not required to provide every aspect of healthcare that patients may demand.

In a review of public policy making on medical-moral issues, Kennedy and Stone (1990) observed that:

"the manner in which we decide whether to make public policy on any medical-moral issue and what form policy should take could (politely) be described as

haphazard. If issues attract the attention of the press, utterances are delivered from those whom the press judge capable of having a view, and then silence, until the next crisis/climax/breakthrough"

On some occasions media publicity may trigger the government to set up a working party or committee. However, the report that is produced may or may not address the issue of how, by whom or what public policy is to be established. Even if the report does make recommendations, they may or may not be acted upon. Eventually some frustrated individual or group will approach the courts:

"the difficult questions about whether we need any public policy and the role of law are swept aside. The law is invoked and must respond. Public policy is made. The courts will determine it, regardless of their suitability for the task".(Kennedy and Stone, 1990)

Courts in the UK have been critical of the way decisions have been made, for example if health authorities have not consulted widely, or have not adequately communicated with those affected by the decisions. However, as illustrated in the previous chapter, in the UK as in many other countries, the courts have been reluctant to interfere with the process of healthcare prioritisation, and so decisions have rarely been overturned.

Seedhouse illustrated how clear statements of purpose could affect the choice of priorities with the NHS. He proposed two possible basic statements of purpose:

"The purpose of the NHS is to provide medical services (i.e. those clinical processes which are the specialist knowledge of the medical profession) efficiently and without discrimination to all people who are in need of them."

"The purpose of the NHS is to improve the quality of life of all members of the population who might be helped."

The first of these statements would require considerable streamlining of the NHS with the removal of responsibility for the social aspects of care to other public services, to the private sector or to the patient and their family. The NHS with this objective would be more accurately called a 'national ill-health service'. In contrast, the second statement would require agreement on the meaning of quality of life, but result in a shift of emphasis from treatment to prevention and from the acute to the community/primary care sector.

THE RECOGNITION OF THE IMPORTANCE OF QUALITY OF LIFE

Many healthcare workers now realise that when elimination or cure of a disease is not possible, a major aim of therapy must be to limit the complications of the illness so that the patient is able to carry on a comfortable, functional and satisfying life style (Wenger *et al*, 1984). In the past, medical practitioners were primarily concerned with alleviation of symptoms and prolongation of their patients' life (Siegrist, 1987). Currently, there is a growing awareness that in the treatment of disease, relief from symptoms is not the only criterion for success. Perhaps even more important to the patient is the effect that different treatments have upon their quality of life, particularly in the treatment of chronic disorders (Charlton *et al*, 1983). Even in situations when therapy is effective in removing disease, such as in many surgical procedures, residual limitation in the patient's ability to function may bring about the necessity for quality of life to be considered (Schipper, 1983; Schipper & Levitt, 1985; Fletcher *et al*, 1987). In consequence, in the evaluation of routine management or new therapy, consideration should be given to the impact that the regime has upon the "total wellness" or quality of life of the patient (Levine & Croog, 1984), this being based on a certain critical level of physical and psychosocial well-being necessary for an enjoyable life. This level is the foundation on which a meaningful and satisfying social and psychological status in daily living is built, providing a sense of fulfilment which is generally referred to as quality of life (Kottke, 1982).

Needless to say, quality of life has been defined and studied in a variety of disciplines (Bubolz *et al*, 1980). Perhaps the most important stimulus for conducting quality of life studies has been the patients' desire to live rather than survive (Jones, 1977; Kottke, 1982). In addition, studies in recent years have failed to demonstrate strong associations between objective and subjective measurements in determining patient response to therapy. This led to policy changes with respect to social programmes based on factual indicators rather than on people's subjective responses (Berg *et al*, 1976; Alexander & Williams, 1981; Najman & Levine, 1981; Flanagan, 1982).

Improvement in therapies for different diseases may affect a patient's quality of life, either for better or for worse. Thus, it becomes essential to acquire an understanding of the concept of health-related quality of life so that the impact of disease and the efficacy of therapies can be measured in more than biomedical terms (Flanagan, 1982). Ware *et al* (1981) emphasised the need to distinguish objective from subjective meanings of quality of life and to differentiate between objective and subjective evaluation of outcomes of therapies. Indeed, there is a genuine concern as to which measures, objective or subjective, are more valid (Najman & Levine, 1981; Ware *et al*, 1981).

Promoting the patient's best interests is the ethical approach to the concept of quality of life and is shared by both clinicians and research scientists. However, the competency of the health professional to assess or evaluate a patient's quality of life has been called into question (Cohen, 1982; McCullough, 1984). During the last 25 years the historic claim of physicians to be the sole arbiter of the patient's best interests has been challenged by patients who consider that they should be permitted to play a part in the therapeutic decision-making process. This subjective approach is traditionally considered to carry less weight than objective measurements although there would appear to be little reason for not treating them equally.

Health is viewed by some professionals in terms of simple, ordinary, normal or good physiological function. Others, such as the WHO Expert Committee, define health in terms of "complete physical, social and psychological well-being and not merely the absence of disease or infirmity" (World Health Organisation, 1947; World Health Organisation, 1957; World Health Organisation, 1976; World Health Organisation, 1984). According to this definition, the concept of quality of life must include more than just the incidence of mortality and morbidity. It should encompass all functional activity of daily life whereby the incorporation of the autonomy model significantly enriches the concept of quality of life. Furthermore, subjective dimensions of quality of life if coupled with objective measures could broaden the patient's apparent state of well-being. The absence of such an approach in some cases may raise doubts about the validity of claims regarding changes in the quality of life caused by illness and therapy. Attempts should be made to enhance the autonomy for those patients whose competency is diminished prior to assessment of their quality of life (McCullough, 1984). This decline in competency, and hence autonomy, is usually caused by a number of new experiences such as hospitalisation, forthcoming surgery, family crisis, retirement, job dissatisfaction and financial difficulties. In these circumstances the investigator should initially help the patient to understand the experience and then be able to assess their quality of life. In situations where a patient has downgraded his expectation for certain daily activities as a result of long-standing chronic disease (e.g., asthma, bronchitis), subjectively the patient may consider their quality of life satisfactory despite a low level of physical and psychosocial function. Thus, increased levels of activity as a consequence of a new therapy might go unrecognised as such (Guyatt et al, 1987). On the other hand, from an objective viewpoint the level of function would indicate a poor quality of life. Subsequently, the patient should raise their subjective expectation if an appropriate level of physical and psychosocial activity is to be maintained.

MEASURING QUALITY OF LIFE

Review of the Concepts

Historically, social forces have played a major role in the development of operational measures of function such as restricted activity measures. For example, at the time of the famines in Ireland and Australia 1851-1891, prevalence of sickness and associated restriction in work activity were the two most important elements surveyed (Collins, 1951). Similarly, as a result of the increasing number of elderly subjects and patients suffering from chronic diseases over the last 50 years, restricted activities and other dysfunctional behaviours were introduced into surveys carried out in Canada, Finland and United States in the 1950's and 1960's (DBSDNHW, 1956; National Centre for Health Statistics, 1963; Kalimo et al, 1968). These formed the foundation for future work. Their usefulness was enhanced by concurrent theoretical and applied studies including those of construct validity, reliability and sensitivity (Katz et al, 1963; Lawton, 1972; Ware et al, 1979; Gurland,

1980; Spitzer et al, 1981; Lawton et al, 1982; Katz, 1983). Thus, the importance of function and social forces became recognised as major components of well-being and operational measures of function.

Both Ware (1979) and Gurland (1980) contributed to the concept of mental health in an effort to minimise confusion between mental health and mental illness. Ware (1979) also distinguished between psychological manifestations such as mood, and physiological manifestations such as psychosomatic symptoms. Furthermore, Ware et al (1979) proposed that "changes in any aspect of health should be reflected in personal ratings of health in general, which are expected to capture a general health status factor common to all components". Health-related quality of life should be considered to be multidimensional. In the view of Spitzer (1987) we are not in the domain of either quality of life or health status measurement unless we include physical and social functions, emotional or mental states and perception or sense of well-being.

The range of quality of life studies published to date demonstrates a considerable variation in purpose. Some deal with understanding the origins and underlying dynamics of well-being while others address methodological issues or focus on clinical and/or social usefulness. Studies on clinical usefulness have recently concentrated on evaluating the impact of chronic diseases and their treatment on patients' quality of life. However, there is an urgent need for research on the clinical usefulness and validity of the measuring tools employed. This need was expressed by Spitzer et al (1981) who wrote, "the process of validation of any measuring tool for research or for clinical practice, seldom ends". A review of quality of life literature shows how true this statement is (McDowell & Newell, 1987).

Working in a field of applied science, the ultimate goal of measuring health status and quality of life is to achieve improved ways of caring for the sick, with or without drugs, and improved ways of protecting the health of those who are well (Spitzer, 1987). Although medicine has been improving over the years, there is still a long way to go in finding the missing pieces of the jigsaw puzzle of health. No doubt a better understanding of the concept of health-related quality of life, with valid and practical techniques to measure it and clinically sensible methods of incorporating the measures into various therapeutic strategies, will most certainly be of assistance in finding such missing pieces.

Benefits

The concept and study of quality of life has generated much controversy and scepticism both about its relevance and feasibility. Advocates of quality of life measurement in both practice and research point out that quality of life should represent the final common pathway of the healthcare process and that some refocusing of our goals for healthcare delivery away from objective assessment of laboratory results and towards functional outcomes is necessary if society's health is to be maintained in accordance with the WHO definition of health (Schipper, 1983). Those opposing this practical viewpoint argue that measuring quality of life is simply not feasible and are further concerned that so called "soft data" will replace objective measurements. Despite these views, many workers believe that traditional medical assessments and quality of life measurement are complementary and together contribute to rational prescribing and improved healthcare.

Schipper (1983) considered that there are three essential criteria which if met ensure successful treatment. First, treatment has to be delivered to the patient in the real world. Second, there must be measures of outcome that are understandable and relevant to the patient, whose perspective is emotional and personal, in contradiction to that of the detached scientist. Third, the net effect of a treatment must be perceived by the patient to be of functional benefit, both physical and psychosocial. In other words, patients are unlikely to accept a treatment, whatever its scientific merit, if they see no tangible benefits. If there were no effective treatments, then the aim would be to reduce symptoms (Wenger et al, 1984). Similarly, if treatments were curative and of short duration with negligible residual side effects, then quality of life considerations would be of little importance. For example, there would be no need for quality of life assessment during treatment of pneumococcal pneumonia with penicillin. However, where treatment is toxic, of substantial duration and only partially curative, then quality of life must be seriously considered as the outcome measure. Furthermore, if there were no scientific knowledge concerning the concept and the measurement of health-related quality of life, then those treatments providing increased survival time would become the new standard and would ultimately receive the patients' acceptance. As a result, we might be faced with effective treatments that produce a cure but functionally disable the population or lead to non-compliance (Meenan, 1985). Availability of quality of life data will remove these inadequacies and provide the scientist with relevant information that would indicate a modification of treatment in order to produce maximum improvement in the patient's functional behaviour.

Aaronson et al (1986) in their economic approach to the treatment of bladder cancer observed that despite an enormous investment of resources, survival rates for the major cancers remain static. The continued search for effective treatments has led to the use of increasingly toxic regimens. Since the benefit of the treatment must outweigh the cost, the use of quality of life measures may be seen as an attempt to introduce more comprehensive specifications into the cost-benefit equation and further highlight the fact that there is more to life than money. In other words, a person's quality of life may be more important than material wealth (Teeling-Smith, 1982; 1985).

Quality of life scales/profiles

A wide range of instruments (**Table 2.1**) possessing a range of attributes thought to affect a patient's quality of life such as physical and psychosocial functioning and ability for self care, is available (Salek and VandenBurg, 1988; Salek and Luscombe, 1992). These include the following major methods: the Sickness Impact Profile/UK Sickness Impact Profile (Bergner et al 1976, 1981; Salek, 1989) which largely measures the impact of illness on the patients functional behaviour; the Nottingham Health profile (Hunt et al, 1980, 1986) which evaluates the symptomatic evidence of sickness and its impact on daily activity and was also used in an economic

Table 2.1: Summary of major quality of life assessment methods.

Measure	Categories	Items	Completion time (mins)	Mode of administration
Sickness Impact Profile/UK Sickness Impact Profile	12	136	20-25	Interviewer or self-administered
Nottingham Health Profile	6	45	10	Self-administered
McMaster Health Index	13	59	20	Self-administered
SF36 (MOS Short Form)	8	36	10-12	Interviewer or self-administered
Spitzer Quality of Life Index	5	5	1-2	Self-administered
Quality of Well-being Scale	8	50	12	Interviewer
Psychological Well-being Index	6	22	10	Interviewer or self-administered
General Health Rating Index	6	29	7	Interviewer or self-administered

evaluation of the heart transplant programme in the UK (Buxton *et al*, 1985); the McMaster Health Index Questionnaire (Chambers *et al*, 1982) which is concerned with physical, social and emotional aspects of life without relating them to the symptoms of the patient; the SF–36 (the Medical Outcome Study Short Form) (Ware and Sherbourne, 1992) which is designed to survey health status in clinical practice and research by evaluating health-related dysfunctions in eight areas of daily activity; the Spitzer Quality of Life Index (Spitzer *et al*, 1981) which is aimed to identify the components of quality of life and primarily intended for monitoring cancer patients before and after therapy; the Quality of Well-Being Scale (Kaplan *et al* 1976) which measures performance and preference with regard to limitation of physical, self-care and social activities; the Psychological Well-Being Index; and the General Health Rating Index (Ware *et al*, 1978) which deals with a patient's perception of health and the impact that disease has on physical activities.

Which quality of life measure?

The most important task in measuring quality of life is the selection of a proper quality of life instrument. A desirable scenario is to be able to select one from existing measures which has already been shown to possess an acceptable level of psychometric properties such as *reliability* (the ability of the instrument to measure quality of life is a reproducible and consistent manner), *validity* (the ability of the instrument to measure what is intended to measure) and *sensibility/responsiveness* (the ability of the instrument to detect small but clinically important changes).

However, if a new instrument needs to be developed, these properties are the minimum requirement which must be demonstrated before it is to be implemented in the study.

The big debate, 'generic vs. specific' instrument, continues to be a central issue in the selection of a quality of life measure for use in clinical drug research. Generic or general instruments are designed to have a broad application across different conditions and treatment, and one comprehensive in their coverage of quality of life aspects of daily activity in particular physical and psychosocial domains. Generic measures also allow comparisons across chronic diseases and broadly speaking, they are divided into two major classes: 'profiles' and 'measures of utility or indices', which are fully described in the above sections. Single index measures are useful for cost-effectiveness and cost-utility analyses, although may not be responsive to change.

In contrast, specific measures are designed to assess the impact of specific disease states or areas of function on a patient's quality of life. Specific measures can be divided into two major classes: 'disease state-specific' and 'function or therapeutic specific'. Function or therapeutic specific measures are the more recent approach in the development of specific instruments. They should possess a high degree of discriminant validity if they are to differentiate between different disease states within a therapeutic area. For example, a cardiovascular–specific measure must be capable of discriminating between hypertensive, angina and cardiac failure patients; a renal-specific quality of life instrument must be capable of discriminating between different modalities for end-stage renal failure (i.e. haemodialysis, continuous ambulatory peritoneal dialysis, kidney transplant patients). In fact, they would provide ideal tools for routine patient monitoring as well as being suitable for clinical drug research, since they have a wider scope than the disease-specific measures and one that is in general more comprehensive.

Specific measures are generally more respondent-friendly and may be more responsive to change, but unlike the generic measures, they cannot be used to compare across different disease and medical interventions (Patrick de Deyo, 1989; Patrick, 1992). Obviously, there is a trade-off between the simplicity of specific measures and loss of information due to lacking score whereas generic measures are very useful for comparison across different diseases states and, in particular, single indices for utility measurement in subsequent economic analysis. In clinical drug research, when comparing a drug with placebo or with a alternative treatment, we would recommend the use of both specific and general measures which not only may complement each other but also may be useful for validation purposes (Salek et al, 1993; Croog et al, 1986; Bombardier et al, 1986).

Administration of quality of life instruments, like measurement of the physiological and biomedical outcomes in clinical drug research requires great care and close monitoring if serious claims are to be made on the strength of the collected data and should not be looked upon by the investigators as just another questionnaire, particularly in situations where quality of life is considered as a primary end-point. Among the methods of administration, self-administered instruments are the most reliable and preferred and certainty less expensive to undertake (Salek & VandenBurg, 1988; Salek, 1990; Salek & Luscombe, 1992). In particular, personal domains such as sexual behaviour and family life are best assessed by self-administered measures. Furthermore, they are free from inter-rater variability or bias. However, these advantages of the self-administered instruments should not be taken for granted and respondents should not be left to their own devices throughout the completion of the questionnaire. Standardisation of their presentation and delivery to patients by trained personnel, to positively motivate the patients in order to comply with every single item, and their presence throughout the completion of the questionnaire would ensure the reliability and quality of the results (Bergner et al, 1981). Finally, it should be born in mind that the choice of the method of administration very much depends on factors such as the disease state, and the study patients' acceptability based on socio-cultural differences. For example, an interviewer-administered method may be more suitable for patients with cognitive decline and older respondents.

Before quality of life measures are selected, a number of issues must be considered in the early stages of the plan for quality of life studies:

1) the reason for studying health status or quality of life must be identified and quality of life defined in the context of the study being developed (Ware et al, 1981);
2) the conceptual framework of the quality of life aspects of the study (whether as a primary or secondary end-point) should be described, meaning that initially the full picture of the disease model reflecting the health status to be addressed by the clinical drug research must be confirmed;
3) a thorough review of the available instruments must take place prior to selection and issues such as whether a general/generic or specific (disease state vs. therapeutic area) instrument and methods of administration/data collection (e.g. interviewer-administration, self-administration) should be considered;
4) after selection, the potential valuer (e.g. reliability, validity, responsiveness) must be carefully assessed;
5) a pilot study to assess the practicality of the instrument (i.e. the time required to complete the questionnaire, the resources needed for administering the instrument and collecting the data) before the full implementation of the clinical drug research, is absolutely crucial.

UTILITY MEASURES

Utility measures on the other hand are those favoured by economists in assessing the relative value for money from healthcare interventions. Thus, the desire for a single unitary value of health status on a utility score (Kaplan & Bush, 1982; Torrance, 1987) led them to look for a generalisable global index of quality of life which can then be combined with survival data to calculate the QALYs gained from treatment. Such utility scores are expressed on a 0.0 to 1.0 scale, in which 0.0 is the quality of life of the state of death and 1.0 is the quality of life of the state of perfect health.

Measurement of utility values

There are two methods of measuring the utility of health states:

1. to approach subjects with the health state under investigation and measure their utility for their condition based on their own judgement (Sackett & Torrance, 1978)
2. to approach members of the general public who do not have the condition under investigation and measure their utility for it by giving them a short written description of the condition. Alternatively, people who are already knowledgeable of the health states concerned, such as physicians, nurses etc. could be used (Torrance, Boyle and Horwood, 1982). There are certain advantages and disadvantages attached to these two different approaches.

Cost-utility analyses are often used in public policy decisions and therefore appropriate utilities are those derived through the second method described above (i.e. those of an informed member of the general public). However, the way in which a health state is described to people who do not have the condition and the way in which the question is structured can bias the answer. The best way to partly eliminate this bias in measuring utility on the general public is to avoid cognitive overload by way of using abbreviated descriptions and wording the question in a balanced manner (i.e. positive and negative) (Drummond et al, 1992). On the other hand, using patients as the source of utilities for cost-utility analysis has, of course, the advantages of avoiding the problem of health state description, but, instead, it may introduce other biases as the result of potential conflict of interest. In general, patients suffering from a condition have a tendency to exaggerate the disutility of their condition in order to enhance the cost-utility of the targeted treatment programmes. In addition, the use of patients restricts the measurement to one health state utility per subject, whereas measurement on members of the general public allows collection of many health state utilities during the one interview. Nevertheless, patients are an appropriate group to use, particularly, where the alternatives being compared are all targeted at the same disorder and the primary intention is not to compare the results to programmes targeted at other disorders.

Finally, the most accurate way to obtain utility values for any given study will be to measure them directly on a sample of subjects rather than to use judgement to estimate the values or to use existing values available in the literature. There are at least three instruments available: the rating scale, the time trade-off and the standard gamble (Drummond, 1992). The rating scale is usually based on a visual analogue scale with the most preferred health state placed at one end of the line and the least preferred at the other. The remaining health states lie between these two extremes, as indicated by the respondent's perceived preference proportional to the distances between the locations on the line. In the second approach, the time trade-off, which is mostly relevant to chronic health states, subjects are assessed to consider a health state (e.g. osteoarthritis of the hip) and to find out how many of their remaining years of life in that state they would be willing to exchange in return for full health. The logic is that the worse a particular health state, the more years of life an individual would be willing to trade and this forms the basis for comparing different health states. In the third instrument, the standard gamble, subjects are given the choice between the certainty of living the rest of their life in a particular health state and a gamble of an intervention which would return them to full health if successful and kill them if unsuccessful. The probability of the gamble is then varied until the subject becomes indifferent to the gamble and the certainty. As with the time trade-off approach, the logic here also is that the worse a particular health state, the greater the gamble an individual would take.

Each of the above three methods has its strengths and weaknesses. The rating scale is the least costly mainly because it does not require interviewers. On the other hand, the standard gamble technique is considered to be the Gold Standard as it is based on the general principle of utility theory. Different combinations of these techniques can be used in economic appraisals which would have the added benefit of examining the validity of the data and the techniques.

QUALITY ADJUSTED LIFE YEARS (QALY)

The underlying rationale for QALY concept is that it is no longer relevant to measure life expectancy in unadjusted years because a single year of perfect health, in terms of utility, may be equivalent to more than one year of impaired health. An individual may well prefer a shorter but healthier life to a longer one with diminished health. Thus, the traditional approach to determining life expectancy has to be modified by adjusting the number of years by a factor based on their quality. If we were to assign an arbitrary value, of one to an extra year of healthy/good quality life-expectancy, then an extra year of unhealthy/poor quality life-expectancy must be worth less than one. In order to determine how much less than one an unhealthy year of life-expectancy is worth, it is necessary to produce a second fixed point in the valuation scale and that being dead is worth zero, bearing in mind that quality of some living states may be perceived worse than being dead.

The Rosser Utility Valuation Matrix

Health is a multi-dimensional concept. Perhaps one way of not adding to the complexity of this concept is to abandon any attempt to produce an index on which to base healthcare decisions. However, the reality is that we live in a world of ever increasing demands on resources which forces us to make choices. Until recently, such decisions were primarily based upon the value judgement of physicians, usually without a rational appraisal of options. However, it is essential that trade-offs between quality and quantity of life to be encompassed in any forms of policy decisions for health services appraisal. Rosser and Kind (1978), in an attempt to describe dimensions of health, asked 60 physicians about the criteria considered in assessing severity of a patient's condition, other than prognosis. Two principal dimensions for quality of life emerged from this exercise: disability and distress. They then devised a matrix where each cell represented a health state corresponding to a

Table 2.2: Rosser's Valuation Matrix (scale of values: perfect health = 1, dead = 0).

Disability state	Distress state			
	1 none	**2** mild	**3** moderate	**4** severe
1 None	1.000	0.995	0.990	0.967
2 Slight social	0.990	0.986	0.973	0.932
3 Severe social work	0.980	0.972	0.956	0.912
4. Severe work	0.964	0.956	0.942	0.870
5 Unable to work	0.946	0.935	0.900	0.711
6 Chair bound	0.875	0.845	0.680	0.000
7 Bed bound	0.677	0.564	0.000	−1.486
8 Unconscious	−1.028			

given combination of disability and distress. Utility scores were derived for each health state by asking a sample of 70 people (i.e. patients, health volunteers, doctors, nurses) to score each state on a scale where 1 = perfect health and 0 = dead. For measuring QALY (i.e. measure of health gain), then, individuals are placed into one of 29 cells. Rosser's Classification of Illness States and its associated valuation matrix (**Table 2.2**) has been used to measure the QALY gain and thus priorities can be determined by cost per QALY (unit of health gain).

Calculation of QALYs

In terms of utility, a single year of better health may be equivalent to a longer period of impaired health (i.e. with pain and physical/social disability). This means that two years with a score of 0.5 QALYs per year would be equivalent to a single year of perfect health. For example, based on the matrix values in **Table 2.2**, a health state with a score of 0.564 would define a person confined to bed suffering from a mild pain. Twenty-three months in that condition has the same utility as one year completely free from disability and distress. Taking this one step further, a treatment that has the prospect of producing four years of healthy life rather than four years in a health state with a utility value of 0.75 would have the advantage of providing one extra QALY. By the same token, a treatment that improves a patient's health state from 0.25 to 0.75 in four years would be worth two extra QALYs.

A medical intervention that costs £1400, which allows a newborn child, who would otherwise have died, to have a normal life would collect 70 QALYs, at a cost-per-QALY of £20. If the child has residual complications such as distress, disability or shortened life expectancy, the number of QALYs will be reduced and thus the cost-per-QALY rises. The discount rate (see Chapter 3) is applied to costs and benefits projected in the future. The cost-per-QALY may vary widely, as illustrated in **Table 2.3**.

Table 2.3: Treatment Costs at 1990 prices in £ sterling.

Treatment	Cost/QALY (£)
Cholesterol testing and diet only (all adults aged 40-69)	200
Neurosurgical intervention for head injury	240
GP advice to stop smoking	270
Neurosurgical intervention for subarachnoid haemorrhage	490
Antihypertensive therapy to prevent stroke (ages 45-64)	940
Pacemaker implantation	1,100
Hip replacement	1,180
Valve replacement for aortic stenosis	1,410
Cholesterol testing and treatment (all adults 40-69)	1,480
CABG (LMD severe angina)	2,090
Kidney transplant	4,710
Breast cancer screening	5,780
Heart transplantation	7,840
Cholesterol testing and treatment (incrementally, all adults aged 25-39)	14,150
Home haemodialysis	17,260
CABG (one vessel disease, moderate angina)	18,830
Hospital haemodialysis	21,970
EPO treatment for anaemia in dialysis patients (assuming 10% mortality reduction)	54,380
Neurosugical intervention for malignant intracranial tumours	107,780

CABG = Coronary artery bypass graft; LMD = Left main disease; EPO = Erythropoietin.

QALY league tables

Recently, comparisons between healthcare interventions in terms of their relative cost-effectiveness per quality adjusted life year (QALY) gained have been used to help policy decisions about the allocation of resources in healthcare. Information on QALYs has been combined with costs of different treatments (cost-utility analysis) to produce cost-per-QALY league tables (Williams, 1985; Gudex, 1986; Gudex & Kind, 1988). The QALY league table is based on the principle that a beneficial treatment programme is one that generates positive QALYs, and that an efficient treatment programme is one where the cost per QALY is as low as it can be. Thus, a high priority treatment programme is one where the cost per QALY is low, and a low priority treatment is one where cost per QALY is high (Williams, 1985). Then in the QALY league table the intervention providing the greatest benefits in terms of cost-per-QALY is placed at the top of the table and decreasing priority is placed on the less cost-effective interventions as proceeding to work down the league table. Clearly, interventions at the bottom of the league table would fare badly if the health budget becomes stretched.

In general, such league tables have a certain inherent attractiveness to healthcare decision makers such as the Department of Health in the UK (Parsonage & Neuburger, 1992; Mason *et al*, 1993). Recently, they attracted the interest of officials concerned with the allocation of public health resources in the State of Oregon which led to the Oregon Experience project (Eddy, 1991; Hadorn, 1991). However, the use of QALY league tables in rationing healthcare and the use of scientific methods for solving its inherent problems have been much criticised on ethical grounds. Taking the decision making away from those involved (i.e. physicians and their patients) takes away sensitivity from the clinical procedures. Moreover, QALYs create a means of choosing between patients which potentially leads to unjust results. Naturally, the cost-effectiveness approach to the prioritisation of healthcare applies utilitarian maximisation principles, which will always tend to favour patients whose age and disorder have the prospect of longer and better survival.

The EuroQol

This instrument has been developed jointly by a multidisciplinary group (EuroQol Group) from a number of Northern European countries (i.e. United Kingdom – 3 centres, Finland – 2 centres, Sweden, Norway, The Netherlands – 4 centres) as an alternative means for generating QALYs. The EuroQol Group has members from a variety of disciplines such as health economics, mathematics, medicine, nursing, philosophy, psychology and sociology. The researchers involved are actively engaged in practical experimentation and share a common interest in the evaluation of healthcare services. This small group of researchers from centres in five European countries started their collaboration with a common interest and a common vision in the valuation of health-related quality of life and met for the first time in May 1987. The principal aim of the group was to test the feasibility of jointly developing a standardised non-disease-specific instrument for describing and valuing health-related quality of life. Of particular importance to the group was the capacity to generate cross-national comparisons of health state valuations. It was envisaged that this in turn would facilitate the exchange of data on methods and lead to standardisation in the collection and reporting of common quality of life data for reference purposes.

The original descriptive classification system which formed the basis for the EuroQol instrument encompassed six distinct dimensions (i.e. mobility, self-care, main activity, social relationships, pain, mood) with two levels or categories on three dimensions and three levels on each of the other three. These dimensions were selected following a detailed examination of the descriptive content of existing health status measures including the Quality of Well-Being Scale, the Sickness Impact Profile, Nottingham Health Profile and the Rosser Index. The resultant descriptive system defines a total of 216 possible health states. In order to provide relative valuations for these states, the group conducted a rating exercise in which a number of subjects were asked to rate 16 of the possible 216 health states on a visual analogue scale (thermometer design) ranging from 0 to 100 (the EuroQol Group, 1990). As a result of further developmental work, the original six-dimension descriptive system has been reduced to five dimensions with three levels in each and a total of 243 possible health states. Although the EuroQol instrument is still going through the developmental process, members of the EuroQol group are keen to use it for providing a set of weights which could be used to calculate QALYs in place of the Rosser matrix. The EuroQol is gaining popularity and is increasingly being used in current research. Further work is being carried out concerning the EuroQol validity, reliability and its clinical application as both a profile and index.

ALTERNATIVE MEASURES OF QUALITY OF LIFE

Economic Measures

The Healthy Years Equivalent (HYE)

The HYE has been developed by economists as an alternative measure of outcome to the QALY. This measure is based on the utility theory and is derived from the individual's utility function and therefore fully reflects that individual's preferences (Mehrez and Gafni, 1989, 1992). The authors of the HYE claim that it combines outcomes of both morbidity and mortality and can therefore serve as a common unit of measure for economic appraisal of all health interventions (including drug interventions). This is encouraging because it allows comparisons across different interventions. It is also suggested that the HYE, by fully representing individual preferences, avoids some of the major problems of the QALY, yet preserves the appealing intuitive meaning that QALYs have.

The HYE is based on the same general economic principles as QALY but differs essentially in that the HYE seeks valuations of health profiles over time as opposed to valuations of specific health states independent of time. The HYE uses the standard gamble (classical method for obtaining individual preferences) to determine the utility of a specified health profile over time rather than a health state (Mehrez and Gafni, 1991). A second gamble is then set up to identify an alternative profile which gives the same total utility as the original, but also entails H years of perfect health followed by death. H is varied until indifference is achieved. Thus, in summary, the HYE approach seeks equivalence between the certainty of an imperfect health profile of given length and a shorter (H) profile of perfect health. The higher the utility of the imperfect health profile, the higher is H. The QALY and HYE are both intended to capture the individual's remaining life expectancy and also the quality (utility) of life in each remaining year. These two approaches may, in certain circumstances, yield the same result. However, the debate between supporters of the two approaches is over which better captures true preferences.

Saved young life equivalent (SAVE)

This fairly recently developed method (Nord, 1992) of cost-utility analysis is conceptualised on the basis that in health programme evaluation society should evaluate different healthcare outcomes relative to each other. In other words, one can simply choose one particular healthcare outcome as the unit of measurement and let people compare other outcomes directly with this unit. Nord (1992) offers the following example to illustrate the above concept.

"Saving the life of a young person and restoring him or her to full health. This outcome is suggested as the unit of measurement on the ground that most people will probably regard it as the maximum benefit that a single individual can obtain. Thus, this value assigned by society to this outcome is regarded as a saved young life equivalent, or one SAVE, for short."

Perhaps some of the properties of the SAVE method can be better explained by drawing a comparison with QALY.

1) The SAVE method is presented as being a much more direct way of estimating the social values of healthcare interventions than calculating QALYs and hence easier for lay people to understand.
2) Nevertheless, it yields value assessments in terms of numbers just as QALYs do.
3) Similarly, it allows comparison of different interventions in terms of cost utility ratio.
4) Unlike QALYs, the SAVE method allows consideration of various distributional and ethical rules.
5) The SAVE method is more comprehensive than the QALYs, since it allows judges to take account not only of the amount of health produced by each intervention but also of any distributional or ethical consideration they might find relevant. To clarify this, Nord (1992) offers the following example:

"Consider three health states, A, B and C that are on a health status index score 0.3, 0.5 and 0.9, respectively. In terms of QALYs, an improvement from B to C would carry a greater value than an improvement from A to B (0.4 vs. 0.2). But as noted above, on the grounds that severity is an argument in itself, people may very well consider it more important to help a person progress from state A to state B than help another person progress from state B to state C. In the SAVE method, people could express this by selecting a lower equivalence number (relative to saving a young life) for improvement from A to B than for improvement from B to C. Similarly, in terms of QALYs, taking one kind of patient from A to C carries more value than taking another patient from A to B (0.6 vs. 0.2). However, society may very well find that the two kinds of patients should have equal priority on the grounds that both would be significantly helped and both are equally entitled to treatment. In the SAVE method. people could express this by choosing the same equivalence number for the two kinds of improvement."

The SAVE does not suggest QALYs should become redundant or make them invalid, but it is intended to provide the decision makers with an alternative method to QALYs. In fact, in situations where decision makers are interested in the amount of health produced by different health services or different therapeutic interventions, the QALYs may prove to be a useful procedure (Nord, 1992).

The SAVE measures social values which includes distributional as well as ethical consideration and therefore is suggested as an aid to decisions concerning allocation of scarce resources to different healthcare programmes. Moreover, the SAVE method may also prove useful as a guide in decisions concerning the distribution of resources between known patients. If operating in this context, other ethical rules such as the "rule of rescue" (Hadorn, 1991) (i.e. the obligation to save human life regardless of cost) should be applied.

The reliability of responses to equivalence of numbers needs to be studied. In the few rare studies that the technique has been used (Patrick et al, 1993; Nord, 1991; Nord, 1992) no reliability tests have been performed. Testing of a first version of the model on a set of hypothetical healthcare outcomes has shown a high discriminant capacity. However, the real test of validity of the model is to see whether the equivalence numbers it predicts for different outcomes correspond with the equivalence numbers that people would suggest if asked directly (Nord, 1991; Nord, 1992). There is evidence to suggest that perceptions of health-related quality of life are much the same in Norway as in other Northern European countries (EuroQoL Group, 1990; Nord, 1991). However attitudes towards distribution may differ, and so may health perceptions outside the Northern European region. Thus, other countries interested in adopting the SAVE method will probably need to develop an estimation model of their own.

Disability-Adjusted Life Years (DALYs)

The DALY is a new indicator of the burden of disease which is mainly based on four key social choices. First, giving due consideration to advantages and disadvantages of various methods of calculating the duration of life lost due to a death at each age, DALYs use a standard expected-life lost based on model life-table West level 26. Second, the value of time lived at different ages is captured using an exponential function which reflects the dependence of the young and the elderly on adults. Third, the time lived with a disability is made comparable with the time lost due to premature mortality by defining six classes of disability severity (a severity weight between 0 and 1 is assigned to each class and the years not lived or lost due to premature mortality are assigned a value of 0). Fourth, a 3% discount rate is used in the calculation of DALYs (Murray, 1994).

As is evident from the above the DALY methodology uses the basic scheme for evaluating the cost-effectiveness of health interventions as a comprehensive assessment of ill health related to specific diseases. However, there are a number of features which are unique to the DALY:

1. The objective of measuring the total burden of disease from all the important diseases combined. This requires a great deal of effort in estimating the incidence, prevalence and mortality of a large number of diseases by using a model to produce estimates with high internal consistency.

2. The use of disability weights. Six classes of disability severity were identified. Expert panels were used to estimate the number of disabled people with a certain disease and their level of disability. No doubt this approach to obtain disability weights, as in QALYs, has some weaknesses.

3. The use of age-weights. Both economic and social role arguments have been used to justify valuing lost years of life due to mortality and morbidity differently by age.

4. The use of one standard life-table worldwide and not different regional life-tables. The author argues that this is necessary to compare 'like with like' and not to value a death at a given age more in a high life-expectancy than a low one.

5. The discounting of future years. It is not a generally accepted concept in the health sector that future years of life should be treated in the same way as with other commodities.

Non-economic health status measures

The Sickness Impact Profile (SIP)

In the early Seventies, development of methods for evaluating healthcare services was considered to be one of the most urgent concerns in the field of health services research (Gilson et al, 1975). This was primarily due to a change in emphasis in the developed countries from the curing of disease to minimising the impact of illness on everyday activities. Efficacy and efficiency of treatment could no longer be judged by just morbidity and mortality rates (Bergner et al, 1981). Instead, estimates of the actual performance of activities were needed to provide a relevant and sensitive indicator for evaluating medical care and its impact on patients' quality of life, assessing needs and determining the allocation of resources. Thus, the SIP was developed to provide an appropriate outcome measure for use in assessing healthcare services. It was conceptualised as a measure of sickness-related dysfunction designed to produce a reliable, valid and sensitive measure of health status. The SIP was also designed to reflect a subject's perception of his performance of daily functions, both physical and psychosocial.

Originally, 1250 statements describing sickness-related dysfunction relating to everyday life and encompassing the areas of social activities, emotions and physical function were collected from patients, carers (who were apparently healthy), healthcare professionals and from a review of the literature. After applying standard grouping techniques, the SIP in its preliminary form contained 312 statements in 14 domains of daily activity. Subsequently, it was reduced to 235, 189 and finally 136 which was grouped into 12 areas of daily activity. The SIP can be either interviewer or self-administered. The statements are presented in a tick-box format, allowing the individual to specify which descriptive statements are applicable to them and are related to their health. An equal-interval category scaling method was used to rate the relative severity of dysfunction of each questionnaire item within a given category. This was firstly done with a group of 25 judges and subsequently with a larger group of members of a prepaid group practice (108 persons).

The scaling of the SIP items was based on the following considerations. First, coverage of a broad range of functions and a diversity of severity within each subject area provides intuitive evidence suggesting the SIP items should not be equally weighted. Second, because of its comprehensiveness, the impact of sickness on the behaviour of two persons could be quite different even if they both ticked the same number of descriptive items. Third, the possibility of social or cultural differences in the perception of health-related behaviour (i.e. individual items may be valued differently by different subgroups of the population). Thus, scaling provides an opportunity to test the extent to which a single instrument is valid across social and cultural groups. Fourth, the criticism that has been made of many previous attempts at evaluating outcomes of healthcare, that of sensitivity. Therefore, scaling was applied explicitly to increase the SIPs precision and sensitivity in accounting for variance (Carter *et al*, 1976).

Like the QALY, the SIP has been developed out of a concern for the importance of the role of indicators of health status in resource allocation decisions but with the concept of a social consensus. The SIP is more a product of societal opinion since the health state descriptive statements which it uses were derived from a wider consultation than was the case for the Rosser Index. With regards to the scoring systems, both can be accused of employing a relatively restricted group of judges. However, the two consecutive scaling tasks conducted for the SIP (as described above) yielded very similar results, despite the differences between the two groups, suggesting that the values may be relatively insensitive to variations in cultural groups. Thus, there appear to be a few differences in the underlying philosophies of the two techniques.

The SIP uses a category rating method to develop an interval scale, whereas the magnitude estimation method was used by Rosser to develop a ratio scale. Furthermore, there is evidence for consistency of the initial valuations with an interval scale. The overall impression is that the scaling method used for rating the SIP is superior to that associated with the QALY. There is also better evidence for reliability and validity of the SIP compared with that of the Rosser matrix.

The United Kingdom adaptation of the SIP, UKSIP, developed by Salek in 1986 has retained all the properties of the original SIP, including the scale values (weightings). The UKSIP has been tested for validity, reliability and sensitivity in a variety of clinical situations. The classification system of each instrument is similar, although, the format and presentation of the UKSIP is different to that of SIP in order to make it more patient friendly and more suitable for self-administration.

The Medical Outcome Study (MOS) 36-Item
Short Form Health Survey (SF–36)

The MOS 36-Item Short Form (SF–36) was constructed to survey health status in clinical practice and research, health policy evaluations and general population surveys (Ware and Sherbourne, 1992). The SF–36 is a multi-item scale that assesses health-related dysfunctions in eight areas: physical; role limitations due to physical problems; bodily pain; social functioning; general mental health (psychological distress and psychological well-being); role limitations due to emotional problems;

45

vitality (energy/fatigue); and general health perceptions. The SF–36 items have been adapted from instruments that have been used for 20 to 40 years or longer. The content of various instruments used to measure limitations in physical, social, role functioning, general mental health and general health perceptions was reviewed. The SF–36 was designed for self-administration by persons 14 years of age or older and for administration by a trained interviewer in person or by telephone. The scores for SF–36 items and scales are easy to compute using the Likert method of summated ratings which permit scoring of a set of eight scales presented as a profile of health status concepts.

THE USE OF ECONOMIC AND QOL INFORMATION BY THE PHARMACEUTICAL INDUSTRY

It has been argued that there is already undue scrutiny of the cost of medicines, particularly in countries such as the UK where it represents only some 16% of the total annual NHS expenditure (OECD, 1997). The argument to exclude medicines from 'value for money' assessments is difficult to sustain, not only because of the nature of this cost but also because the medicine bill represents the second largest element of NHS expenditure (Wells, 1992a). In addition, all aspects of healthcare provision are being increasingly looked at from a 'value for money' context under the purchaser/provider split.

Pharmaceutical companies themselves are also recognising the weakness of such arguments and this is reflected by an increasing number of companies generating economic and/or quality of life data in support of their products (Wells, 1992b). Indeed such activities are positively encouraged by the Department of Health in their NHS reforms document, "Improving Prescribing" in which they state that "the pharmaceutical industry can play an important role by providing clear cost-benefit and cost-effectiveness evidence for new products which are brought to the market" (Department of Health, 1990).

The Centre for Medicines Research (CMR), one of the offices of ABPI, has undertaken a survey of activities in 55 pharmaceutical companies (Europe = 29; Japan = 11; USA = 15) relating to the socioeconomic evaluation of medicine. Eighty-five per cent of invited companies responded to the survey (Europe = 86%; Japan = 100%; USA = 73%). The questionnaire was divided into three sections, including company policy and organisation, current practices in quality of life assessments and economic evaluations, and future strategic and regulatory requirements. The findings of this survey can be summarised as follows (Kunze *et al*, 1993).

The pharmaceutical industry is increasing its activities in quality of life assessment and economic evaluation of medicines. Quality of life assessment is generally part of the clinical department whilst economic evaluation is part of marketing. Although the lack of top management commitment appears to be a major obstacle to conducting socioeconomic evaluation studies in European companies, most companies in Europe operate a central strategy for socioeconomics. At a global level, the industry is moving towards a greater reliance on in-house expertise by increasing the recruitment of qualified staff. In addition, there are a number of automated databases available for health economic evaluations. However, a more recent survey conducted by CMR International (Lumley, 1997) suggests that there is generally no consistent approach to the selection and use of any data sources for health economic studies carried out by the pharmaceutical industry. This survey has also shown that the automated databases lack quality of life information/data required for health economic evaluations.

Socioeconomic evaluation studies are conducted throughout clinical evaluation of a drug and during post-marketing surveillance (PMS). The level of activity is greatest during Phase IIIa, Phase IIIb clinical trial and during PMS. At a regional level, European and American companies are more active than Japanese companies during the latter three stages of clinical evaluation (including PMS). The performance of socioeconomic evaluation studies during Phase IIIa and b trials and PMS shows that companies conduct these both prospectively (perhaps as part of clinical trials)and retrospectively. Socioeconomic data are used in a number of ways, including price setting, new price and reimbursement negotiations and marketing. They are also used in the selection and termination of R & D projects. Surprisingly, however, European and American companies also use economic evaluation data in new drug applications. They do this although there is no formal requirement for the inclusion of such data. Pharmacoeconomic data obtained in one country are often used in another country. Japanese companies do not employ generic quality of life instruments commonly used by European and American companies. A majority of European and American companies expressed an interest in collaborating with other companies to develop disease-specific quality of life instruments. The majority of respondent companies suggested that there is a need for the formulation of "good socioeconomic practice", akin to good clinical practice, and for drafting standard methodologies in pharmacoeconomics. At the same time, it was felt there is an urgent need for the pharmaceutical industry to ascertain government expectations in different aspects of socioeconomic evaluation.

3

Technical criticisms and resolutions

Ethical concerns about the QALY can be of two distinct types. The first relate to the fundamental economic principles upon which QALYs are based. Ethical objections to any of these principles thus represent objections to the basic economic approach to healthcare resource allocation and can be debated independently of any reference to the QALY as a specific resource allocation tool. The second refer to technical issues surrounding how QALYs are derived e.g. their reliability and validity. (For a recent discussion of technical issues see Johannesson et al, 1996). This chapter will demonstrate that many of what appear to be ethical criticisms of QALYs per se are in fact criticisms of the technical aspects of how QALYs are derived – or misunderstandings of how cost/QALY information is intended to be used. This chapter begins by presenting, but not debating some fundamental principles.

"QALY methodology" refers to a broad approach to measuring and valuing the health output (health gain) resulting from healthcare interventions. There is no strict prescription as to how this should be done and a variety of different measurement and valuation techniques can be accommodated within a broad QALY approach. Criticisms of specific techniques (how QALYs are derived) must therefore be separated from criticisms of the approach itself (should QALYs be derived). To quote Mooney (1992) "I have found so often that the measurement issues get in the way of the issues of principle with QALYs. If the reader becomes obsessed with the measurement issues, he or she may fail to appreciate the beauty of the principles incorporated in QALYs."

The (economic) principles referred to can be summarised as follows (see for example Drummond, 1980, or Cohen and Henderson, 1988):

1. resources for producing health gains are scarce;
2. prioritising is inevitable;
3. prioritising on the basis of explicit criteria is preferable to prioritising without, and,
4. maximising the health gain from available resources is a good criterion (this does not imply it is the only valid criterion).

Despite the intuitive attraction of QALYs and their apparent conceptual simplicity, the controversy and scepticism surrounding them remains. Whilst the ethical dilemma of using a QALY-based system as a rationing device must be faced explicitly, there is a danger of overlooking the technical problems of the QALY. Here, some of these problems will be briefly discussed.

MAXIMISING THE HEALTH GAIN FROM AVAILABLE RESOURCES IS A GOOD CRITERION

The efficiency criterion is based on an objective of maximising the benefit to. available resources. This is explicitly a utilitarian objective taking no account of the distribution of those benefits. Moreover, prioritising on the basis of cost per QALY assumes that health gains are the only benefits from healthcare. This raises two related but separate issues.

First, while people are clearly concerned with the outcome of treatment (QALYs gained) they may also be concerned with the way in which healthcare is delivered. Economists distinguish 'process utility' (the utility derived from the process of being treated) from 'outcome utility' (the utility attached to the outcome of treatment). By adopting a consequentialist approach and only considering the latter, the QALY approach may prioritise a less preferred form of treatment over a more preferred one.

Second, equating QALY gain with 'benefit' ignores all other possible outputs of healthcare including non-health benefits such as productivity gains to those who receive treatment, and all 'external' benefits such as to the wife who no longer has to stay at home to care for her now healthy husband. Nevertheless, health gains to those receiving healthcare are normally regarded at least as a major output, if not the most important output, of healthcare.

Stating that efficiency is a 'good' criterion, however, does not suggest that efficiency should be regarded as the only criterion. There is much scope for debate concerning utilitarianism versus the alternatives, but accepting the QALY methodology does imply accepting utilitarianism as a good principle. It must be stressed, though, that cost per QALY information, is only advocated as an aid to resource allocation decision making and never a replacement for it. This means that accepting the QALY methodology does not mean accepting that utilitarianism should always take precedence over alternative approaches.

There is no shortage of critics of the economic approach to resource allocation – and no shortage of debate on the ethical aspects of applying economic principles to healthcare decision making (see for example Mooney and McGuire, 1988). The ethical debate surrounding the use of QALYs is clearly a legitimate part of that broader debate, but as suggested above many of the criticisms which have been levelled specifically at the QALY relate to the broader economic principles and are not in fact criticisms of the QALY at all. However, the QALY methodology can be used to overcome some of these ethical objections e.g. by using different methodologies to derive the utility matrix, weighting or discounting.

DERIVING A MATRIX OF HEALTH STATES

In its early development, the QALY approach became associated with the "Rosser Matrix" (Rosser and Kind, 1978) of 8 rows representing different degrees of 'disability' and 4 columns representing different degrees of 'distress'. In principle any matrix will do, providing the health states are mutually exclusive (it is not possible to be in two health states at the same time) and exhaustive (together the matrix represents all possible health states).

To be effective for its intended uses, the matrix should be capable of demonstrating changes in an individual's health over time i.e. any treatment judged to have improved a patient's health, should be represented by a movement between cells. Since more cells means more narrowly defined health states, bigger matrices, particularly multidimensional matrices, will always in this sense be superior to smaller ones.

At the same time, however, the matrix has to be operationally feasible and a matrix with thousands of cells would be wholly impractical. The advantage of the Rosser Matrix is that it is easy to manage – but it should be noted that any criticism of the Rosser Matrix based on the small number of cells or how they are described, is not a criticism of the QALY *per se*.

DETERMINING THE UTILITY SCORES OF HEALTH STATES.

Health status is difficult to measure because it is value laden. The inability to climb a flight of stairs cannot 'objectively' be a better or worse than being in pain of some given degree. All health status measures must therefore incorporate some notion of the utility attached to that health state.

Whose values should be used?

As indicated earlier in Chapter 2, there is considerable debate surrounding the issue of whether the appropriate values should be those of individuals currently experiencing each health state or those of society more generally. Some economists (e.g. Williams 1985) support the view that since choices have to be made about how to allocate society's scarce resources, then *social* valuations are most appropriate. Since expansion of any programme will have opportunity costs in the form of forgone health gains across other programmes, then society should decide what values should be attached to the various gains and losses. Counter arguments to the social approach include the fact that attaching social utilities to health states implies that not only is life in a wheelchair less healthy than life without disability, it is also of less value. This position is ethically highly controversial (Harris 1987) and disabled people may find it repugnant. It is worth stressing, though, that the focus of the QALY approach is on the size of a health improvement rather than the starting point and end point.

At the same time, many economists (e.g. Torrance 1986) argue that QALYs should be based on individual preferences – a view more consistent with the individualistic foundations of welfare economics. Accepting the QALY methodology, however, does not demand accepting this or any single view of whose values are most appropriate.

How should utility values be elicited?

The main ways that valuations have been sought have essentially tried to determine how people feel about specified static health states – as opposed to health profiles over time. An early attempt to do this was by Rosser and her colleagues using a sample representing patients, health professionals and healthy individuals. Values for the 29 states of the Rosser Matrix were determined by a magnitude estimation scaling exercise with the aim of producing a ratio scale. This approach can be criticised because a distortion may occur when converting the unconstrained results of magnitude estimation on a 0–1 scale, and this was observed in the Rosser study where scores were clustered at the upper end of the range. Alternative but related methods, such as visual analogue, may be superior.

Non-related methods of obtaining scores can also be used. In particular the standard gamble is an attractive alternative because it is based on the theory of decision making under risk (expected utility theory), and is thus, at least within economics, regarded as the classical method for obtaining individual preferences. As before, however, the point is that the QALY methodology does not prescribe any technique to elicit utility scores. Criticisms of any particular technique cannot be regarded as criticism of the QALY methodology.

Valuing health states independently of time

The Rosser approach elicits values of static health states and then combines these with estimates of duration The implicit assumption is that the utility of any given state is independent of time.

This can be criticised in a number of ways. First, the utility of any state may depend on how long a person expects to remain there. Human beings tend to develop tolerance towards their diminished health states as time passes and hence change in their value judgement, usually for the better (Harris, 1991; Mason et al, 1993; Petrou et al, 1993). Second, the utility of any state may depend on whether a person is moving up from a lower health state or moving down from a higher health state. The static approach may thus give distorted preferences.

This 'problem' though, relates to the most commonly used approach to QALYs. Other techniques such as time trade off or standard gamble take a different approach to determining utilities, and thus may be considered to be more appropriate. While there is clearly much room for debate here, the questions relate to *how* utilities are derived. There is nothing in the QALY methodology that would preclude any method being used.

Stability of utilities between cultures and over time

Systematic reviews of clinical as well as economic studies in any areas of healthcare have to take account of factors such as differences in methodologies employed and cultural differences in the study populations. There is thus nothing unique to cost per QALY league tables (e.g. Maynard, 1991) being based on information from studies carried out in different countries at different times but there may be additional factors which need to be borne in mind.

For example, Gudex (1986) combined information from studies carried out at different times (17 years) and in different places in a single league table. Such an approach would not take account of the fact that both costs and benefits from medical interventions can change over time as a result of technical improvements and economies of scale. It is thus possible that results of older studies may not be strictly comparable with more recent studies – even if, strictly, the clinical effectiveness of the intervention is unchanged. Moreover, costs may also vary from one nation to another and perhaps even between regions within nations, suggesting that the results of studies not carried out in the same geographical location may be affected by extraneous factors (Petrou et al, 1993; Mason et al, 1993). For example, attitudes to the trade-off between length of life and quality of life may not be constant across cultures. Similarly, since discounting is based on 'social' time preference, the most appropriate discount rate in a study in one country might be inappropriate for another.

These factors suggest that research is needed to examine the effects of cultural differences and the stability of utility values over time. More importantly perhaps, they suggest that care must be taken in interpreting cost/QALY information. Again, these cannot be seen as problems of QALYs per se. Rather they raise concerns that cost/QALY information might be misused and in particular, warn against using cost/QALY data as a substitute for, rather than an aid to, decision making.

In light of the ethical and technical controversies surrounding the QALY concept and cost-per-QALY league tables, one should use a QALY league table with caution and mainly as an aid to resource allocation decisions in seeking to shift resources away from activities that are less efficient in terms of the health benefits they generate and towards activities that are of relatively higher efficiency (Robinson, 1993; Williams, 1987).

IS A QALY OF EQUAL VALUE REGARDLESS TO WHOM IT ACCRUES?

The preceding section was concerned with the issue of measuring QALYs. Here we turn to the related question of whether a QALY to one person should be regarded as being equal to a QALY to another.

In standard QALY usage, an egalitarian stance is adopted in the sense that a unit of benefit is of equal value no matter to whom it is provided. By implicitly incorporating this particular rule, the standard QALY can be defended on the grounds that it treats each individual equally. Thus, it does not discriminate between people according to any 'irrelevant' criteria such as age, sex, social class, wealth, race, lifestyle and so on. In its unweighted form the QALY ascribes equal importance to everyone regardless of their personal or other characteristics. However, as with all implicit judgements, there are other viewpoints which can give rise to arguments justifying unequal weighting so that a given unit of benefit defined in purely health terms may be valued, or weighted, differently for different people.

Although the QALY is non-discriminatory in the manner outlined above, it can be argued that QALYs implicitly discriminate against older people because they are likely to have less gain from medical care than their younger counterparts, at least in survival terms. It can also be contended that QALYs discriminate against certain groups in society with conditions which are not easily amenable to treatment or for which medical technology can provide little benefit. A systematic pattern of disadvantage according to either race or sex may, it can be claimed, become established.

A response to these arguments is that, if so desired, the QALY can be used to discriminate against or in favour of any group that may be identified, by the application of a set of weighting factors. Accordingly, if it is felt that a particular group is being unfairly treated under the conventional QALY, the situation could be redressed by favourably weighting the QALYs provided to that group relative to other groups in society. Resource allocation based on weighting QALYs would result in more resources being devoted to the treatment of that group and would also improve their access to treatment. In this way, equity defined in terms of access to treatment as well as the outcome of treatment may be promoted. Where it is desired to discriminate in favour of those who are the least healthy and have the least to gain from treatment through the vehicle of weighted QALYs, justification might be found in the Rawlsian notion that where inequalities are present, they should favour the most disadvantaged.

INTRODUCING OVERT DISCRIMINATION: THE WEIGHTED QALY

The assumption that a QALY is a QALY regardless to whom it accrues can thus be challenged and, if appropriate, adjusted within the QALY framework by the use of weights. There is no reason why the QALY gain to one type of individual cannot be weighted 1.1 and the QALY gain to another type of individual weighted 0.9. This, of course, opens a great debate discussed above about whether to apply weights and if so what weights to apply, but it should be noted that the conclusion from such a debate can easily be incorporated into the QALY approach. Any criticism that QALYs do or don't, should or shouldn't, discriminate against any particular group can be addressed within the QALY approach, and is therefore not a criticism of the approach itself.

In the following sections, reasons that have been proposed for weighting QALYs are considered in turn.

Weighting in favour of the young

One rationale for weighting in favour of the young, is the 'fair innings' argument. By this reasoning, a younger person should have a greater claim because he or she has not yet had the opportunity to survive for as long a period as an older person, or has had less of a 'fair innings'. Evidence suggests that this may be a widely held view.

The Cardiff Health Survey asked respondents to choose between two patients who were identical in every respect apart from their age (Lewis and Charny, 1989; Charny, et al, 1989). When choosing between a 5-year-old and a 70-year-old, 94% of 721 respondents indicated they would give priority to the child. The overwhelming majority said that it was a very or quite easy decision to make. Only 1% would give preference to the 70-year-old, the remaining 5% were unable to answer. The more elderly respondents in the sample were more likely to choose the child, than any other age group in the sample. The reasons for the preferences included the extra potential years of life that the younger person would have and their greater potential economic contribution to society.

The decision became more difficult, however, as the age differential narrowed. When choosing between identical patients aged 35 and 60 years, 80% gave preference to the younger patient, although over half said that the decision was quite or very difficult. 13% were unable to give a preference. When the range was narrowed to choosing between a 2-year-old and an 8-year-old, 46% could not make a choice. Of those who did indicate a preference, most said that the decision was very difficult. The greater preference (34% v. 21%) was to the *older* child. Reasons for favouring the older child included a wish to protect investments that had already been made and because the 8-year-old was more likely to suffer because they would have a better understanding of their circumstances.

In moral reflection on the question of evaluating the remaining days, months, or years of person's life, Glover (1977) has asserted that it is absurd to place as much value in 'postponing death for ten minutes as in postponing it for ten years'. Harris (1989), however, argues in opposition to this, seemingly common-sense, position. He argues that a person who knows for certain that they only have a short time to live, can place a value on their remaining time equal to that of a person who has a much longer life expectancy, precisely because it is all the time that person has left. Thus, if two patients both say that they value their life highly, no matter how the quality of their lives or their probable life expectancy is judged by a neutral party, then Harris's argument would support an equal entitlement to treatment. The only way to resolve the dilemma of allocating limited resources which are insufficient to meet the needs of all patients, would therefore be the adoption of a lottery, with random allocation of treatment.

Harris in fact modifies this bold proposition by acknowledging the strength of our intuition that there is something unfair about one person living a long and happy life (and thanks to his or her fortune in the lottery, being given treatment that allows him or her to hang on grimly to the end), while another person is allowed (through misfortune in the lottery compounding the misfortune of serious illness) to die young. He is therefore drawn to acknowledge one exception to the strict application of lottery principles: in the choice between one person who has had a fair innings, and one who has not. The person who has had a fair innings still sufferers an injustice from being denied treatment (or indeed, being denied access to the lottery for treatment), for his or her life is cut short. Yet, the other person would suffer the double injustice of being denied a fair innings, as well as having his or her life cut short. Thus, if age is a legitimate criterion for interfering in a lottery, it would seem to be less problematically a legitimate criterion for interfering in such a non-arbitrary allocation mechanism as the QALY.

Weighting by stage of the life cycle

At different stages of the life cycle, individuals may regard the value of good health as more or less important than at others, depending on their activities. For example, periods of family responsibilities when there are children or elderly relatives to look after is a stage which may be seen as particularly significant. In this case, weights may be assigned to QALYs gained by those with family responsibilities.

The Cardiff Health Survey referred to above, also asked respondents to make choices between otherwise identical patients who differed only by marital status. About three quarters of respondents were willing to give a higher priority to the married patient. This preference was only partly related to an assumption that the married person would have children. There was a view that marriage carried with it responsibilities which being single did not, and this was sufficient for some respondents to make a choice. The marital status of the respondent did not bias their preference.

When to choose between patients who differed only in that one was male and the other was female, over half the respondents were unable to make a choice. Of those that were, there was a preference for choosing the woman (about a third). There seemed to be an ambivalence for choosing the man because of his presumed productive worth i.e. to generate an income for the family, and choosing the woman because of her more important parental role in child care.

Glover has summarised these moral intuitions by suggesting that a failure to distinguish between two potential recipients of healthcare on the grounds that one has dependent children and the other does not, is to place no value on the additional misery that the loss of a parent would have on the children. From this, it may indeed be suggested that the calculation of QALY values, by taking into account only the quality of life of the immediate recipients of healthcare, expresses a similar insensitivity to the potential suffering of the patients' dependants.

Weighting according to lifestyle

It is possible to argue that QALY gains from treating ill-health which is brought about as a result of individual's own behaviour (smoking, drinking, engaging in dangerous sports, etc.) should be of lower value than those from treating ill-health for whom the victim was blameless. By the same token, more weight may be given to health benefits provided to those whose health has suffered through factors outside their control such as deprivation or unemployment.

Suggestions that smokers should be given a lower priority for treatment have received considerable criticism. In August, 1993, there was media coverage of the death of a 47-year-old man who had been refused consideration for a coronary artery bypass graft for his angina because he was unable to stop smoking cigarettes (Jones 1993, Anderson 1993). It was argued that the patient concerned had as much right to healthcare as any other patient, not least because of the extra taxes he had paid in the form of tobacco excise duties. However, the doctors involved had correctly pointed out that a coronary artery bypass graft would be unlikely to be effective for a patient who continues to smoke. Thus the smoker was being given a lower priority, not as a result of moral discrimination, but following a decision based on evidence of effectiveness.

As part of the Cardiff Health Survey, respondents were also asked to make choices between individuals who could be 'blamed' to some extent for their illness; 74% of respondents were willing to give preference to a non-smoker over a smoker. Respondents who smoke cigarettes, were just as likely to give preference to the hypothetical patient who did not smoke, as did those who were ex-smokers or non-smokers. The smokers among the sample did however, find this choice more difficult.

Respondents were also willing to use alcohol intake and diet as a priority discriminator for otherwise identical patients; 80% said they would choose a patient with a low alcohol intake rather than a heavy drinker. As with the smoking choice, the frequency of alcohol intake of the respondent did not affect their choice of patient, although frequent drinkers again tended to find the choice very difficult.

A patient who developed a diet-related disease tended to be discriminated against compared with an identical patient who had a genetic basis to their disease; 60% of respondents said that they would give the life-saving treatment to the patient with inherited disease.

The Cardiff Health Survey indicated that the public were willing to consider a patient's lifestyle in micro-resource allocation decisions. The main difficulty with this form of discrimination is deciding on where to draw the line. For example, should a heavy smoker by 'blamed' more than an occasional smoker? Or perhaps more controversially, if we 'blame' an obese individual who develops heart disease should we not also 'punish' a heart attack patient if they have eaten an occasional cream cake? While the degree of risk is important, social values of the form of risk are also influential; for example, it has not be argued that we should turn patients away from accident departments who have sustained their injury whilst mountaineering or even playing rugby.

Weighting by 'social worth'

It would in principle, be possible to discriminate between people according to their skills and abilities, with those whose talents are widely recognised and appreciated being regarded as more socially valuable and so receiving preferential treatment.

In addition to age, dependants and lifestyle, the Cardiff Health Survey demonstrated that other 'merits of the person selected' could be used as a discriminator. In comparisons involving differences in social class, just over half of respondents were unable to make a choice. However, there was a two to one ratio of support for prioritising an employed person over someone who was unemployed. There were similar ratios in favour of the claim for treatment of a company director compared with someone who was unskilled, and for a teacher compared with a lorry driver. These broad preferences were seen across all the respondents' social class groups.

Preferential treatment could be a reward for those who have made a contribution to society. Alternatively, society may be acting from 'selfish' motives, i.e. by protecting those individuals who have valued skills to offer.

Glover (1977) compared choices for treatment based upon moral worth with "a kind of reluctant but retributive capital punishment", since a life or death decision is made according to "a person's desert". While a death sentence for murder follows a judgement that the law has been broken, a patient's desert is "assessed on the much more nebulous basis of a judgement of moral character".

Weighting survival versus quality of life

It can be argued that one weakness of the QALY is its failure to distinguish between 'life-saving' procedures and those which improve quality of life but add nothing to its duration. Some may feel that extending life should be given priority over enhancing its quality. Although the QALY overtly represents a trade-off between length and quality of life, it is possible that combining the values of states at one point in time with estimates of life expectancy may not accurately reflect society's trade-off between life improving and life extending. If this is the case, additional years of life could be weighed more heavily than those which are merely improved if it is accepted that prolonging life is in some way morally superior to raising its quality.

INTRODUCING TIME: IS A QALY OF EQUAL VALUE REGARDLESS OF WHEN IT ACCRUES?

In economic theory, individuals are said to have a "positive rate of time preference", which means that the value they attach to any benefit (or cost) is reduced the further in the future it arises. Positive time preference is said to exist for a number of reasons including uncertainty (the longer the wait before benefits accrue, the greater is the likelihood that something will happen in the meantime to prevent those benefits from being realised, e.g. the individual may die) and myopia (people prefer early benefits simply because they are 'short-sighted'). Since society is a collection of individuals then, according to economic theory, society has a 'positive rate of social time preference'.

Government and other bodies who make decisions on behalf of society need to take account of social time preference in the same way that individuals take account of individual time preference when making their own resource allocation choices (or at least behave as if they did so). In economic evaluations this is done by adjusting all future benefits and costs into 'present value' terms via a process called *discounting*. The present value depends on 1) how far in the future any benefit (or cost) arises and 2) the discount rate applied.

The principle of discounting is universally accepted by economists with regard to monetary cost and benefits. With regard to health benefits, however, some economists dissent from the prevalent view that the same discount rate should be used for QALYs as other benefits, arguing that some adjustment to the value of future QALYs is necessary but that a different (lower) discount rate should be used. A minority feel that future QALYs should not be discounted at all, i.e. that the appropriate rate is zero.

The resource allocation implications of different discount rates can be considerable. Discounting QALYs at a low or zero rate makes prevention and other programmes with long term benefits more attractive than would be the case if a higher rate were used. At the same time, use of higher discount rates, tends to counter the view that QALYs are 'ageist' in that high rates significantly reduce the (present) value of future QALYs, thus bringing the value of a long stream of QALYs to a young person closer in value to the shorter stream of QALYs to an old person.

Those who argue against the QALY approach because they believe discounting health benefits is inappropriate, are simply arguing for a zero discount rate. The issue of whether future QALYs should be discounted at the same or at a different – including zero – rate from future non-health benefits is not germane to the debate on whether or not to accept the QALY methodology. Any rate, including zero, can be accommodated within the QALY approach.

ARE THE TECHNICAL CRITICISMS OF QALY VALID?

The QALY approach to resource allocation is firmly rooted in the principles of economics. It is thus legitimate on ethical grounds to criticise the QALY methodology on the basis of arguments against the economic principles upon which the approach is based.

This chapter has not entered into that broader debate but has focused instead on ethical criticisms directed specifically at the QALY methodology, i.e. the technical aspects of QALYs. The overriding conclusion is that technical issues may have ethical implications, but the QALY methodology is capable of accommodating different technical solutions to ethical problems. This means that many of the ethical objections which have been raised against "the QALY", do not necessarily represent objections to the QALY *per se*. Assuming one accepts the economic principles upon which the approach is based, there is nothing unethical about QALYs.

The following chapter presents a discussion of broader ethical issues surrounding the QALY. Inevitably it will need to return to some of these more technical issues in the context of the broader principles.

4

Ethical criticisms

The purpose of this chapter is to review the major ethical criticisms that have been put against the use of QALYs in healthcare resource allocation[1], and in addition to raise a number of broader philosophical issues that relate to the construction and use of QALYs. The chapter is structured by appeal to two ethical defences. The more familiar is utilitarianism (and thus the argument that QALYs contribute to the efficient use of scarce healthcare resources). The less familiar argument is borrowed from Menzel, and interprets QALYs, and especially the processes of public consultation upon which they depend, in the context of a social contract. Neither defence will be found to be wholly satisfactory, although Menzel's arguments in particular will allow the development of a discourse ethics approach to the problems posed. In short, it will be suggested that the problems of healthcare allocation are not resolved simply by using scarce resources efficiently, nor in consulting the public, but rather in generating a continually unfolding public debate about healthcare.

TWO MORAL JUSTIFICATIONS FOR THE USE OF QALYS

Utilitarianism

QALYs are most typically defended on utilitarian grounds. Where classical utilitarianism, following Jeremy Bentham, seeks the greatest good for the greatest number, the use of QALY, and specifically cost per QALY calculations may be seen to facilitate the greatest health gain, given scarce resources, for the greatest number. Health gain is defined in terms of the net gain in Quality Adjusted Life Years. In so far as QALY values are derived from surveys, it may be held that QALY calculations reflect the aggregate subjective preferences of the population affected by the resultant healthcare allocation. Potential problems with classical utilitarianism, as to the source and legitimacy of the evaluation of consequences, are thereby avoided. As Williams notes, the QALY approach does not, of itself, dictate whose values should be represented in the QALY matrix, nor the weight that should be given to different groups' values (Williams, 1994). Further justification is provided by presenting a unit of health benefit (such as a Quality Adjusted Life Year) as

---

[1] The following list of criticisms is substantially derived from Crisp (1989).

being of equal value, no matter who gets it. This 'standard rule', as Williams calls it, 'has a very strong non-discriminatory egalitarian flavour, it is free of judgements about people's worth, or deserts, or influence, or likeability, or appearance, or smell, or manners, or age, sex, wealth, social class, religious beliefs, race, colour, temperament, sexual orientation, or general or particular life style' (Williams, 1988).

Contractarianism

A contractarian justification of the use of QALYs is provided by Menzel (1990). The burden of this argument lies not on the consequences of implementing cost per QALY calculations, but on the possibility of a QALY matrix reflecting a population's 'prior consent' to a specific allocation of healthcare resources. (QALYs are thus of interest to Menzel precisely insofar as they facilitate public consultation and the eliciting of public views about fair allocations of scarce healthcare resources.) QALY rankings presuppose that individuals may express a preference for a short life of good health to a longer life with some impairment of health. (The presence and precise nature of this preference is elicited through such techniques as time trade-off and standard gamble.) However, one cannot immediately deduce from this that an individual would willingly sacrifice his or her own long life of poor health for somebody else's short healthy life. However, because the QALY calculation is indifferent as to who gets the net QALY gain, consent to this form of trade-off is required if the cost per QALY calculation is to be acceptable. Menzel therefore suggests that a QALY questionnaire should, and indeed could, be so formulated as to make explicit the terms upon which members of a population are willing to gamble upon the availability of healthcare treatment. The 'QALY bargain' as Menzel calls it, 'would expose me to a greater risk of being allowed to die should I ever be an accident victim who could only survive with paraplegia, but in return I gain a better chance of being saved should I ever be a victim with prospectively normal health' (1990). In effect, by presupposing that the respondents are ignorant of their own future health requirements, the questionnaire would seek to establish the precise nature of the bargain into which respondents would be willing to enter.

PUBLIC CONSULTATION

Before embarking on a review of the ethical criticisms of QALYs, a key implication of Menzel's interpretation (and indeed, an important motivation of the general movement towards quality of life measurement) may be introduced. Menzel's emphasis on the use of QALYs to elicit the 'prior consent' highlights the association that quality of life measurement has with public consultation over healthcare policy. Quality of life measurement, and the associated construction of scales and matrices, focuses typically on two aspects of public concern: the way in which the concept of health is understood by a population; and the weighting of different health states (and both of these issues will be discussed further below, as will the question of who should be consulted). A more general question may be posed prior to such specific issues of quality of life measurement: should the public be consulted at all?

Many healthcare systems have expressed a need to involve the public and their representatives in their planning process. Perhaps the most famous, if not notorious, exercise in public consultation was that carried out in the State of Oregon, in the late 1980s, in order to prioritise the funding of medical treatments from Medicaid. The procedure used was significant insofar as attempts to elicit the core values of the community (through community and public meetings, and telephone surveys) were complemented by the use of a quality of life index (Kaplan's Quality of Well-Being Scale) in order to rank 709 'treatment-condition pairs' (i.e. a particular medical condition was linked to each possible treatment, so that a condition could appear more than once on the list, partnered by treatments that differed in terms of their expense and known efficacy). Once treatments were ranked, the total funds available to Medicaid would determine the cut-off point between treatments that would be funded, and those that would not (see Strosberg *et al*, 1992).

The Core Services Commission in New Zealand similarly sought to consult the lay population over the restructuring of the New Zealand Health Service. Part of the consultation process involved workshops with seven groups representing different sectors of the New Zealand population and those seeking healthcare. These groups were high school pupils, the elderly, the rural population, the low income urban population, people with disabilities, Maoris and Pacific Islanders. As part of the consultation process, the representatives were invited to participate in exercises to explore how they would deal with a range of rationing problems (from the division of a birthday cake to the allocation of scarce supplies amongst survivors in a lifeboat) (Campbell, 1995).

While public consultation may appear to be immediately desirable, not least as it would appear to be fundamental to the proper exercise of a democracy, a number of problems may be outlined. In a UK document called *Local Voices*, the NHS Management Executive states that the aim of public consultation 'should be to involve local people at appropriate stages throughout the purchasing cycle: a combination of information-giving, dialogue, consultation and participation in decision-making and feedback, rather than a one-off consultation exercise'. They note, pointedly, that 'developing a dialogue with local people is unlikely to be an easy or quick process' requiring 'perseverance, diplomacy and resources'.

The inclusion or exclusion of some individuals or groups can have significant effects on the content and tone of the opinions expressed, but also the moral legitimacy of the results of the consultation process. Independently of the question of the competence that any individual or group can bring to judging the relative severity of particular health states (an important issues for quality of life measures, and one to be addressed below), one may ask after the moral entitlement that any individual or group, considered merely in terms of their position in society, has in order to be involved in the consultation process. A variety of public groupings could be identified. The general public may have a claim to be consulted not merely as potential users of the service, but also as those who, through taxation and insurance, pay for the service. Rather than consulting the whole population (for example, through some form of survey), respected members of the community who act as opinion leaders (e.g. locally elected officials, primary care health professionals, teachers, local business owners) might be consulted. Conversely, it may be argued that the most relevant group to consult are the current users of the service and perhaps their kin. The work of the Core Services Commission in New Zealand was notable as it sought to identify groups that posed particular challenges to the healthcare system, for example because they might be expected to have cultural values that diverge from the dominant values of white New Zealanders, or because they have a low health status, are routinely excluded from the service, or make relatively high demands upon the service.

Furthermore, until recently public consultation has mainly consisted of questionnaire surveys and public meetings (Jones et al, 1987; Donovan et al, 1994). The public may therefore either not feel themselves to be competent to contribute to policy decision-making, or may lack necessary skills and a reliable knowledge-base. The response to questionnaires and public meetings has been poor. Those views that have been expressed have tended to come from lobby groups, and may not be representative of society as a whole. It may be that many people are apathetic, or do not have sufficient spare time to contribute to healthcare decision making. Of course, public bodies usually have a poor record on considering clients' views and the public may perceive that offering their opinions would be a waste of time because they are likely to be ignored. The general public may be satisfied with the service that they receive or are content to leave health service planning arrangements to the 'experts'. In a BMA/King's Fund survey only 22% of the general public in the UK thought that they should make prioritisation decisions. In comparison, 61% trusted hospital consultants to make prioritisations on their behalf, 49% suggested general practitioners and 25% said local health authority managers (Heginbotham, 1993).

There are additional dangers in allowing the public to make the final decision on which healthcare services should be purchased and at what level. In the past, public pressure may have affected resource allocation most clearly only in the context of specific emotive cases which have generated media publicity. Such publicity frequently involves children, and the intervention requested tends to be expensive and experimental with a low success rate. It may therefore be suggested that there is a tendency for public opinion to be swayed by 'shroud waving', i.e. the publication of emotionally disturbing cases, such as those involving young children, and by their own personal interests or those of their friends and relatives. Thus, for example, the acute sector of healthcare provision (usually provided within hospitals) has tended to be better funded than care for the elderly or the mentally ill (usually provided in the community or long-stay hospitals). This discrimination is partly due to the high profile, technology and glamour associated with acute services which are more likely to attract funding but is also caused by the threat of 'media blackmail' and 'shroud waving'. Donovan et al (1994) have therefore noted that public opinion is most readily incorporated into the decision-making process only where the decisions are uncontroversial. In controversial cases, and especially where unpalatable decisions need to be made, that might require choosing between the old and young, the deserving and the undeserving, or perhaps more concretely, the closure of a long-standing, much loved, but now expensive local hospital, then consulting public opinion may only reveal prejudices and preconceptions.

This leads to a most profound problem of political philosophy, which goes beyond the possibility that individuals hold mistaken or overly emotive opinions (see Lamb, 1989). One of the oldest questions of political philosophy, stretching back at least as far as Plato's disputes with the Sophists, asks whether the principles of justice (and morality) are universal, binding upon all societies and individuals whether recognised or not, or whether systems of justice and morality are relative to particular societies, and thus binding only upon those who recognise them as such? If the latter is held to be the case, then it is incoherent to criticise public opinion as prejudiced, even if, for example it appears to undervalue of the quality of life and importance of the severely disabled, or if it insists on the maintenance of an expensive and inefficient hospital, providing that it is genuinely representative of the dominant view within society.

A non-relativist account of justice and morality (such as that of Rawls' *Theory of Justice*, or most versions of human rights theory) may reply that, despite the fact that a view is dominant and prevalent in a particular society, action based upon that view (such as the lack of adequate provision of healthcare to the elderly or to non-acute sectors,) may be morally wrong. As Bowling has observed, in the context of public consultation by UK District Health Authorities, the first question to be addressed, is what is to be done if one disagrees with the results of the consultation (Bowling *et al*, 1993). A partial response to this question requires consideration of the nature of justice, and the procedures by which prejudiced and ill-informed opinions can, albeit imperfectly, be identified and eliminated from public debate and policy formation. This will be the task of the section below.

At present it is sufficient, on the one hand, to suggest the desirability, in principle, of public participation in healthcare resource allocation decisions (both as part of the democratic process and as a mechanism for legitimising and thereby gaining public support for difficult decisions), and on the other hand, to recognise the dangers that may be inherent in any unconsidered use of public participation.

QALYS PLACE INSUFFICIENT VALUE ON LIFE AND LIFESAVING

To turn to a series of moral criticisms made frequently and specifically of QALYs, the first may be that QALYs fail to give sufficient value to the role of life-saving in healthcare. This criticism responds to Williams' 'standard rule'. Because QALY gain is indifferent to the identity or number of people bearing those QALYs, a treatment that saves the life of one person for 10 good years would be preferred to six treatments (at the same total cost) that would save six people for one good year each.[2] This entails that six lives would be sacrificed for one life. Similarly, QALY

---

[2] To present the QALY application in this way simplifies the issues involved, but is potentially misleading, precisely because QALYs are not designed to decide between individual patients. An example may be imagined in which the decision rest upon the funding of the extension of two hospital units, one of which could save an additional 100 lives for an average of ten QALYs each, as opposed to the other saving an additional 600 lives for an average of one QALY each. It may further be noted that the complexities of discounting are also being omitted. Again, figures could be generated that make the same point and yet discount the later years of the long-term survivors.

calculations would suggest that it is preferable to improve the quality of life, say by 0.5 QALY per year, of a patient who is not terminally ill, than to save the life of a patient who, with treatment, could only enjoy a quality of life of 0.4 QALYs per year (assuming that they both would continue to live for similar periods after treatment). QALYs thereby appear to reverse the moral intuition that saving life is of greater importance than merely improving quality of life. (It may be noted that this criticism is not applicable only to QALYs. Any criterion for prioritisation that takes into account life expectancy will tend to prioritise the one person with a prospect of ten years of life over the six people with a year each. The QALY approach, by taking account of the quality of each year lived, is less culpable than other cruder approaches.)

The utilitarian may respond to this criticism by arguing that life *per se* is of little or no value. Life is of value only instrumentally, in so far as being alive is a precondition of the pursuit and fulfilment of other, intrinsically satisfying goals. Longer and more healthy lives open up more possibilities, and are thus of more value. The fundamental intuition that governs the QALY approach, that a short healthy life is preferable to a longer life with some impairment of health, presupposes this. (This is in stark contrast to a sanctity of life approach, which presupposes or seeks to justify the inherent and infinite value of all innocent human life. Crucially, because the value of human life is held to be incommensurable with any other value, length of life cannot be traded for quality of life. The QALY approach is thereby rendered untenable from this position (see Gormally, 1994).)

Harris provides the most pointed criticism of the QALY approach, not least because he shares the instrumental valuation of life, by arguing that 'it does not follow that where the choice is between three years of discomfort for *me* or immediate death on the one hand, and one year of health for *you*, or immediate death on the other, that I am somehow committed to the judgement that you ought to be saved rather than me.' Because, for Harris, 'the value of someone's life is, primarily and overwhelmingly, its value to him or her'; if someone wants to go on living, then a wrong is done to them by failing to save their life, regardless of the number of QALYs generated elsewhere (Harris, 1987). The utilitarian and Harris thereby appeal to different ethical principles, and mediation between them appears to be difficult, if not impossible (see Williams 1987). Menzel's approach, however, directly answers Harris, precisely in so far as his 'QALY bargain' makes explicit the trade-off between one's own long life of poor health and someone else's short healthy life. Menzel does acknowledge that it must also be possible for the respondents to reject the QALY bargain altogether (1990). This is to accept the possibilities, either that the fundamental intuition governing the QALY approach may not be widely held in the population, or that the extrapolation from an intuition about one's own life, to the bargain between one's own life and an other's life, is not made. (These possibilities raise further questions, to be addressed later, with respect to the discrepancy between economists' expectations of human behaviour and moral judgements, and actual behaviour and judgement.)

QALYS ARE AGEIST

Because younger people typically have a longer life expectancy, treatment of them will generate more QALYs than a similar treatment administered to older people. QALYs are therefore argued to entail a systematic bias against the elderly. Similarly, it may be argued that if a particular gender, cultural or ethnic group was demonstrated, statistically, to have a worse prognosis in QALY terms after treatment for a particular condition, then that group would again be systematically discriminated against. A better prognosis would lead to a discrimination in favour of that group, but in consequence against all others (Harris, 1987).

The accusation of ageism has been challenged by appealing to the 'fair innings' argument. This would hold that discrimination against the elderly in the allocation of healthcare is not intrinsically unjust, because the elderly have already had a 'fair innings'. The moral priority is therefore to do as much as possible to enable the young to enjoy a similar advantage (Lockwood, 1988). One approach to countering this argument attempts to extend the QALY calculation to an apparent absurdity. This argument would hold that, while it may be acceptable, given the 'fair innings' argument, to allow the prioritisation of a 20-year-old over an 80-year-old, it would in principle follow that one should prioritise a 35-year-old over a 36-year-old. The reduction to absurdity does not, however, work, because it rests upon a confusion over the use of QALYs. Because QALYs are not designed to prioritise individual patients, but rather the funding of treatments, the suggestion of prioritising a 35 year old over a 36 year old could only occur if there were at least two treatments, one of which was appropriate only for those up to 36 year of age and the other of which was appropriate only for those of 36 years and over. It seems highly unlikely that any such treatment could ever exist.

The 'fair innings' argument is not obviously of use as a defence against the potential racism or sexism of QALYs. Further, because treatments that are appropriate for only males or only females are numerous, the charge of sexism at least has real import for the use of QALYs. Here an alternative line of reasoning may be employed. It may be noted that 'ageism' entails discrimination purely on the grounds of age, just as sexism is discrimination purely on the grounds of sex. The apparent discrimination in QALYs against the elderly, against a gender or other group, does not occur because of the group members' age, gender, or ethnicity, but because of their short life expectancy or prognosis of a low quality of life (Crisp, 1989). If treatment A was typically used on white women in their 30s, and treatment B was typically used on black men in their 70s, and both treatments gave an average patient an extra 5 QALYs, then given no cost differential, the QALY approach could not discriminate between the treatments. (It may still be argued that a QALY approach would ultimately allocate fewer funds to, say, geriatric services than public opinion would support. While Menzel's contractarian approach makes much of the role of public opinion, such examples raise questions as to the degree of subtlety with which this is opinion can be reflected. This issue will be returned to below.)

THE DOUBLE JEOPARDY ARGUMENT

Illness or injury may leave the patient, even after treatment, with the prospect of a poor quality of life. This is a personal misfortune. The QALY approach imposes a further dose of bad luck by allocating the treatment that could have benefited the patient (albeit to a small extent) to someone else. (Again, it might be argued that the QALY approach is not used to choose between individuals, such as two accident victims. It may, however, influence the allocation of resources to such specialities as heart or liver transplantation, that may not yield many QALYs per patient treated. The bad luck of liver failure may thus appear to be compounded by the non-availability of a liver transplant service.)

The QALY approach may readily acknowledge the tragedy of leaving someone to die (and especially someone who, in Harris's words, wants to go on living fervently (Harris, 1987)). However, given scarce resources, alternative methods of allocation appear to have a greater degree of unacceptability. As formulated above, the criticism implies that healthcare should be allocated in order to compensate for people's bad luck with respect to their health. (It may plausibly be suggested that one purpose behind a national health service is to reassure healthy people that help exists should they fall victim to ill-health in general, or to specific and particularly feared forms of ill-health.) Rigorous application of such a principle would lead to counter-intuitive results. Large quantities of scarce healthcare resources would be drawn, not merely into the saving of the lives of those with poor prognoses, but also into the continued support of those subsequently surviving in poor health. Again, it may be suggested, as was the case for disagreements over the prioritising of life saving, that different and incommensurable fundamental ethical principles lead to the support of different approaches. Menzel's QALY bargain, precisely insofar as it makes this double jeopardy explicit, may serve to mediate between the two approaches.

An alternative to a principle of compensation may lie in a lottery approach. Here prioritisation would still occur, but without one human being appearing to stand in judgement over (the worth of) the life of another (Harris, 1988). Williams replies to this suggestion by noting that such lotteries 'do not fall like manna from heaven, but have to be devised and run by people who have to determine who shall be eligible, when, and under what conditions, for each and every treatment that is on offer' (Williams, 1994). The necessity of judging the worth of others' lives cannot therefore be avoided, for criteria have to be set for eligibility to enter the lottery and for any particular entrant's probability of 'winning'.

THE 'NEEDS' ARGUMENT

It has been argued that allocations of healthcare resources according to QALY criteria are mistaken, insofar as QALYs fail to recognise that resources should be distributed according to need (see Williams, 1988; Frankel, 1991). The claim that healthcare should be given to patients according to their clinical determined needs is attractive, precisely because it has the superficial appearance of resolving complex moral dilemmas of allocation, through appeal to an objective and quantifiable phenomenon.

Rigorous and subtle philosophies of need have been developed, with specific reference to healthcare, by Daniels (1980), Doyal and Gough (1984), and Ramsay (1992) amongst others. At the core of all these accounts is a definition of 'need' as a resource that is required, instrumentally, as a precondition to any other human action. Deficiency with respect to a need 'endangers the normal functioning of the subject of need considered as a member of a natural species' (Braybrooke, 1968). Developing upon an account of justice that is indebted to the work of John Rawls, Daniels holds that society is responsible for guaranteeing the individual a fair share of basic liberties and opportunity. Given that the satisfaction of health needs is a precondition of all other purposes that an individual could pursue, and that variations in health amongst individuals are morally arbitrary (which is to say that they are not typically deserved, as for example variations in income or wealth might be), Daniels argues that social provision for the satisfaction of healthcare needs is a necessary condition for ensuring fair equality of opportunity, and thus justice, within a society (1980).

From an economist's perspective, Williams dismisses the appeal to needs as a 'red herring'. He reduces the philosophy of need to the proposition that 'someone would be better off *with* the 'needed' treatment than *without* it. This leaves open the issue of whose values determine whether (and to what extent) that person *will* be better off, and... how one person's "needs" (i.e. potential benefits) are to be weighted against another's' (Williams, 1988). Two important points are being made here. First, Williams is challenging the assumption that needs claims are inherently objective (and as such to be distinguished from less morally pressing subjective claims, such as desires, wants, wishes or demands). To suggest that there is an issue as to whose values should determine the respective weighting of two competing needs claims, is to suggest that even needs claims entail some element of subjective evaluation (so that the complexities of moral decision making are not avoided after all). Second, Williams ultimately reduces needs to the ability of the patient to benefit from treatment. Given scarce healthcare resources, it is not possible for all healthcare needs to be satisfied immediately, as was shown in Chapter 1. Competing needs claims will therefore have to be prioritised. For Williams, the ultimate criterion of priority of needs will be the patients' respective ability to benefit (for example in terms of QALY gain) from the available medical resources. While significant in linking need to the ability to benefit (and thus to healthcare outcomes), these criticisms may fail to engage fully with the philosophy of need.

With respect to the question of the objectivity of needs claims, Wiggins notes that a needs claim rests upon the way the world is, and not upon the workings of the claimant's mind (Wiggins, 1991). Thus, for example, a hypochondriac may hold the subjective opinion that she needs a specific medical treatment. While she may need some form of psychiatric treatment, she does not, on the best medical opinion, need the treatment she desires. An adequate philosophy of need responds to this problem in two ways. On the one hand, the philosophy of need must be complemented by an epistemology (i.e on account of how knowledge is acquired and tested). The philosophy of science will provide criteria of 'objective' knowledge in medical science (and thus of the currently most acceptable model of the normal functioning of the human species (see Ramsay, 1992)), and will explain the limits of that knowledge. Crucially, as science develops, the medical needs of particular patient groups, or the population as a whole, will be reassessed and modified. At any given moment, objectivity lies with the body of knowledge that is most widely accepted (after due critical scrutiny) within the community of scientists. There will, however, always be dissenting voices. Scientific consensus is rarely complete, precisely because knowledge of the world is rarely straightforward. On the other hand, it must be recognised that the issue of normal human functioning cannot be resolved purely by appeal to natural science, precisely because humans are cultural creatures capable of redefining their 'nature'. This is, in part, to suggest that the medical needs of human beings go beyond the physiological. A healthy human being is a creature that can carry out complex social and cultural functions. (This definition of health will be discussed further below.) Needs will change over time, as cultures, technologies and lifestyles develop. In addition, at any given time, different individuals and groups have particular needs, that are distinct from the needs of the dominant population.

In the light of these observations, the suggestion that needs are 'objective' in any unproblematic sense must be reconsidered. The objectivity of needs cannot lie in their immediate, empirical identification. Objective, perhaps, rather lies in the common or widespread acknowledgement of the legitimacy of a needs claim. This recognition will in turn presuppose a sensitivity to cultural diversity and change, as well as a critical understanding of current scientific research. (One might, for example, consider whether or not infertile couples, in requesting IVF treatment, are expressing a need, rather than a desire, for children. In this debate, much depends upon one's understanding of the role of children in ordinary family and personal life in contemporary societies.) Scope must therefore be provided for the democratic negotiation of needs claims (see Doyal and Gough, 1984). As Wiggins asserts, a needs claim is not the end of a moral argument (as if it resolved all moral problems with the trump card of objectivity), but precisely in so far as it entails a challenge to imagine a realistic scenario in which the claimant is denied satisfaction of the need but does not suffer (or a scenario in which the claim is granted but only at the expense of greater suffering elsewhere), it is part of a continuing process of open debate (Wiggins, 1991).

In addition, in discussing the adjudication of competing needs claims, while a needs deficiency may be briefly defined as something that will endanger the normal functioning of the human being, this does not serve to specify the degree of that danger. Wiggins thereby provides criteria for prioritising needs claims in terms of what he calls their gravity, urgency, entrenchment and substitutability. Gravity is assessed in terms of the amount of harm that will be done if the needy person does not have a needs claim met (and as such suggests Williams' association of need with ability to benefit). However, urgency (assessed in terms of the time that can elapse before harm is suffered), entrenchment (by which one is invited to think of a realistic future in which the needy person is deprived of treatment without being harmed), and substitutability (asking if there are alternatives to a particular treatment or any treatment at all), open up further dimensions for debate and negotiation.

It may, in summary, be suggested that QALY approaches and needs approaches are not competitors in resource allocation, but complements. The emphasis that a philosophy of need places upon the normal (biological and social) functioning of a human being, and thus upon health as a precondition of normal life, may provide material for determining those parameters of health that are most relevant to the delineation of quality of life. Conversely, as Williams suggests, QALYs may serve as effective instruments to measure the degree of gravity of needs claims, and thus to begin to resolve disputes between two or more claimants over a limited resource.

THE PROBLEM OF MAXIMISATION

It has been argued by Crisp that a QALY approach presupposes that QALYs should be maximised, and that this leads to 'repugnant conclusions' (Crisp, 1989; Crisp, 1994). First, the aggregation of fractions of QALYs over time entails that 'sixty years of life of a very low quality (0.2) are better than fifteen years of high quality (0.75)' (Crisp 1994). At one extreme this implies that an extremely long life as an oyster is preferable to an extremely short life as a human being (with full faculties). This conclusion can be avoided if it is suggested that a discontinuity can be established between the very low quality life and the higher quality life. No amount of years spent at the lower level would be allowed to outweigh life at the higher level.

Strictly, in so far as this example rests upon a choice between two individuals, it is not an appropriate test of QALYs. A more suitable choice would be between the provision of additional funds to a treatment that kept patients alive (for an average of 60 years each) at the low quality, and additional funds to a treatment that gives patients an average of five extra years of relatively good health. Here the discontinuity between the two possibilities leads to a second, and for Crisp, unhappy, conclusion: 'Other things being equal... we should remove all but very basic funding for the severely mentally defective, and use it to decrease risks of death for non-defective people' (Crisp 1994). Even minor improvements to the health of those with a relatively good quality of life (including the removal of minimal risks of death and ill-health) would be funded in preference to treatment of those whose quality of life falls chronically below the point of discontinuity.

In reply to this criticism, two points may be made. Firstly, the grounds upon which a point of discontinuity is established may be examined. Crisp, developing from Griffin, suggests that the value of a life cannot be understood in terms of an aggregation of (the quality of) its individual moments. Rather, a 'global view' must be taken, covering the life as a whole. As such, the life of very low quality could never give rise to the same achievements and satisfactions that even a short, high quality life could provide (Crisp 1994, Griffin, 1986). Similarly, Brock appeals to the ability of a person to develop a life plan, and thus to live a meaningful life, or a 'biographical' rather than merely a 'biological' life (Brock, 1993). Such reflections inevitably raise questions as to the relationship between health-related quality of life and more comprehensive conceptions of the quality of human life. Superficially at least, QALYs do not appear to be designed to make the sort of discriminations required in order to decide the point of discontinuity between biographical and merely biological life.

The second point suggests a partial solution to this problem. Crisp's analysis may be criticised in terms of the leap that it makes in the first (repugnant) conclusion, where it deals purely with QALY scores, and the second (unhappy) conclusion, where the condition of those in the poor quality of life is substantively described. Independently of a survey-based QALY matrix, however, one cannot readily assume the condition reflected by any given score. Prior to any interview, the Rosser-Kind matrix presupposed substantive descriptions for only two conditions, corresponding to '1' and '0'. It is, perhaps, '0' that is most significant in the present context, for it provides an inherent point of discontinuity within the QALY scale. If '0' represents a state that is equivalent to death, then it may be suggested that any condition that is judged to be permanently at or below '0', is not worthy of treatment. (No amount of time spent in this condition can ever lead to a positive quality of life, and thus QALY maximisation entails that life-preserving resources should be removed from those condemned to live in any such condition.) It may be suggested that any such implication should be made explicit as part of the 'QALY bargain'. If the public holds that it can be in the interests of certain severely and chronically ill patients not to go on living, then the ascription of '0' or low scores to substantively described health states will reflect this belief. The absence of any such ascriptions in a public survey would indicate the rejection any point of discontinuity, and thus the acceptance of Crisp's first conclusion as acceptable rather than as repugnant.

THE PROBLEM OF WHO TO ASK

It has been argued that because QALYs tend to be grounded in surveys of public opinion, they are open to the danger that they reflect individuals' or groups' mistaken perceptions of what is in their own interests, or prejudiced and ill-informed opinions about the quality of life enjoyed by other groups. QALYs typically avoid making allocation decisions upon the basis of specific characteristics of the patients or their diseases (so cannot record explicit biases for or against genders, ethnic or cultural groups, or for or against certain diseases or diseases with certain causes). However, the descriptions of health states and of the parameters of health used in quality of life instruments contain a good deal of substantial information about the health state, if not about its cause or about the person suffering in it. This description may be enough to spark prejudiced or otherwise ill-informed judges of the worth of life lived in that condition. To take Menzel's example, a response to the condition of paraplegia requires a leap of the imagination that may be guided as much by stereotypes and misinformation as by any profound contact with people with paraplegia. It may therefore be suggested that those who have not experienced a particular condition cannot accurately predict the impact that the condition will have upon their quality of life, and that other factors, such as the stigma suffered by those with physical disabilities, may influence assessments.

Williams may be seen to deal with this problem, in part, by noting that the QALY approach does not dictate who should be consulted in the development of a matrix (or the weighting of items within a profile). If it was held that only patients could provide accurate evaluations, then only patients need be consulted. (The calculation of index numbers as median averages rather than means would also serve to exclude extreme and unrepresentative evaluations.) Williams expresses his personal preference for a populist approach, and thus for consulting all the people (Williams, 1994). It may be added that such populism is more coherent with an original presupposition of many QALY and QALY-type indexes and profiles: to allow the voices of patients and the public to be heard against that of the medical expert (see Hunt et al, 1986). To exclude the voice of certain sections of the public is to impose anew a paternalism that QALYs initially sought to challenge. Menzel's contractarian approach is equally explicit in consulting all (or at least a representative sample of all) people within the society. The QALY bargain requires that the respondent is able to anticipate living both a short life with mild disability and a long life with severe disability after an accident, and as such respondents to the bargain cannot be restricted to those who have experienced one or other (let alone both) of the prospects.

These approaches still tend to beg the question of whether or not people are capable of accurately anticipating the effect that illness might have upon them. As a matter of personal biography, and thus of the way in which illness impacts upon one's life-plans and prospects, this will be discussed in detail in the section below. As a matter of judging the impact that illness has on other people, or upon some useful if mythical average person, it may be noted that both the utilitarian and the contractarian approaches presuppose that the individuals consulted in weighting exercises have pre-given opinions about the severity and impact of health states on normal functioning. At worst, it is assumed that the respondents need only exercise their imaginations in order to clarify or finalise their judgements. Such an approach ignores the inherently social nature of human existence. A healthy individual will not come to understand or empathise with the position of a person with sickness or disability simply by imagining what it is to be like in that position. Rather, understanding and empathy will depend upon the direct and indirect contact that the person has had with that condition.

In general, it may be suggested that the more intimate the experience of the condition, the more accurate the healthy person's judgement of its value will be. From this, it may follow that in order to elicit accurate QALY weightings, it is inappropriate to question individuals in isolation, for the resultant responses will be tainted by the stereotypical and simplified presentations of illness and disability current in the respondents' culture. An alternative may be for weightings to be elicited from mixed groups of people, bringing together diverse experience of health, illness and disability. Any individual within such a group would be asked not simply to express his or her evaluation of a series of health states, but to justify and if necessary modify these judgements in the face of the experience and criticisms of others.

JUSTICE

The six criticisms of the QALY approach given above may all be construed as the accusation that QALYs are inherently unjust. A precise and generally agreed definition of the concept of 'justice' is, however, elusive. Gillon, in discussing justice as one of the four principles of medical ethics, summarises it as: 'the moral obligation to act on the basis of fair adjudication between competing claims' (Gillon, 1994). From this broad definition, the claims of the first three criticisms and the fifth may respectively be summarised as: QALYs fail to adjudicate according to the morally relevant fact that individuals may fervently want to go on living; QALYs adjudicate according to the morally irrelevant characteristics of age, sex, and ethnicity; QALYs adjudicate according to the morally irrelevant fact of a patient's (poor) prognosis; QALYs adjudicate according to the morally irrelevant fact of a patient's chronic low quality of life. While these criticisms assert that QALYs are unjust, they entail no single alternative account of justice that could be used to allocate healthcare resources. (These criticisms may be integrated through reference to the violation of patients' rights, either to healthcare, or to entry into a lottery. Diverse theoretical grounds could, however, be given to such rights claims, with diverse implications for health policy and the proposed alternatives to QALY-based allocation.) In contrast, the fourth criticism pits an explicit theory of justice, that of allocation according to need, against the QALY approach. (Here a 'right' to healthcare can be explicitly based on the public and professional recognition of a 'need', and, for Daniels, in the relationship between health and fair equality of opportunity.) The sixth criticism demands an explicit theory of justice, but in terms of the procedures by which allocation decisions are arrived at, rather than the rights (or morally relevant characteristics) of the recipients of care.

Two forms of reply to the six criticisms have been proposed. Both can be explained in terms of the claim that QALY-based approaches are just. The two forms of reply appeal to distinct theories of justice. A pure utilitarian theory of justice presupposes that 'the sole ground for allocation of goods... is the maximal promotion of the utility of the members of society, so that "each is to count for one and no one for more than one"' (Elster, 1992). The justice of such a position therefore rests both upon the moral intuition that the efficient use of scarce resources is desirable, and that the preferences or satisfactions of no individual can override those of the group as a whole. Notably QALY matrices, by being non-disease specific, prevent the respondent from allocating resources according to what may be morally irrelevant characteristics, such as the disease suffered (e.g. AIDS), or the cause of that disease (e.g. smoking). Williams' replies to his critics have been seen to focus upon the squandering of resources that would occur if alternative principles of allocation were adopted. The rights arguments that criticise this approach typically point to the possibility of maximal utility being achieved only at the cost of minimising the utility enjoyed by the individual (or minority group).

Contractarianism, in Scanlon's formulation, presupposes that an 'act is wrong if its performance under the circumstances would be disallowed by any system of rules for the general regulation of behaviour which no one could reasonable reject as a basis for informed, unforced general agreement' (Scanlon, 1982). Thus, Menzel's defence of the QALY has been seen to rest upon its potential for eliciting unforced general agreement. As such, greater emphasis is placed upon the procedures by which any method of allocation is established. Maximal efficiency is not necessarily assumed to be the overriding ethical principle (although, as Scanlon concedes, there is no *prima facie* reason why utilitarian principles should not emerge from contractual agreement). Contractarianism was seen in general to provide a more effective reply to the six criticisms, because it formulated the allocation problem in explicitly moral terms. By presupposing that maximal efficiency is morally desirable, the utilitarian approach jumps from the eliciting of individual evaluations of health states, to resource allocation. Menzel is more careful in describing the problematic nature of the link between evaluations and allocation, and thereby allows an opportunity for the QALY-based allocation to be modified in favour of other, communally held values, or even for the QALY bargain to be rejected altogether.

Menzel's account of the QALY bargain still falls short of Scanlon's formulation of contractarianism. Scanlon calls for 'informed, unforced general agreement', and thus for the rational negotiation and justification of the regulations governing healthcare allocation. Menzel, by focusing on existing QALY survey techniques, seems content with the eliciting of the pre-existing opinions of isolated individuals. For Menzel it appears that agreement is unnecessary, beyond the acceptance of majority opinion. While it may be argued that such sampling elicits the results of current, informal debates on healthcare resource allocation, this cannot readily be presupposed. Menzel is thus left in danger of falling prey to the same accusations of injustice as hamper simple utilitarianism, by allowing the majority to suppress minority views. Scanlon's contractarianism explicitly gives each individual, not merely a vote, but a rational voice in the formulation of regulations, whereby minority preferences, interests or needs cannot simply be overridden by the majority.

In effect, while Menzel's contractarianism treats those who subscribe to the contract as isolated individuals, each of whom brings a pre-formed set of preferences to the contract, Scanlon's approach allows a move forward into what has come to be known as discourse ethics (Edgar, 1997). Here, individuals are not treated as isolated persons, but rather as cultural beings who form and crucially reform their opinions through discussion with and experience of other persons. As the discussion of needs, above, may have begun to suggest, justice lies in the institutionalisation of procedures that allow all of a society's members to enter into discussion, putting forward their views, criticising the views of others, and being given reasoned replies to those criticisms. No individual then has a *prima facie* right to have his or her views adopted by the collective, but he or she will have the right to expect those views to be considered and respected.

This more demanding formulation of procedural justice allows some comment to be made on two remaining problems in the above account and defence of QALY-based approaches. Firstly, it was noted that the fundamental values that underpin QALYs can be, apparently, incommensurable with other value systems. (The tension between the instrumental evaluation of life that justifies QALYs, and the sanctity of life doctrine was noted.) Precisely because it invites rational debate of and comparison between such value systems, even if the debate is unable to overcome actual incommensurability, discourse ethics prevents the overriding of a value system merely because it is a minority position, or (worse) because maximal utility is assumed to be the most acceptable moral principle. An incommensurable value system presents a continuing challenge to the dominant system of resource allocation, requiring it to defend itself and thus to reflect critically upon its own foundations. Secondly, concern was expressed that appeal to public opinion as the ultimate arbiter of resource allocation might lead to allocations, or rules of allocation, that would be unacceptable on certain universal accounts of ethics and moral reasoning. The non-disease specific nature of QALY matrices does not rule out the possibility that the parameters by which health and disease are defined leave scope for prejudices and stigma against disability or disease in general to be recorded. Scanlon's formula of 'informed, unforced general agreement' suggests that any views that are grounded in prejudice (e.g. against the disabled), and thus which appeal to morally irrelevant criteria of allocation, would be eliminated from the debate.

HEALTH

Two remaining philosophical issues may be addressed in order to conclude the ethical consideration of quality of life measurement and application. These issues concern the definition of 'health' that is most appropriate to health-related quality of life measurement, and the understanding of personhood and personal identity (and in consequence, human nature) that may strongly influence quality of life measurement.

There is no single agreed definition of 'health'. Four concepts or theories of 'health' that have wide currency will be reviewed: the bio-medical theory; the sociological theory; the ideal state theory; and the humanist theory. The inherent viability and scope of each theory will be considered, as well as its relevance to the conceptualisation and measurement of quality of life.

The bio-medical model of health and illness is typically articulated in terms of the normal functioning of a member of the species. Given an understanding of the normal functioning of the species, disease (including infectious syndromes, deformities, injuries and genetic defects, be these symptomatic or asymptomatic) may be defined as 'a state of an individual which interferes with (or prevents) the normal functioning of some organ or system of organs of the bearer of the state' (Boorse, 1976). Health is thereby defined negatively, as the absence of disease. For Boorse, the definition of 'disease' is complemented by one of 'illness' as the felt experience of disease. A person is thus ill 'if and only if the person has a disease which is serious enough to be incapacitating, and therefore is

i   undesirable to its bearer,
ii   a title to special treatment and
iii a valid excuse for normally criticisable behaviour' (Boorse, 1975).

As Nordenfelt has demonstrated, a series of conceptual problems occur in the definition of normal functioning, culminating in the ultimate circularity of the definition of 'disease' (i.e. the definition of 'disease' turns out to be no more than 'disease' means 'disease') (Nordenfelt, 1993). Thus, normal functioning cannot be defined in purely biological terms. What is normal for an individual within a species will vary according be certain parameters. Such parameters include age and sex, but more problematically also environment and activity. Physiological functions of human beings will vary according to the society (and thus environment) within which they live. Similarly, the individual's activity will influence physiological functions. Thus, the normal pulse rate of an athlete after a race is different to that of a non-athlete at rest. This entails that there are an enormous number of conditions that must be documented before 'normal functioning' could be adequately defined. (Bernard takes this problem further, by suggesting that there is an inevitable discrepancy between statistically based normal functions and the functioning of the individual. He observes that 'no two patients are ever exactly alike; their age, sex, temperament and any number of other circumstances involve differences, with the result that the average, or the relation deduced from our comparison of facts, may always be contested' (Bernard, 1927).) Nordenfelt points to the ultimate circularity inherent in the definition of health as normal functioning, by observing that the diverse conditions in which an individual may function normally may be expanded to include, for example, viral infections and physical traumas. One may then specify the normal functioning of a member of the species when ill. Yet these conditions (of illness or injury) cannot be separated from other conditions or environments according the criterion of normal functioning. Hence the circularity: the definition only appears to be informative because it presupposes an existing understanding of what 'health' and 'illness' mean. Models of health that try to avoid this problem do so, in part, by criticising the negative definition of 'health' that is assumed by the bio-medical model, and so by generating a positive definition of 'health', that is independent of the definition of 'disease'.

While the concept of 'health' was not initially well defined in Rosser and Kind's original QALY matrix, the authors may be seen to attempt to move away from the biomedical definition of health and disease, precisely by focusing upon the 'subjective' dimension of distress, as well as upon the 'objective' dimension of 'disability'. (Indeed, the rejection of the adequacy and exhaustiveness of a purely bio-medical model is a pre-requisite of quality of life measurement.) It may be suggested that the scores of each cell within the QALY matrix attempt to capture something akin to the experience of 'illness', as defined by Boorse. Yet 'health' and 'disease' within the Rosser/Kind matrix are ultimately only negatively defined. Crucially, the matrix is concerned with divergence from a state of 'no disability' and 'no distress'. Quality of life measures that have been developed since the Rosser/Kind matrix have explored increasingly diverse and subtle conditions of health and disease. This suggests that a positive definition of health and disease is required, precisely insofar as such a definition serves to articulate what dimensions are relevant to the measurement of health- related quality of life.

A sociological model focuses upon the social and cultural environment of health and disease. Health and disease are typically understood in terms of the individual's competence, or otherwise, to function as a social agent. Some degree of physical (and mental) health is a pre-requisite of the agent's ability to function in domestic and family life as well as in work and in a public setting. More precisely, the actions of an agent who is unwell will deviate from the socially accepted norms. The 'sick role' (in Talcott Parsons' theory) thereby becomes a form of positively sanctioned deviance. Once an agent is accepted as being 'sick', he or she may legitimately withdraw from his or her normal obligations to society, and is not held to be responsible for the condition (albeit that there will be an obligation upon the sick to seek competent medical help). This model may be seen to focus upon what Boorse terms illness. Insofar as each culture will have different expectations of normal agency, what is actually acknowledged as disease will vary from one culture to another. Further, it may be suggested that what counts as disease may vary from one social role to another.

The Parsonian model of sick roles is explicitly a functionalist model (in that it is concerned with the normal functioning of the social agent), and so raises the question of whether or not Nordenfelt's criticism of the circularity of the bio-medical model is applicable. Crucially, normal functioning is defined in terms of the expectations of the agent's ambient culture (and thus the roles and tasks for which the agent has been socialised). The agent is thus healthy as long as he or she continues to function, or to act, as others expect, and as he or she expects of him or herself. The distinction between health and illness thus rests upon the prior definition of normality and deviance. More subtle approaches within the sociological tradition would, however, recognise that the boundary between normality and deviance (and thus between health and illness) is typically contested. (Parsons too readily accepts the authority of benevolent medical expertise, and that a society will be unified by the general acceptance of a single, all-encompassing set of cultural norms.) The classification of a particular pattern of behaviour as disease (as opposed to laziness, malingering, criminality, sinfulness and so on) may more adequately be understood as the result of a struggle between sufferers, medical professionals, scientists, employers, trade unions, the legal system and the state (see for example Turner, 1989 on Repetitive Strain Injury). In summary, the sociological model holds that disease is socially constructed. No biological phenomenon is self-evidently a disease (or injury), but must be interpreted as such, drawing upon the (scientific, technical and political) resources of the culture, and responding to the obligations placed upon agents within that culture.

Sociological reflections upon the nature of health and disease are of relevance to quality of life measurement insofar as they serve to clarify relevant dimensions of health, and to explore, not merely the cultural divergence in disease, but also the cultural divergence in the experience of similar diseases. Those quality of life measures that do not merely establish the weighting of health states through surveys of sample populations, but further derive the descriptions of health states from descriptions elicited from those populations, incorporate much of the sociological model. Divergences in the weightings of items within quality of life measures (such as the Nottingham Health Profile) between countries may, thus, in part, be understood in terms of the different demands placed upon agents carrying out mundane activities in those cultures.

Problems do remain with the sociological model, and with its applicability to quality of life measurement. First, as noted above, the older versions of the sociological model (associated with Parsons) presuppose that there is a dominant culture within society. This is to suggest that there is a predominant understanding of health, and similarly predominant evaluations of health states. Menzel's contractualist defence of the QALY bargain makes a similar assumption, expressed in the notion of 'prior consent'. Later versions of the sociological model question this. While an anti-paternalistic ethos is presupposed by much research into quality of life measures, (because such measures serve to challenge the authority of the medical profession's (bio-medical) definition of health and healthcare priorities), it remains as yet unclear how the diversity of understandings and evaluations within a single society is to be adequately expressed and represented in a quality of life measure.

Second, and to make a parallel but opposite point, both older and more recent versions of the sociological model may legitimate an extreme form of cultural relativism. The health or illness of an individual may be presented as being wholly dependent upon the particular society within which he or she has been socialised, or in which he or she lives and works. The problem for quality of life measurement lies less in the interpretation of a particular physical (or mental) condition as disease, but rather in the evaluation of that condition. To follow up the final point made earlier, it was suggested that quality of life measures may encode the prejudices inherent in a culture against certain disease states (including severe disability). An understanding of sickness as legitimate deviance is revealed as being too limited in the light of this problem. While adoption of the sick role may exempt the agent from certain social obligations, this exemption may not be without a cost, in terms of the stigma associated with the disease or disability. The encoding of such stigma into a quality of life index may compound the cost, by directing scarce healthcare resources away from persons in such stigmatised states. The sociological models, as discussed above, appear to offer no scope for challenging such evaluations. Again, it may be suggested that the problem lies in an ultimately negative definition of 'health'. While the sociological model may be capable of giving greater substance to the concept of 'health' than can the bio-medical model (and crucially may do this without circularity), 'health' remains subordinate to the prior definition of 'disease'.

The World Health Organisation's definition of health as 'a state of complete physical, mental and social well-being and not merely the absence of disease and infirmity' is the most frequently cited and widely supported version of an ideal state theory of health. While the definition does recognise that health may be understood as more than the mere absence of disease or injury, and that health encompasses more than just physical well-being, key concepts within the definition are left vague. It is thus unclear how 'complete' well-being is to be understood, and how disputes over the precise nature of 'physical', 'mental' and 'social' parameters are to be resolved. This imprecision ultimately makes the definition inappropriate for quality of life measurement.

A humanist model of health can be summarised by seeing health as 'an ability to adapt positively to the problems of life' (Seedhouse, 1986). Health is thereby understood in terms of the capacity of the individual to pursue self-chosen (or at least voluntarily accepted) goals, and to overcome barriers to the achievement of those goals. In contrast to the bio-medical model, health is not understood in terms of the normal functioning of a typical member of a species (nor even a typical member under specific circumstances). Rather, emphasis is placed upon the individual's grasp of his or her own life, environment, and resources. As such, health and disease are not simply defined in opposition to each other. A person may have a physical (or mental) disease, injury or disability, and yet still be understood as healthy. Something of this superficially paradoxical position is expressed by Canguilhem's observation that: 'To be in good health means being able to fall sick and recover; it is a biological luxury' (Canguilhem, 1978) To be healthy is thus to have the capacity, resources and will to respond positively to challenges, and to changes in one's self and one's environment.

The humanist may suggest that disease and injury are themselves to be understood as amongst the problems and challenges confronted in mundane activity. The individual does not thereby stand passively before his or her illness, but rather engages with it, and incorporates it, more or less well, into his or her pursuit of other goals. In consequence, the physical and mental requirements for being healthy do not merely vary from one individual to the next, so that it might be said of two individuals with the same physical injury or disease that one is healthy and the other not, but rather the difference between health and illness may rest upon the individual's attitude to his or her disease or disability. The person who, after injury, is confined to a wheelchair, and who yet continues to lead a fulfilled and purposive life, by modifying goals or by adopting new goals appropriate to his or her physical condition, is not, according to the humanist definition, unhealthy. The person confined to a wheelchair who sees this as an insuperable obstacle to any further development is unhealthy. Similarly, a person without any biomedical abnormality may still be unhealthy, if he or she is failing to exploit the capacities he or she has, by setting too limited or minimal goals. A person with unrealistically high goals, and who is distressed by his or her inability to realise goals that go beyond his or her physical or mental capacity, is again to be understood as unhealthy. Crucially, such a model should not be taken to place the full burden of health and illness upon the attitude of the individual. Environmental factors, including the availability of effective medical help, advice and counselling, and a built environment that does not further frustrate the person's use of his or her capacities, will significantly affect the degree to which he or she can be healthy.

The humanist model, on the preceding account, presupposes a very strong normative model of human nature. At the core of this is an Aristotelian view of humans as purposive creature, such that the failure to pursue more or less challenging goals entails forsaking one's true human nature. This model is fundamental to the dominant forms of Western liberalism. While this account of human nature emphasises the importance of personal autonomy (and thus a value that has already been suggested as fundamental to the ethos of quality of life research (in Chapter 2)), if taken too seriously, the model can become problematic in at least two respects. First, it is questionable whether it can be applied readily in all cultures. As such, its incorporation into quality of life measures may inhibit their trans-cultural applicability. Second, the normative nature of the model may prejudge those who do not appear to be actively pursuing good health (by eating 'unhealthy' food, or failing to take exercise). As such a new form of the 'double jeopardy' criticism of QALYs could be engendered, whereby those in chronically unhealthy lifestyles (on the humanist definition) are given a low priority for treatment, despite the fact that their bio-medical health is liable to deteriorate. This in turn raises the question of whether a person who has merely set him or herself minimal goals (or even self-destructive goals) is to be understood as ill, and as being in need of some form of medical help (be it health education, counselling or other more interventionist measures).

Two further problems may be noted with the humanist model. First, to judge certain goals to be too ambitious or too modest, indicates that 'health' is not defined purely with respect to the subjective preferences (and thus goal setting) of the individual. The source of the judgement that a person's freely chosen goal is in some way inappropriate may remain obscure. Second, it is not clear that the failure to achieve one's goals will always be due to health problems. In order to account for the difference between health related and non-health related failure, Nordenfelt suggests, as part of his definition of 'health', that the healthy need only achieve their goals under 'standard circumstances' (Nordenfelt, 1993). Standard circumstances thereby rule out non-health related factors that may interfere with the pursuit of one's goals. Non-standard circumstances might include war, or severe weather conditions. (While such factors, precisely because they entail stress or physical danger may subsequently affect a person's health, a person living under such conditions is not perceived as being unhealthy *per se*.) However, to establish that standard circumstances are not health-related presupposes a prior definition of health. (It is not then clear that Nordenfelt has avoided the circularity of which he accused the bio-medical model.) It may be suggested that light can be thrown upon both of these problems by returning to the sociological model. The more subtle versions of the sociological model entail that the boundaries between sick and healthy-but-deviant behaviour are under continual negotiation by groups and individuals within society. From this it may be argued, not simply that the substantive definition of 'standard circumstances' (and thus of 'health related failure') will depend upon negotiations within particular cultures, but also that the substance of 'normal' personal goal-setting will also be relative to a particular culture.

The humanist model remains of crucial relevance to the development of quality of life measures, precisely insofar as it facilitates the derivation of a comprehensive and positive definition of 'health'. The humanist model focuses upon the impact that physical (and mental) disease, disability and injury may have upon the pursuit of mundane (but to the agent valuable) goals. Health is thereby understood, not merely as a biological (or possibly psychiatric) phenomenon, but rather as the result of a complex interplay of physical, cultural, environmental, and attitudinal elements. This suggests that quality of life measures, ideally, need to be sensitive to these diverse parameters, recognising both variations between cultures (in the expression and weighting of health states), and variations between individual respondents. Specifically, the weighting of health states may reflect the presence or absence within a given society of physical, environmental and cultural resources (including the degree to which the health state was stigmatised), that affect the degree to which a physical or mental incapacity is a burden upon the agent. A quality of life measure presupposing a humanist model would thereby record illness in terms of the impact that it has upon the individual's ability to pursue a minimally fulfilling lifestyle. Nordenfelt suggests that Sickness Impact Profile approximates to such an ideal, by taking into account a wide range of mundane human activities, and thus the impact of sickness upon these activities (Nordenfelt, 1993).

PERSONHOOD

Issues of personal identity serve to shed light on a number of problems within quality of life measurement, not least with respect to the under-researched area of the impact of temporal considerations upon the evaluation of a health state. A number of interrelated themes may be addressed. A core issue concerns the instability of personal identity over time, so that an individual's judgement of what is in the interest of his or her own future self is revealed to be of questionable reliability. This is compounded by the impact that sickness has upon a person's normal or usual judgements, evaluations, and thus personality.

Through a series of more or less surreal thought experiments, Parfit has sought to challenge orthodox ideas concerning personal identity. Within the philosophical tradition (at least since Descartes and Locke), it has been assumed that a person is one and the same person throughout his or her life, and that some set of criteria (typically expressed in terms of memory and intentions) can be established by which identity might be judged. Parfit succeeds in offering a plausible response to the short-comings of this account . At the centre of his model of personal identity is a distinction between psychological continuity and psychological connectedness (Parfit, 1975). Person A at time t and person A at the later time t+1, is psychologically connected if there is direct contact between these two states. Here, A at t+1 would carry out intentions formulated by A at t (and importantly, A at t+1 carries out these intentions, not accidentally, but because he or she shares the motivations and priorities that caused A to formulate them at time t), and similarly, A at t+1 would remember A's experiences at t. A at t and at t+1 would thereby be the same person, insofar as they share a common stock of memories, attitudes, intentions, evaluations and beliefs. Psychological continuity presupposes the breakdown of this direct connection. A at time t, and A at (the considerably later) time t+3, may no longer be psychologically connected. A at t+3 may no longer share the attitudes and beliefs of the youthful A at t. As such, A at t+3 will have no inclination to carry out the plans that A at t formulated for his or her future self. Similarly, A at t+3 may no longer remember (completely or as intensely) the experiences of A at t. This need not entail that the two selves are radically sundered (for example by amnesia or mental illness). Rather, stretching between the two will be an infinite series of other selves. Any two selves closely related in time will be psychologically connected, sharing the bulk of their experiences and attitudes. Yet, through greater or lesser cumulative changes, the more temporally distant selves will share less. Thus, while A at t+3 may remember and identify with a great deal of the personality of A at t+2 (so that A at t+3 and at t+2 are psychologically connected), and A at t+2 may be similarly psychologically connected with A at t+1, these overlapping relations may be the only link between A at t+1 and A at t+3.

The recognition of such changes in personality over time poses problems for assessing the reliability of any anticipation of experiences that may befall a future self. Living wills provide a relevant illustration. The healthy, competent person is asked to anticipate how he or she will evaluate the worth of his or her life in the case of a severe injury. It is not clear, given Parfit's model, that the severely injured person and the healthy person will share the same values, and thus will agree upon the judgement of when life is no longer worthwhile. The disagreement can come about either through the mundane ageing process (so that, for example, one's conceptions of indignity and worthlessness change through widening experience of the world), or, possibly more crucially, because the injury itself will so impact upon one's personality (possibly through injury to the brain, but also, more significantly, through the impact that the very experience of the injury has upon one's perception of the world and one's place in it), that one will no longer share the values of the young and healthy self. This has implications for the weighting of quality of life health states, firstly insofar as such weighting may involve a person carrying out a process of anticipation, very much akin to that required in writing a living will, and secondly, insofar as not just the experience of illness *per se*, but also the anticipated duration of that illness will impact upon one's evaluation of it.

It has been suggested above that a 'biographical' account of a person's life is preferable to a purely biological account. As such, human beings are understood as being 'embedded', such that personal identity cannot be separated from the fact that a human being is a physical and social creature. Personality will be mediated by a component of the continual struggle to make sense of one's body, its functions, and of one's physical and cultural environment (see Taylor,1993). This is, indeed, coherent with the humanist model of health, is so far as it entails that health impacts upon a person not simply as a biological organism, but rather as a complex social-psychological being, with plans, desires and obligations to be fulfilled. Sickness challenges the meaning that a person has ascribed to his or her life, and thus the 'biography' that could be written, precisely because sickness delays, undermines or otherwise hinders the fulfilment of certain goals. Chronic (or terminal) illness may require a fundamental reassessment of the biography, and crucially its anticipated conclusion. In terms of Parfit's model, this may be articulated by saying that the healthy A at t formulates a series of intentions to be carried out by the equally healthy, and psychologically connected A at t+1. Illness disrupts this psychological connectedness. On the one hand, A at t+1 may be frustrated because A at t's intentions cannot be fulfilled. Psychologically, the illness would then have affected A only slightly. On the humanist definition, A would be unhealthy, precisely because of the discrepancy between his or her intentions (and thus goals) and his or her ability to pursue them. A's quality of life would then be low. On the other hand, and as noted above, A may develop a tolerance to the illness. Cutting the psychological connectedness between A at t and A at t+1, A at t+1 may abandon his or her earlier intentions, and formulate new ones, more in keeping with his or her illness. (As Canguilhem notes, 'to be sick means that a man really lives another life' (Canguilhem,1978).) A's quality of life would thus be relatively high. This throws into question the possibility of giving any simple, uniform and stable value to a health state. The actual impact that the health state has upon the patient's quality of life will be mediated by the ability to revise one's goals, but also by anticipation of how long the health state will last (and thus the degree of impact that it will ultimately have on one's mundane activity, and anticipated biography).

These issues may, in conclusion, be seen to reflect back upon the problem of who to ask in developing a quality of life measure, and particularly in weighting health states. The above reflections superficially suggest that a healthy person will not, with any accuracy, be able to anticipate the experience of being in a given state of ill-health. Yet, it has also been noted that someone currently suffering in a given health state (or indeed, identifying him or herself as such a sufferer, so that his or her biography is constructed around the experience of the disease), may lack the ability to draw an accurate comparison between that health state and any other. To pose the problem in such a way is to understand it as a problem of epistemology i.e. a problem of how knowledge about health states and quality of life can be acquired. That is to say, it is to presuppose that the purpose of quality of life measures is to provide an 'objective' measure of the experience of health states. (Implicit to such a project is the assumption that quality of life exists independently of its measurement. However, the exact ontological status of quality of life – i.e. what sort of thing quality of life is – remains obscure.) While quality of life profiles may indeed seek such objective measures, the primary purpose of economic measures, such as the original QALY, is that of resource allocation. As has been seen with reference to Menzel's 'QALY bargain', the objectivity of the measure is not of direct relevance to moral and political questions of allocation. If, for example, the purpose of a health service is seen to be the giving of reassurance to the healthy, then the evaluations of the healthy anticipating future illness, even if these evaluations are inaccurate, may be of the greatest relevance. Healthcare resources would, as a consequence of such consultation, be so allocated as to reassure the healthy that adequate treatment is available for the diseases they most fear.

A final implicit assumption, of individualism, in the above account needs to be explained. While it has been suggested that human beings need to be understood as social creatures, drawing upon the cultural (as well as medical) resources available in their society in order to make sense of illness, this suggestion can be taken further (in line with the comments already made above on discourse ethics). A human being does not live and respond to illness in isolation from other humans. Cultural resources are drawn upon through co-operation and negotiation with others. This insight raises two key issues for quality of life measurement. First, as to the weighting of health states, it throws into question any methodology that merely asks discrete individuals to suggest weightings. This may presuppose that the weighting is a pre-existing opinion or judgement, that the question merely elicits. It is more plausible to suggest that the evaluation of the health state is created as a response to the question, which is to suggest that respondents need have no views on health states prior to the question being posed to them. If so, then at best the evaluation given may be treated as an initial suggestion, not as a definitive and objective fact. As such, it may be challenged, and the respondents may be asked to defend and provide reasons for the evaluations given. Crucially, such challenges may serve to identify cases in which an evaluation is based upon unacceptable prejudice (Edgar, 1995). Second, if human beings are understood thus, as discursive creatures, then it may be suggested that an individual's competence to evaluate a health state he or she has not experienced may be enhanced through discussion with those who have experienced the state. While no individual can experience all health states, he or she can be expected to listen sympathetically to those who have experienced the state, and to discuss, and if necessary challenge, the evaluations given by such sufferers. The methodological individualism inherent in both the epistemological and moral approaches to quality of life measurement is thereby questioned.

5

The ethical QALY

The first section of this chapter is constructed out of the original objectives of 'The Ethical QALY' application for funding by the European Commission. After each objective, there is a summary of the groups' response to the problems and issues posed. This section is followed by a series of suggestions for the use of QALYs in healthcare allocation, and areas that may require further research and reflection.

OBJECTIVES AND RESPONSES

I. To investigate the ethical issues that arise in the derivation of QALYs and the ethical consequences of existing methods used in the construction of QALY scales, in terms of potential injustice in the representation of different groups through:

1. *Consideration of the temporal aspects of quality of life valuation, by investigating the degree to which existing scales fail to take account of a number of problems posed by the temporal nature of disease states, including:*
   (a) the possible instability of an individual's valuation over time;
   (b) the potential change in valuations due to different durations of disease states.

Response: Empirical evidence on these issues was found to be sparse and of little value. Philosophical reflection upon these issues centred upon the concept of personal identity, and the recognition that parallel issues had arisen in debates over 'living wills'. Two approaches to personal identity will be defended as relevant. First, the work of Parfit has provided an important stimulus to questioning the degree to which there is strict identity of the person over extended periods of time, and the implications that predictable or unpredictable changes in personality (and thus on personal identity) have for decisions made by a younger 'self' that may affect an older 'self' of the same person. Second, the recognition that a person is necessarily embodied (in the work of Taylor and others) entails that changes to the body (including changes through disease and illness) will lead to changes in the person (as to the way in which they will act and make evaluations). Current quality of life measures do not appear to be sufficiently aware of these philosophical problems, and further study of the implications of these theories for quality of life measurement, and the just application of such measures, is necessary.

2. *Consideration of the use of discounting in quality of life calculations, including:*
   (a) *the rationale for discounting and the validity of its analogous relationship to economic discounting;*
   (b) *the degree of correspondence of discounted valuations to the actual behaviour and experience of disease over time;*
   (c) *the appropriateness of applying a common discount rate across cultures which may have different rates of social time preference.*

Response: In view of the fact that society displays a positive rate of time preference, it is appropriate to use a discount rate greater than zero when evaluating public expenditure programmes. For consistency, decisions for public expenditure should utilise a common discount rate. However, there is to date insufficient evidence of both the degree to which society's time preference can be converted to a discount rate, and whether or to what extent time preferences are consistent between different areas of public expenditure. It may therefore be appropriate to apply different discount rates within each area of public spending providing the same rate is applied to all evaluations within that area. This 'different' discount rate need not exclude a rate of zero (no discounting). A zero discount rate however, implies that society is indifferent to when health benefits (QALYs) arise and would, for example, willingly sacrifice one life today in exchange for one life saved in the distant future. The group does not consider this to be a tolerable argument either intuitively, or on the basis of evidence from healthcare decision making.

3. *Investigation of the conceptualisation of health in existing quality of life measurement-scales, by:*
   (a) *investigating the degree to which existing scales incorporate only a negative concept of health, defined in terms of the absence of disease;*
   (b) *investigating the degree to which existing scales are slanted towards physical rather than psychological or cultural states;*
   (c) *investigating the possibility of modifying quality of life scales through examination of the cultural mediation of the concepts and valuation of health, health states and death as used in the scales.*

Response: Various concepts of 'health' and 'illness' were reviewed. These included the 'negative' definition of disease, as criticised by the WHO, as a divergence from perfect health; the bio-medical model of disease; the social functioning model; the humanist (or 'positive') definition of health in terms of the individual's response to bodily and environmental conditions. It was concluded that the humanist concept is the most adequate definition of health, although the precise definition of health may be contested under different circumstances and to different purposes. A principal objective of many quality of life measures is to give the patient a say in the medical evaluation of their own health state (so challenging unnecessary professional paternalism). An open humanist definition is coherent with this objective, because it allows recognition of the complexity of the individual's perception of their own health and well-being, and their ability to make sense of, and give value to, their physical condition.

While the Rosser-Kind scale only weakly theorised its implicit concepts of health and disease, other measures demonstrated the use of more subtle and wide ranging definitions. It was therefore concluded that there were no technical inhibitions that would prevent the development of a scale that takes due account of a humanist definition of health, and thus of the psychological and cultural aspects of health that will be important to the individual's understanding of their condition.

With particular reference to objective 3.c), the group reviewed the extensive literature on the use of measures in cross-cultural contexts, and the translation and modification of measures for diverse national and cultural contexts. (Particular attention was paid to the Nottingham Health Profile.) Philosophical work on the way in which individuals express and justify general preferences, led to the conclusion that cultural differences may be important in giving individuals diverse conceptions of the 'good life', and different ideas of what is normal and acceptable. It was concluded that ideally the construction of quality of life measures should take account of the way in which preferences for and against different health states are generated and defended by respondents.

4. *Consideration of the nature of the valuations used in the construction of the quality of life measurement-scales, including:*
   (a) the degree to which existing scales fail to take into account potential differences that may occur between the valuations given by actual sufferers of the state in question, medical practitioners, and the general (tax-paying) public;
   (b) the degree to which a given group (e.g. sufferers from a given disease) has use of and access to the process of defining quality of life;
   (c) the degree to which a group is controlled through subordination to given and potentially inappropriate definitions of the quality of life.

Response: With reference to 4 a), it followed from our discussion of objective 1, that individuals' anticipations of the quality of life of a health state that they have not yet experienced will not necessarily correspond to their actual quality of life in that state. It was argued that this result, in itself, does not require that only those who are currently experiencing a health state (or have experienced it in the past) should be consulted. If quality of life measures are to be used for the allocation of healthcare resources for a population as a whole, the objectives of the healthcare system need to be clarified, before the question of who should be consulted is resolved. (For example, if a healthcare system is perceived as having the primary objective of reassuring the healthy that adequate treatment is available for the diseases they fear, then non-patients comprise the most relevant response group.)

With reference to objective 4 b), it was concluded that the construction of quality of life scales does not, in principle, entail the exclusion of any particular group (although this may be a fault – or for disease specific measures, a virtue, of particular scales).

With reference to objective 4 c), it was recognised that much of the ethical debate concerning QALYs focused upon their alleged bias against the elderly, the chronically ill and those with a poor prognosis. The group concluded that none of these objections is conclusive, and indeed that non-disease specific measures (such as the original QALY), by separating health gain from specific diseases, conditions or patients, served to filter out what may be morally irrelevant prejudices against certain diseases (such as AIDS), or patients (such as smokers thought responsible for their illness). It was concluded that there remains a danger (which follows from the group's reflections on objective 3 b),) that cultural prejudices against perception of disease and especially disability in general may adversely influence the evaluation of certain health states. (Underlying this is the argument, that is also entailed in our response to objective 1 a), that one person cannot accurately judge the quality of life of another. At an extreme, there is the danger that quality of life judgements are deployed to justify the abortion or infanticide of the mildly disabled, on the grounds that their potential quality of life is unacceptably low.) This raises the prospect that quality of life measures could be used to diminish the value of certain groups. The group strongly disapproves of any such use of quality of life measures.

General response to objective I: Our concern in formulating this objective was to explore the injustice that may be inherent in the derivation of quality of life measures. To articulate adequately such a concern, and our response to it, it is necessary to clarify the most appropriate concept of 'justice' to use, and from this the forms of ethical defence that are suitable for quality of life measures. Our final report will review various approaches to justice, including utilitarianism, distributive justice and discourse ethics. Utilitarianism calls for the greatest happiness for the greatest number, and thus the greatest health gain possible given available resources. This provides the most common defence of the QALY (as used, for example, by Williams). Problems with this approach centre upon the danger that high aggregate health gains may conceal unacceptable allocations of resources about the population.

Menzel's contractarian defence of QALYs provides an attractive complement, and is strongly recommended by some members of the group. This approach to distributive justice focuses on the use of surveys to establish QALY values, and thus the need to formulate QALY questionnaires appropriately, so that the full implications of evaluations are made clear to respondents, and further that respondents are given the option to reject the QALY approach altogether. A discourse ethics approach develops from this, by arguing that respondents to questionnaires and surveys need not be treated as isolated individuals, with pre-given preferences, but rather as subjects who can debate, defend and revise their preferences. This allows a response to certain problems identified with reference to objectives 3 and 4. Specifically, the problems of making judgements on behalf of others (whose health states one has not experienced), and the potential prejudices that emerge against certain groups, would be mitigated. Extreme and indefensible views could, to a degree, be marginalised through the involvement of a range of groups, representative of the population as a whole, not merely in the expression of preferences, but in the discussion and defence of any preferences, and in the derivation of the parameters of the quality of life matrix.

II. To identify the ethical problems arising from the application of QALYs in the distribution of healthcare resources, through investigation of the rational planning of healthcare and the use of quality of life measures in the context of such planning, by:

1. *Considering the geographical patterns of preference for the rational planning of healthcare within Europe.*
2. *Considering the divergences between the approaches to rational planning in the participating countries.*

Response to (1) and (2): Empirical data has been compiled, from existing sources and from material available to group members, in order to provide a overview of the state of rational planning across Europe. Specifically, the structure of the health service in the project's participant countries; the explicit (legal) or implicit objectives of the health service; the degree to which prioritisation is being debated or enshrined in government consultation and policy; and the level of public debate on prioritisation, were considered to be the key issues for documentation and analysis.

3. *Considering the desirability of rational planning with specific reference to the weighted QALY, and the possibility that weighting may reflect potentially unjust social preferences.*

Response: This objective focuses a number of key ethical concerns about the use of QALYs, and the underlying emphasis that they place upon cost-efficiency in the provision of healthcare. While the group accepts that cost-efficiency is an ethically laudable objective for any planning of healthcare prioritisation, especially given the inevitability of scarcity of resources for healthcare, the group does not regard this as the only possible objective, or even, necessarily, the most important. Following from our response to objective 4 a), the group accepts that health services may have diverse objectives (grounded in the nature of the public perception and support of those health services). Certain objectives, or more significantly moral principles, may be incompatible with a straightforward cost-efficiency approach to healthcare allocation. The public may give overt support, for example, to disproportionate funding of neo-natal services, emergency services or life-saving treatments. The group can see no reason why a QALY approach cannot be subordinated to such concerns. (More fundamental problems are posed by ethical principles that are inconsistent with the QALY. The clearest example of this is the sanctity of life doctrine. In so far as the QALY approach presupposes that life is only of instrumental value, it is fundamentally incompatible with an approach that presupposes that life is of intrinsic and overriding value. The implication of the sanctity of life doctrine in a particular culture, may seriously limit the relevance of the QALY approach to that culture.)

The possibility of weighting QALY scores was debated, and subsequent discussions recognised the potential that weighting gives for responding to a number of ethical objections to QALYs, precisely insofar as weighting can be used to recognise other moral principles than those implicit in the basic QALY methodology. (For example, if public opinion expresses a strong preference for prioritising the young over the elderly, the QALY scores of the young can be weighted accordingly.)

In view of the cultural differences within and between countries, data within QALY league tables should not contain assumptions about weighting or discount rate. However, the data should be available in a form that will allow modification of QALY league tables to reflect the specific requirements and weighting/ discount rates of each country.

It may be recognised that there is a continuing debate as to which technique is most appropriate for deriving utility scores (e.g. time trade-off, standard gamble) and as to which tool should be used (e.g. QALY, EuroQol, SAVE, HYE, SIP, etc.). It is held that it is possible to derive a more ethical resource allocation tool by including a moral perspective in such considerations . It may be argued that the more important ethical considerations are in the context in which such tools are used. While the decisions on the best technical methodologies are largely outside the remit of the group, a consistency of approach in the way in which QALYs are derived is important otherwise QALY league tables will be difficult to interpret. It would be helpful if a European institution were given responsibility for approving the methodology used to derive QALY data. This institution could have also have a role in ensuring that data remain valid e.g. by updating costs as economic environments change. Without such safeguards on the quality of data the ethical debate on the use of QALYs will be distracted by technical issues such as the number of subjects used to derive the utility matrix.

RECOMMENDATIONS

1. An explicit mechanism is required for resource allocation.
2. If quality of life measures are to used for the allocation of healthcare resources for a population as a whole, the objectives of the healthcare system need to be clarified, before the question of who should be consulted is resolved.
3. The mechanism should be derived following discussion with professionals, patients and general public. A discourse ethics approach argues that that

respondents to questionnaires and surveys need not be treated as isolated individuals, with pre-given preferences but rather as subjects who can debate, defend and revise their preferences.

4. This mechanism should be reviewed on a regular basis to consider challenges to allocation decisions and to reflect changes in societal preferences.

5. Moral considerations should be included in the construction and the use of QALY like tools. However the decisions on the best technical methodologies are largely outside the remit of the group.

6. The group believe that the more important ethical considerations are in the context and the way that the QALY and similar measures are used. We believe that QALY league tables are of value to the prioritisation process but that they must never be regarded as the only consideration.

7. Weighting could be used as a means of adjusting QALY scores to reflect societal preferences.

8. Ideally the construction of quality of life measures should take account of the way in which preferences for and against different health states are generated and defended by individuals.

9. There should be a debate as to what extent limits should be placed on the implementation of societal preferences in order to guard against discrimination. There is a prospect that quality of life measures could be used to diminish the value of certain groups. The group strongly disapproves of any such use of quality of life measures.

10. A European Institution should be given responsibility for accreditation of cost-per-QALY data prior to inclusion within league tables to ensure consistency of methodological approaches.

11. Cost per QALY scores should be reviewed on a regular basis to reflect changes in economic environment.

12. Data should be provided with different assumptions concerning discount rates, weightings etc, which would allow the tables to be interpreted in different cultural settings along with the other factors that impinge on prioritisation decisions. This is in keeping with subsidiarity. The group strongly feel that there would be benefits in using the same rates in each European country, for example in allowing easier comparison between countries and exchange of data.

13. A humanist model of health is the most appropriate model since it allows recognition of the complexity of the individual's perception of their own health and well-being and their ability to make sense of, and give value to, their physical condition.

FURTHER RESEARCH

1. To analyse the ethical, social and legal issues raised by integrating the public more fully into the public policy deliberations involved in resource allocation.

2. To promote a rational and balanced dialogue between the key players including experts from medicine, philosophy, economics professionals involved with

healthcare management and the social sciences; and to involve the general public in this debate.

3. To understand public attitudes and diversity of viewpoints, including the fundamental values which are the basis of the differences and similarities in the perception of ethical issues.

4. To elucidate public understanding of justice: including distributive justice in terms of utility, desert or need; and non-distributive theories of justice of public participation in decision making.

5. To explore the concept of the 'quality of life' in public understanding of the objectives of healthcare.

6. To establish and interpret public understanding and preferences for life extension and quality of life improvement as fundamental objectives of a health service.

7. The elucidation of concepts of risk in terms of the likely effectiveness of an intervention and the probability of achieving health gain, and their place in public understanding of healthcare priorities.

8. To recognise and appreciate the range of viewpoints which arise from cultural differences between and within countries due to a diversity in cultural, social and health experiences, and to analyse the possible impact of the assessment of medical and health research discoveries on societal values.

9. To identify the fundamental values that could be a basis for a possible consensus, and to explore the institutional structures that would serve to manage or resolve differences in values.

10. To fulfil a prospective role, anticipating problems and providing early warnings for new ethical and social issues that might arise from discussing resource allocation issues with the public.

LIBRARY
THE NORTH HIGHLAND COLLEGE
ORMLIE ROAD
THURSO
CAITHNESS KW14 7EE

Appendix I

Country Reports

NORWAY

The 1987 Lonning Commission Report was one of the first attempts at setting healthcare priorities at a national level in Norway. The Commission argued that the main criterion to be used in rationing should be the severity of the patient's condition, and proposed five levels of priority.

In April 1996, Professor Inge Lonning was asked to chair a second committee, which subsequently published its report in May 1997. In addition to severity, this second report included effectiveness and the cost-effectiveness of the proposed intervention as prioritisation criteria. The Committee recommended that a greater emphasis should be given to health technology assessment and economic evaluations in order to inform the prioritisation process. The 1997 report identified four categories of priority: basic health services, supplementary health services, health services of low priority and services that should not be offered by the public health service. Care of people with mental illness, rehabilitation, and caring services in the community were identified as areas requiring higher priority. It was recognised that waiting times for treatment continued to be a problem. A guaranteed maximum waiting time for basic health services of three months was considered but this recommendation did not achieve majority support. The Committee did recommend that the use of charges and patient payments should be kept under review, especially for low priority services.

It was also recommended that a permanent prioritisation board should be established with responsibility for setting treatment thresholds for different conditions and interventions to ensure a consistent approach was taken to the prioritisation process. It was envisaged that specialists would be asked to advise on priorities in their particular fields, but that the Board would decide which services should be included in each of the four prioritisation categories. It was hoped that this proposal would enhance the quality of the debate on healthcare prioritisation, incorporating a top-down and a bottom-up approach.

NETHERLANDS

In 1990, the Netherlands Government Committee on Choices in Healthcare

(Government Committee on Choices in Healthcare, 1992) was asked

"to examine how to put limits on new medical technologies and how to deal with problems caused by scarcity of care, rationing of care and the necessity of selection of patients for care".

In laying out the tasks for the Committee, the State Secretary for Welfare, Health, and Cultural Affairs posed three questions: why must we choose? what kind of choices do we have? and how should we make the choices? The Committee was expected to propose strategies to improve choices at different levels of healthcare: national (macro), institutional (meso) and individual caregiver (micro).

The Committee expressed a clear opinion that

"choices in healthcare are unavoidable and necessary".

A community-orientated approach was preferred in which individual rights and professional autonomy were limited in the interests of equity and solidarity in healthcare. The Committee advised that the basic package of the mandatory health insurance should contain only care that meets the following four criteria: the care must be necessary, effective, efficient and cannot be left to the individual's responsibility. The Committee applied its criteria to different types of health services and, as in many other countries, it was concluded that it was not feasible to exclude complete services and treatments from the basic healthcare package since effectiveness of care has to assessed in relation to characteristics of each case. The importance of health professionals in determining whether treatment will be effective meant that the Committee concluded that physicians have the primary role in ensuring that healthcare was appropriate. However, health professionals should be

"accountable for the quality of their actions, and for the financial implications thereof".

Treatment choices would have to be made in the context of standards and guidelines drawn up by professional organisations although the Committee recommended that the Government encourage extensive public discussion on choices in healthcare.

Stronks *et al.* (1997) examined how different groupings may apply the Dunning criteria in the prioritisation of ten healthcare services. In addition to these four criteria for public funding of a service (necessary care, effectiveness, efficiency and individual responsibility) the panels were also given information on the nature of the service, the number of people affected (now and in the future), costs, and current restrictions. The panels comprised individuals from five different groupings: the public (university students and civil servants); patients; health insurers, and two groups of healthcare professionals (general practitioners and medical specialists). The panels were asked to economise nearly one third of the total budget.

Both panels of health professionals thought most services were necessary. The general practitioners tried to achieve the budget cuts by limiting access to services to those most in need of them or to those who cannot afford to pay for them. The specialists emphasised the possibility of reducing costs by increasing efficiency within services and preventing inappropriate utilisation. The patients mainly economised by limiting universal access to preventive and acute services. They thought that healthcare for patients with long-term illness should be publicly funded because the chronically ill have no other option but to rely on healthcare. The public panels excluded services that were relatively inexpensive for individual patients or where there were alternative solutions. Moreover, they emphasised the individual's own responsibility for health behaviour and the costs of healthcare and hence advocated the use of co-payments. The health insurers distinguished health risks (for which one can be insured) from inevitable healthcare needs that will eventually be experienced by most of us (e.g. home care and homes for elderly people) and hence should be paid for through taxation. They also emphasised the feasibility of implementation.

As with studies which compared the healthcare funding priorities of different groupings in the UK, this Dutch study found that there were substantial differences in the way the different parties approach the rationing of publicly funded health-care. The main differences in the Dutch study seem to be the extent to which the various groups considered the principle of equal access.

DENMARK

Denmark has experimented with the use of an internal market in healthcare similar to that in the UK. In order to increase competition, Denmark removed the administrative barriers that prevented patients from obtaining treatment in hospitals outside of their own county. It was hoped that patient choice would improve standards as hospitals competed with one another for business. The counties and the Ministry of Health chose a reimbursement mechanism between counties whereby payment took the form of a fixed sum per treatment day. This established a number of perverse incentives for healthcare providers and administrators. For example, the length of stay for out-of-county patients was longer than that for local county residents. Local residents were also given a lower priority on waiting lists because they did not generate the same visible income as out-of-county patients. Some hospitals have been given specific instructions to give priority to out-of-county patients with specified targets for each department to generate income from cross-border flow.

This experience was similar to that in the UK in the early years of the internal market, when a higher priority was given to patients from fund-holding practices. Such injustice in the UK was reduced by political pressure and an expansion of the number of fund-holding general practitioners which reduced the economic leverage that fund-holding GPs had when they were the exception rather than the rule. It has therefore been suggested that the Danish reforms have created more problems than they have solved (Holm, 1995).

In 1997, the Danish Council of Ethics produced a report on "Priority-setting in the Health Service". The Danish Council of Ethics believed that the purpose of the debate on priority-setting is to stimulate thought and dialogue among people who make decisions on a daily basis in the health service, at the general political/administrative level as well as at the clinical level. The purpose of the debate was not to reach a once and for all list of priorities, although it would be expedient if there was a consensus as to how priorities should be set.

The Danish Council proposed that the general goal for the Danish health service should be:

"The furtherance of health and prevention of disease, fighting and relieving suffering related to health with the aim of ensuring the possibility for self-expression for all irrespective of social back-ground and economic ability."

This goal should be seen in connection with a set of "crucial values" which apply to the health service and the welfare state as a whole: Equal human worth, Solidarity, Safety and security; Freedom and self-determination. They also set four partial goals for operation of the health services: Social and geographical equality; Quality; Cost-effectiveness; Democracy and consumer influence.

While the Danish Council felt that everyone would wish that optimum treatment should be provided immediately someone is taken ill, they recognised that this would not be possible in the present Danish health service and that in practice it was impossible to prevent, treat and relieve all suffering. They did not believe that allocation of more funds to the health service would solve this problem, without examining how resources may be used more effectively. They stated that :

*"any **choice not to act**, any **giving a lower priority**, any **disregard** of a patient's needs is repugnant to us, even if it can be justified with somebody else being given help. It sounds like discrimination, like cynicism, like ruthlessness and lack of understanding for the suffering of others"*

The Danish Council did not believe that these characteristics should be connected with the welfare state and the health service. They were unable to agree to a model where one group was given lower priority than another. They specifically rejected rationing based on age, personal responsibility for the illness and social status. Instead they wished to foster an ethical awareness of:

"the value aspects of different patterns of action".

For example, the Council recognised that there had been an increase in the demand for health services and:

"in some cases there may be an overconsumption".

They therefore suggested that there should be an investigation of the factors that stimulate the demand for health services and means for reducing this demand. They questioned whether doctors, patients and the medical industry contribute to high and unrealistic expectations of the health service. They also queried whether general practitioners are adequately fulfilling the gate-keeper function.

They recommended that more research on the effectiveness of interventions was required, in order that treatments that have no particular effect or are *"downright harmful"* are withdrawn.

They belived that Danish Politicians should not attampt to produce a model for priority setting similar to that in Norway, Netherland or Sweden. They felt that experiences in these countries indicated that such models are of:

"limited value in the daily priority-setting effort in the health service because they are formulated at a very general level".

The Danish Council also rejected the implementation of guarantees of patients' rights for waiting times etc., as had been introduced in the Patients' Charter in the UK. The Danish Council belived that such rights would entail an imbalance in the health service. They did believe, however, that some general guidelines of what a patient may reasonably expect would be helpful.

FRANCE

Global, prospective budgeting for public hospitals was introduced for larger hospitals in France during 1984, and the remaining hospitals in 1985, with the aim of cost-containment. Prior to this, public hospitals were funded on the basis of a standard daily rate, which was the same regardless of the treatment given or the length of stay. Under global budgeting, public hospitals are expected to stay within the annual prospective budget that they have been allocated. The budgets are based on the previous year allocation with variable allowances for inflation and projected changes in activity. Any capital requirements are met by the sick funds.

SWEDEN

The Swedish Parliamentary Priorities Commission published its report on priorities in healthcare in 1995. The Commission had been established by the Government to consider the responsibilities, demarcation, and role of publicly-funded healthcare services, to identify fundamental ethical principles which would facilitate a public debate and to recommend guidelines for healthcare prioritisation. The members of the Commission were drawn from central and local government, representing each of the five leading political parties. Between June 1992 and November 1993, the Commission consulted with various experts and other authorities and collected information on international approaches to priority setting. A discussion document was published in November 1993. The Commission subsequently conducted a widespread consultation process that included a series of regional meetings and four attitude surveys.

The first survey was sent to 1500 members of the general public aged 18-84 and asked about the relative value that should be placed on different forms of care and the care for different age groups. A second questionnaire examined attitudes of health professionals (300 doctors and nurses). A third survey explored ethical values among 168 politicians, 144 administrators and 259 doctors. The fourth questionnaire asked doctors and nurses about the impact of changes in health service management.

The Commission felt that similar attempts to prioritise healthcare in other countries had not paid sufficient attention to ethical considerations or to methodological problems in measuring efficiency. The Swedish Commission established three ethical principles as the basis for its final report, the most important of which was respect for human dignity: everyone should have equal dignity and rights irrespective of their personal characteristics or place in society. They therefore rejected rationing whereby access is influenced by contribution to society or to responsibility for their illness. The Commission rejected any weighting based on age, even though the public consultation indicated a preference if all else were equal for treating the young rather the old. The second most important ethical principle was the combination of the concepts of need and solidarity. Solidarity is important in order to protect the interests of those less able to express their needs or to demand their rights. The final ethical principle used by the Commission was cost efficiency since there should be a "reasonable relation" between cost and effect. However, the Commission believed that comparison of interventions was only possible for treatments for a particular disease. They thereby rejected utilitarian approaches such as the QALY.

The Commission used these ethical principles to identify client groups who should be given particular priority, derived mainly from the seriousness of the illness. Ten categories were identified which were placed in the following hierarchy for political or administrative priority:

1. Treatment of life-threatening acute diseases and disease which, if left untreated, will lead to permanent disability or premature death. Treatment of severe chronic disease. Palliative terminal care. Care of people with reduced autonomy.
2. Prevention with a documented benefit. Habilitation/rehabilitation etc., as defined in the Health and Medical Services Act.
3. Treatment of less severe acute and chronic diseases.
4. Borderline cases.
5. Care for reasons other than disease or injury.

An almost identical list was derived for clinical priorities.

A number of services were identified in the borderline category where there was uncertainty about the appropriateness for public funding. For example, treatment for infertility, growth hormone supplementation for short stature of unknown cause, and psychotherapy where evidence of psychiatric illness was doubtful. On balance, the Commission thought that treatment for infertility was justified, but that the other two were not. The Commission also recommended that care for reasons other than disease or injury should not be communally funded.

The Commission explicitly rejected the use of guidelines or financial incentives. Instead it believed that successful implementation would depend on changing the awareness and attitudes among administrators and clinicians.

NEW ZEALAND

In New Zealand a new government was elected in 1990 which had promised to reduce public debt while not increasing taxes. It was necessary to reduce public spending, including that on healthcare, in order to fulfil these election pledges. This economic policy was associated with an increasingly widely held pro-market ideology and belief that the public health system was failing. A Task Force established to make recommendations rejected a radical shift from a tax-funded system to one based on private insurance. In July 1993, the 14 Area Health Boards were replaced by four publicly funded Regional Health Authorities. The document that laid out the reforms stated that:

> "in the past, rationing has been done informally and often without public scrutiny or control. Defining a set of 'core health services' more explicitly will help ensure that the services the public believe to be the most important will be provided. It will also acknowledge more honestly that there are limits to the health services we can afford."

The statement of core services was meant to act both as a guarantee of a minimum entitlement that the individual could expect, as well as a way of capping the risk to the State of spiralling healthcare costs. The individual was expected to take additional insurance to cover those services outside the core. The National Advisory Committee on Core Health and Disability Support Services was charged with independent advice to the Minister of Health about the "kinds, and relative priorities, of public health services, personal health services, and disability services that should, in the committee's opinion, be publicly funded" (Health and Disability Act, 1993, as amended 1995). The National Advisory Committee was later renamed the National Advisory Committee on Health and Disability

The Department of Health invited a public debate on how the core services should be defined. There was discussion as to whether the core would specify those services that would be provided or those that would not. In practice, the process proved to be too problematic. Instead, the National Advisory Committee abandoned the concept of a definitive list in favour of a 'qualified list' which sets out clinical circumstances in which a given treatment is deemed appropriate. The Committee recommended that the core contain all services historically provided but with treatment protocols controlling their use, determined by:

> "when they provide a benefit, when they are cost-effective, when they are a fair and wise use of available resources, and when they are in accord with the values of communities".

The National Advisory Committee and the four Regional Health Authorities jointly sponsored a national project to develop standardised priority assessment criteria for elective surgical procedures (Hadorn and Holmes, 1997a). As part of this project, criteria were developed for cataract extraction, coronary artery bypass graft surgery (Hadorn and Holmes, 1997b), hip and knee replacement, cholecystectomy and tympanostomy tubes for otitis media with effusion. The criteria were used to:

a   assess patients' relative priority for surgery,
b   to ensure consistency and transparency in the provision of surgical services across New Zealand, and
c   to provide a basis for describing the kinds of patients who will or will not receive surgery under possible levels of funding.

In addition to clinical criteria, several social factors were considered and to some extent incorporated into the priority criteria. For example, age was used within the coronary artery bypass graft surgery criteria as a proxy for co-morbidity. Age was not used in the other criteria because of concerns that services would be denied to many elderly patients who had the capacity to benefit as much (or more than) younger patients. Two public meetings were held to discuss whether to incorporate work status, whether patients were caring for dependants or whether there was a threat to independence. Following these meetings it was felt that these factors should be included provided they were given relatively little weight compared to clinical factors. Time spent on the waiting lists was rejected as a criteria because people who wait a long time for treatment have usually not been treated early because they are low priority.

REFERENCES

Government Committee on Choices in Health Care (Chairman: Dunning) (1992) Choices in health care. Rijswijk: Ministry of Welfare, Public Health and Cultural Affairs.

Stronks K Strijbis A-M Wendte JF Gunning-Schepers LJ (1997) Who should decide? Qualitative analysis of panel data from public, patients, healthcare professionals, and insurers on priorities in healthcare. *BMJ* **315**: 92–6.

Holm S (1995) "Socialized Medicine," Resource Allocation and two-tiered health care – The Danish Experience. *J Med Phil* **20**: 631–637.

Danish Council of Ethics (1997) Priority-setting in the Health Service". Copenhagen: Danish Council of Ethics.

Swedish Parliamentary Priorities Commission (1995) Priorities in healthcare: Ethics, economy, implementation. Stockholm: Ministry of Health and Social Affairs, **5**.

Health and Disability Act 1993, as amended 1995; Sec 8, par 2, p5.

Hadorn DC and Holmes AC (1997) The New Zealand priority criteria project. Part 1: Overview. *BMJ* **314**: 131–4.

Hadorn DC and Holmes AC (1997)The New Zealand priority criteria project. Part 2: Coronary artery bypass graft surgery. *BMJ* **314**: 135–8.

Appendix II

The Healthcare System in Greece and the Implementation of QALYs

Nicholas Koutouvidis

INTRODUCTION

The population of Greece is 10,256,464 (Source: NSS Census of 1991) and has similar demographic patterns to other EU countries. The population is concentrated in urban centres, with 30.2% of the population living in Athens. Life expectancy at birth is one of the longest in Europe (74.1 for males and 78.9 for females).

Individuals are tending to marry later, the birth rate is declining and the population is becoming increasingly more elderly.

Additional problems such as increased unemployment, loneliness in the big cities (Athens, Thessaloniki), and immigration from Albania, former Yugoslavia, Turkey and Eastern Europe have generated a series of needs and demands that cannot be met by the existing services. These changes require consideration of an increase in healthcare resources and for their redistribution. In the long term more effective, efficient and humane strategies should be developed in respect to both the healthcare system and to the education of health professionals and users of health services.

Implementation of QALY measures of quality of life in adherence to a given financial framework could be of great value in improving the Greek healthcare system. The "weighted QALY", thus accepted, should in any case be well defined and properly adjusted to social and medical care in Greece. A major prerequisite for this is a reliable presentation of the existing organisation and financing of the Greek healthcare system. This is the aim of the subsequent analysis.

PUBLIC SECTOR HEALTH SERVICES

The structure of public health services is mainly determined by the structure of the National Health system (NHS), established in 1983 by the Socialists, as an intermediate and transitional form between a system of social insurance and a National Health Service system. The basic principles of the NHS are:

1. The country is divided into nine health regions. At least one regional university hospital is planned to serve each region for tertiary medical care. At least one

hospital in each prefecture (nomos) covers the needs for secondary medical care and is linked with the regional hospital and with primary medical care units. In 1987, secondary and tertiary level public hospitals numbered 141, with a total number of over 35,000 beds. However, serious problems arise as the regional distribution of beds and doctors is extremely uneven (e.g. Athens and Central Greece: 6.9 beds and 5.0 physicians per 1000 inhabitants; Thrace: 2.3 beds and 1.5 physicians per 1000 inhabitants).

2. Primary healthcare in rural and semi-urban areas is planned to be provided by health centres but certain difficulties in staffing and equipping of these centres cause the provincial population to seek health services in the large urban centres.
3. There are no geographical restrictions within the system, a factor that also leads to the aforesaid phenomenon.

PRIVATE SECTOR HEALTH SERVICES

Despite the accomplishments of the public sector health services, the private sector has shown a remarkable adjustability with a substantial expansion in the field of modern biomedical technology and in primary healthcare. Today the private sector consists mainly of several large modern private hospitals and many diagnostic centres, leaving the public sector mainly to deal with serious cases requiring prolonged hospitalisation and intensive treatment. Unfortunately precise data concerning the private sector health services are still not available.

Over time, the relation between the public and the private hospital sectors has changed. The NHS law of 1983 prohibited the creation of new private hospitals. Most private non-profit beds were nationalised; profit-making hospitals were not allowed to expand, invest, or change the kind of services provided. Many closed down due to the low fees they received from the health-insurance funds. During the decade of the '80s the proportion of the private hospital beds fell by 12% to 30% which is still one of the highest in Europe.

A new law introduced by the Conservatives in 1992 dealing mainly with the relation between private and public sectors as well as with the industrial relations of doctors working in public hospitals, lifted restrictions on the activities of the private sector.

MEDICAL MANPOWER

It is estimated that 57% of all doctors are situated in Greater Athens and a further 15 % in Thessaloniki. Over 70% of medical specialists are also situated in these two cities, while some of the 53 prefectures (nomoi) in Greece have an insufficient number of physicians with certain basic specialisations. This fact partly explains the movement of patients from the provinces to urban centres for hospital treatment. Therefore, despite the high ratio of 300 inhabitants per doctor, health services are unevenly provided. Another critical point is the lack of general practitioners and the related problem of insufficient programming of family healthcare.

The maldistribution of medical personnel and the quality of health services could be partly improved by a rational development of the QALY implementation. The same may be said for a series of other problems, such as the varying efficiency of health services, the increasing phenomenon of supply-induced demand as well as the significant differences related to insurance coverage (a considerable number of people still have no insurance cover).

The NHS law of 1983 forbade private practice for doctors working in the public sector. The new law (2071/1992), introduced by the Conservatives, also affects the terms of employment of public hospital doctors by enabling doctors to be employed in the NHS full time or part time or on a per-case basis. The second and third categories receive lower salaries but can practice privately. However, public doctors may also receive gratuities (known locally as "envelopes") from patients, which according to a report from the Institute of Economic and Industrial Research (1987) can amount to an average increase of 78% of their official incomes.

FINANCING BODIES

Primary Healthcare is financed by:

1. The insurance funds
2. The patients themselves
3. The state budget

The financing of the Public Hospital Sector is carried out by a mixed and complex form of financing characterised by the involvement of many different bodies, the absence of well-defined criteria and many non-rational procedures. Financing bodies for public hospital services are:

1. The Social Insurance fund, through the mechanism of daily hospitalisation fees that are administratively defined and usually grossly inadequate;
2. The prefecture and the Ministry of Health, using funds from the state budget, but without utilisation of modern methods and criteria;
3. The private insurance companies and individuals to a low but increasing percentage.

The fees paid by the social-insurance funds for the treatment of their members have been kept considerably below cost. Public hospital budgets have been subsidised by the Ministry of Health. In private hospitals, patients have had to bear the cost of the deficit. The fees paid by the funds to both public and private hospitals have now been increased by 220% to 300% depending on the type of facilities available. The fees will cover only "hotel" costs. The funds will be expected to pay extra for any diagnostic or therapeutic procedures. These changes mean that the funds will bear the brunt of financing hospital services, although it is doubtful whether they have the resources to do so. The overall effect of these measures may increase health spending as there are no policies for controlling the growth of hospital expenditure.

Hospital-financing systems remain open-ended and hospitals have no incentives to increase efficiency.

ALLOCATION OF HEALTH EXPENDITURES

The public sector is predominantly concerned with hospital care. In 1991, expenditure on inpatient care accounted for 63.5% of the total public health budget. In contrast, care in the private sector tends to take place outside the hospital setting (in-patient expenditure in 1987 accounted for only 16.0% of total private health spending).

For the time being, however, there is neither any specific state health policy nor any obvious co-ordination between public and private sectors. Additionally, several studies have recorded substantial divergence between the health needs of each region (as expressed in mortality rates) and available resources. This can be attributed to the lack of rational criteria and inadequate utilisation of research and managerial techniques and to the unequal regional distribution of funding.

State health expenditure in 1987 was up to 4.0% of the GDP, while another 1.3% of the GDP was spent by the private sector. This means a deviation from the analogous indicators of the European countries belonging to the OECD (total health expenditures: 7.3% of the GDP in 1987), which can create certain difficulties in the course of convergence between Greece and the rest of EU countries in the field of healthcare. Differences which occur between Greece and the rest of Europe are for example also the rate of beds per 10,000 inhabitants (Greece: 51.6, Europe: 82.7) and the rate of bed coverage (Greece: 74.4%, Europe: 82.0%).

RESTRUCTURING HEALTH POLICY AND QALYS

A common problem in Greece is the lack of clear aims and objectives and the divergence between scientific directions and political choices together with administrative discontinuities. This especially affects complex domains such as health policy and the health system. A subsequent fact on microallocation terms, is also patients' almost exclusive dependence on his/her physician's decision making which altogether cannot be always controlled by rational criteria.

Since the "weighted QALY" ultimately tends to minimise the cost available per effective treatment, its implementation in Greece could contribute to a pragmatic redistribution of health resources, independent from political or personal desires. This may be an objective basis both for financing and organising the health system with reference to the actual needs of the Greek society. Prerequisites for this are further studies of resources per medical speciality, per hospital or health centre, per insurance funding etc, in relation to effectiveness of treatment.

THE SOCIOCULTURAL CONTEXT IN GREECE

Recent debate on QALYs has been much concentrated on the social and cultural environment. Since ethical evaluation is to a great extent socioculturally bound, acceptability and feasibility of rational techniques in reallocating scarce health resources should depend on intervention both on social and cultural levels.

Modern Greek society awards top priority to healthcare, at least as much now as in ancient times (Siegrist, 1977). The rise in the standard of living after World War II, the subsequent adoption of consumer models by the majority of the population (frequently due to mere imitation of the developed Western societies) and the emphasis on quality of life, restored health to a prominent position within modern social and political thought. The upgraded social prestige of the medical profession, the increase of health expenditure as percentage of the GNP and the repeated demand for an increase of available resources for health in the national budget (Kyriopoulos & Niakas 1994) – as well as the exploitation of this demand on the part of the politicians, all contribute to making health a central issue.

In this context, Greek society is very much alike other European ones. However, major differences become apparent when one investigates underneath the surface. It is well known that social prioritisation and modern Greek life style do not always coincide with corresponding economic developments. Greece is slowly but increasingly deindustrialised, hidden economy absorbs a big percentage of the total economic product – also influencing the delivery of health services to a large extent. Administrative bureaucracy seems inadequate to deal with and solve crucial social problems such as irrational distribution of health resources and services or the resulting unequal access to healthcare services (Niakas, 1993).

On the other hand, traditional social structures and conceptions (like the dominant role of the nuclear family or female inferiority) seem to be rapidly changing, if not collapsing, under recent financial and technological evolution. With them, other traditional features of Greek society are under pressure such as social solidarity, interest in politics and in intellectual life, concepts of self-esteem, ways of expressing feelings, etc.

In this changing social context, Greek NHS plays an increasingly significant role. Political debate is nowadays focused on improvement of the NHS not only owing to its importance in healthcare services consumption and demand (Kyripoulos & Niakas 1994) but also due to unethical practices that have a negative impact on its efficiency and effectiveness, along with political interventions and administrative malfunction (Abel-Smith, 1994).

On the other hand, ethical education and research seems rather poor in Greek medical schools. Recent efforts have been made by medical scientists to fulfil such educational purposes but the outcome is still far from those ultimately desired. Thus, moral thought is still governed by the disciples of the Hippocratic Oath alone, moves within the frames of a rather abstract, i.e. not clinically oriented, way of old-fashioned deontological thinking, and much resembles some strict "Kantian-like" moral context. Simultaneously, certain behaviours are heavily characterised by unethical practices such as illegal bypassing of waiting lists and hidden economy, which are exacerbated by the low salaries of health professionals, the lack of a code of practice and the absence of safeguards and of explicit targets (Abel-Smith, 1994). The result is a major divergence between theory and practice which coincides with the absence of certain ethical and clinical criteria in programming strategies for diagnosis, cure and prevention.

There is increasing recognition in Greece of the need to reallocate medical resources, both financial and human. Health economists and other specialists have acknowledged the significance of rational distribution and existing resources while not abandoning the perspective of their increase. Similar voices are also heard on the part of some politicians, and it seems possible that specialists' suggestions will finally be accepted. Consequently, research on biomedical ethics and health-related quality of life measures is urgently needed (Kyriopoulos & Niakas 1994). Discussion in the media and education of laymen is also required if the public is to participate in processes concerning the future of society as a whole.

REFERENCES:

Abel-Smith B *et al* (1994) Report on the Greek Health Services. Greek Ministry of Health and Social Welfare, Athens. *Pharmetrica*, 26-28.

Kyriopoulos D and Niakas A (1994) Topics of Health Economics and Policies. Athens, Centre for Health and Social Sciences, 207-208.

Niakas DA (1993) Health and Regional Development; Regional Health Policy in Greece. Centre for Health and Social Sciences. Athens, 120-129.

Sigerist HE (1977) The special position of the sick. In Landy D (ed) Culture, Disease and Healing: Studies in Medical Anthropology. New York, MacMillan. 388-394.

Appendix III

Inequalities in Health: What are the Alternative Scenarios for Slovakia?

Martin Rusnak

INTRODUCTION

Health status is of vital importance to all those interested in the well-being of human life. In the 1990s, as we look forward to a new century, the burden from chronic, noncommunicable diseases poses the greatest challenge to the health status of populations with mature age structures.

Finding ways to reduce the loss of life, the sickness, suffering, lost productive years, and the irreversible disability from diseases such as heart disease, cancer, chronic respiratory illness, and diabetes, is the essence of that challenge.

The goals of the public health community are to understand the nature of the problem, the scope of the health burden, the personal, social, and environmental factors associated with the development of chronic illness, and then find ways to prevent or effectively treat these illnesses.

There has been much scientific activity directed toward this goal in the past few decades. Professionals from a variety of fields using such tools as vital statistics, population-based surveys, case-control studies, and longitudinal cohort studies have provided us with a vast amount of new information on the frequency and nature of chronic illnesses and the factors associated with those diseases.

What have we learned? In most developed countries more than seventy percent of all deaths are attributable to a handful of conditions; heart disease, cancer, stroke, diabetes and chronic respiratory diseases. In nearly all societies, no matter how poor and underdeveloped, more adults die of chronic than infectious diseases. The historic record shows that some common chronic diseases such as lung cancer and diabetes were not nearly as prevalent in the past as they are now. They are to a great extent illnesses of the 20th Century. We know that these diseases and others such as musculoskeletal diseases, vision and hearing loss, dementias and Parkinson's disease, cause great suffering and rob the world's growing elderly population of quality in their last years of life.

We also know that inequality characterises the burden from chronic disease: men are much more likely to die of premature heart disease; smokers are far more likely to die of lung cancer than non-smokers; black men in the United States have exceptionally high rates of cerebrovascular disease; elderly women are far more likely than elderly men to be disabled by osteoarthritis. Some of these differentials can be at least partly explained by personal behaviour or risk factors (smoking and lung cancer), some by environmental hazards, some perhaps by biological factors and some by different access to effective healthcare.

At a practical level, national and local governments are faced with the evermore costly task of caring for those suffering from chronic, noncommunicable diseases. Some healthcare systems have been or are being restructured, such as those in the UK, Sweden, and the nations of Central and Eastern Europe. Others are now criticised for their costliness and inequities. How the changes, past and future will affect the performance of the healthcare system is a vitally important question. To answer these questions in any country we need to first understand the nature of the change in its healthcare system, then identify the relevant performance indicators (mortality rate, incidence rate, hospital discharge, etc.) and monitor these indicators over time.

SLOVAK REPUBLIC

The turn of the decade saw significant changes both in the politics and in the economies of various countries. The changes in Central and Eastern bloc countries had found a vast amount of relatively new information, previously hidden because of political reasons. One of the most astounding pieces of evidence for both health professionals as well as for ordinary people were that their health condition is generally worse than that in Western European neighbours. The inequality could be documented by differences in standardised mortality or longevity. A new-born boy in Slovakia had an average life expectancy of about 68 years, compared with 72 years for his neighbour in Austria. Less pronounced was the difference in female longevity: 76 in Slovakia versus 78 in Austria. When investigating inequalities within the country itself, the differences are even more striking. The difference between the district with the highest life expectancy for males (70 years) and the lowest (60 years) is 10 years (**Table 1**). The difference for females (77.6 maximum and 71.6 minimum) is 6 years. Potential years of life lost (PYLL) from cardiovascular (**Table 2**) and oncological (**Table 3**) diseases suggest, that those are the most prominent causes of the inequalities. The situation demands a re-examination of the frequently unrealistic expectations for curative medicine and the support of preventive programmes.

The Slovak Republic with its newly emerging democracy is facing a complicated task: to define the role of the state in health policy. In the past, the leading ethical principle in health was based on the notion of need. To apply this principle for the whole population is not only unrealistic in any society, but to measure any fulfilment of this principle is dubious, too. Therefore it seems unavoidable to introduce a new principle to base the state's health policy on. The principle of equity, advocated by the WHO, possesses both positive and negative features. Nevertheless, there are attempts to apply this principle in various countries of Europe (Gunning-Scheppers, 1989). The economic recession in many countries has alsosignificantly changed the situation in healthcare system performance in respect to the equity principle, (Letica

110

Table 1. Life expectancy (LE) at birth.

Rank	Female		Male	
	Region	LE	Region	LE
1	Cadca	77.62	Prievidza	69.97
2	Dolny Kubin	77.17	Topolcany	69.24
3	Bratislava	76.82	Bratislava	69.07
4	Lipt. Mikulas	76.80	Trencin	68.28
5	Prievidza	76.79	Bardejov	68.08
34	Roznava	74.28	Nitra	64.91
35	Dunajska Streda	74.24	Michalovce	64.91
36	Lucenec	73.63	Dunajska Streda	64.79
37	Trebisov	73.43	Trebisov	64.51
38	Levice	71.64	Levice	59.94

Table 2. Potential years of life lost (PYLL) due to cardiovascular diseases per 1000 inhabitants in 1990

Rank	Female		Male	
	Region	PYLL	Region	PYLL
1	Nove Zamky	32.78	Levice	36.67
2	Galanta	23.87	Galanta	35.75
3	Trebisov	23.87	Nove Zamky	34.06
4	Levice	23.56	Ziar nad Hronom	32.32
5	Lucenec	22.96	Banska Bystrica	31.44
34	Dolny Kubin	11.74	Bardejov	15.81
35	Banska Bystrica	11.68	Presov	15.40
36	Nitra	9.63	Dolny Kubin	14.91
37	Kosice	9.28	Komarno	14.72
38	Svidnik	6.94	Kosice	11.57

& Lang, 1989). Slovakia has to follow the line described – however the question remains, how to accomplish this.

POLICY IMPLEMENTATION

The process of building up and applying the state policy on health based on equity consists of an assessment of the extent of the problem, subsequent decision on the policy goals and objectives and the identification of possible points of intervention. The process is complemented by appropriate organisational arrangements and financial requirements as well as developing a monitoring and evaluation system.

Table 2. Potential years of life lost (PYLKL) due to oncological diseases per 1000 inhabitants in 1990.

Rank	Female		Male	
	Region	PYLL	Region	PYLL
1	Levice	171.9	Nove Zamky	73.3
2	Velky Krtis	144.7	Velky Krtis	72.9
3	Nove Zamky	142.0	Komarno	71.6
4	Trenton	140.6	Seance	68.8
5		140.6	Roznava	68.3
34	Rimavska Sobota	31.7	Bardejov	15.81
35	Humenne	27.0	Presov	15.40
36	Cadca	24.7	Dolny Kubin	14.91
37	Bardejov	24.6	Komarno	14.72
38	Dolny Kubin	22.7	Kosice	11.57
38	Svidnik	6.94	Kosice	11.57

Assessment of the health status inequalities

The comprehensive evaluation of all aspects of health and healthcare performance was done on the basis of data from the Health Statistical Office and on cause-specific mortality data. The inequalities between regions were found in both healthcare performance and health status indicators. **Table 1** documents some of the most prominent differences in life expectancy by sex and administrative region. Regions with the lowest values cluster in the south of the country, while the ones with the longest life expectancies are mainly from the northern parts. Why the situation has developed that way is not fully understood. Therefore more detailed studies are being carried out. Most of them are addressing quantification of risk factors and their prevalence in the Slovak population. Studies of smoking habits, nutrition, physical activity, cholesterol and elevated blood pressure are complemented with surveys of soil, water and air pollution, socio-economic and behavioural factors and related effects on population health. Analysis of death certificates by multiple causes promises to bring an insight into quality of death reporting as well as into specific mortality patterns in regions. The performance of the healthcare system is evaluated from the point of view of hospital networks, hospital admissions and discharges, manpower and budgeting.

Decisions on the policy goals, objectives and the interventions.

Approval of the National Health Promotion Programme (NHPP) in November 1991 laid the foundations for everyday implementation of its principles and aims in practice not just in the health sector, but in all other sectors as well. In agreement with the strategy outlined by the World Health Organisation (WHO) the main goal of the NHPP is the implementation of measures to enable WHO Target 1 to be achieved (WHO, 1985). Bearing this in mind, the adjusted main goal of the NHPP is to decrease, within six years, the interregional differences in health status of the population of Slovakia by at least 25%.

Owing to the fact that the implementation of this principle started relatively recently, this goal will probably not be fully achieved in all the regions and groups in Slovakia. Implementation of the Programme consists of a set of interventions procedures, selected on the basis of global scientific knowledge of their efficacy in improving health status of the population. It is necessary to point out that education and research are considered integral parts of this effort. The activities will primarily concentrate upon the following intervention areas: support of non-smoking, promotion and propagation of healthy nutrition, support of physical activity, reduction of elevated blood pressure. The goals in these four areas are to be achieved through several ongoing projects as well as through projects that are being prepared, such as CINDI (Countrywide Integrated Noncommunicable Diseases Intervention), Healthy Cities, Healthy Schools and Healthy Workplaces.

Organisational arrangements and financial requirements.

To develop programme activities, the National Centre for Health Promotion has been established. The plan to transform Institutes for Hygiene and Epidemiology into Institutes of Public Health is currently being designed. They will be responsible for realisation of public health activities within the National Programme of Health Promotion. This system is conditioned by co-operation between local, other than state healthcare providers, local Health Insurance Fund and the local Institute of Public Health. Councils of directors and legally binding contracts between them could assure co-ordination of activities. The institutions will then become more autonomous, with abilities to reflect local differences in health requirements and on the other side, the state health policy will also be accomplished.

Evaluation and monitoring

To establish an effective system of evaluation and monitoring of the activities and accomplishments is an unavoidable precondition for success. To maintain or further develop a health information system with other information systems for data collection is not enough. There must be certain investment into research and development in the evaluation and use of existing statistical methods complemented with design of new methods of building attributable risk health burden models. This phase should be followed by the implementation of attributable risk and burden models to produce estimates and projections of mortality, morbidity, and functional disability for a set of major chronic diseases and conditions. The models should provide decision-makers with results in terms of financial and technological requirements as well as resources and work force options based evaluations of alternative scenarios. For this purpose new approaches to the utilisation of information from multiple sources of data should be developed.

CONCLUSIONS

The revised and updated National Health Promotion Programme sets the priorities for decision making regarding the support of projects. Based on the above three items of crucial importance for the support of the NHPP are necessary to stress:

1. NHPP is an intersectoral programme, approved by the Government and the National Council of the Slovak Republic as the leading programme for improving the health of the population of Slovakia;
2. NHPP represents a major part of the state policy in health – a fact necessitating its concordance with all interventions in questions concerning population health. This applies both, to the development of the National Insurance Company and to improvement of the whole network of healthcare –providing facilities, including diagnostic and treatment process;
3. The situation when the State declares its support of the NHPP while its financial support is of only symbolic nature must not repeat itself in the next year. Reductions in the healthcare budget may lead to saving money in healthcare performance itself, but failing to allocate the required resources for the NHPP would unequivocally lead to the NHPP remaining hardly any more than a declaration. It would thus follow the fate of similar programmes as documented by experiences of the past. If, however, the development is to follow such direction, an honest confession on the part of politicians to abandoning the idea of the NHPP seems to be the only alternative.

REFERENCES

Gunning-Scheppers LJ (1989) How to put health on the political agenda. *Health Promotion* 4(2), 149-150.

Letica S and Lang S (1989) Economic crisis and equity in health. *Health Promotion* 4(2), 87-90.

WHO (1985) Targets for Health for All. European Health for All Series No. 1. Copenhagen, Regional Office for Europe.

Appendix IV

Choosing Core Health Services in the Netherlands

Hen ten Have

INTRODUCTION

The current debate on healthcare resource allocation in the Netherlands is being conducted in a social context in which two values – solidarity and equity – are generally accepted as fundamental (Boot, 1990; ten Have and Keasbury, 1992; Verkerk, 1990; and Wachter, 1988). Since World War 2 the guiding principles of all Dutch governments, conservative or progressive, have been 'equality of access to healthcare' and 'solidarity in sharing the financial burden proportionate to income'. These principles are reflected in the healthcare system. Access to healthcare is not limited either by geography or financial considerations. Since the Netherlands is a small country, there is no problem of distance. Physicians and hospitals are distributed fairly evenly throughout the country. Practically no-one is without healthcare insurance; two thirds of the population (below a specific income level) are covered by mandatory national healthcare insurance, while the others are privately insured. For those insured through the state (not including the privately insured) the burdens of paying for healthcare distributed evenly (since the premiums are proportional to income).

Towards the end of the 1970s an increasing tension was felt between the values of equity and solidarity. The foundational nature of these values was not questioned but the ensuing political debate concentrated upon their implication and range. Over the last 25 years, the relative investment of the national product in healthcare has risen markedly from approximately 4% to 9%. Per capita healthcare expenditure has shown an average annual growth of 0.6% since 1980 if the price level of 1980 is taken as the standard. (Government Committee on Choices in Healthcare, 1992). Such increases have occurred in spite of cost-contracting measures (such as the introduction of budgeting systems in hospitals and the reduction of specialists' salaries) applied to various points of the healthcare system.

SEARCHING FOR FUNDAMENTALS

In the Netherlands the main issue has not been the question of how to distribute scarce resources, but how to find a (new) balance between individual interests and the general welfare (ten Have, 1988). Although there is a stronger tendency not to focus on financial aspects, it is important to realise that the problem of resource allocation is usually discussed within a broader framework than the economic one, since proper deliberation must also involve inquiry into the political and philosophical foundations of the welfare state.

For three reasons, developing a more fundamental approach became politically relevant, especially for government, political parties and healthcare advisory bodies in the 1980s and 1990s.

A welfare state which emphasises equal access and solidarity has its price. The population's willingness to support the collective financing of healthcare services is lessening, but compensating for increasing costs requires higher taxes and premiums. Roughly 36% of each individual's personal income goes into taxes and premiums for social security and healthcare. If continued, this policy will further erode general willingness to apply the principle of solidarity – already under pressure through increased emphasis on individual responsibility in healthcare (ten Have, 1990) – to the financing of healthcare.

The government has introduced a series of proposals to reorganise the healthcare system to introduce a system of basic health insurance for all, thereby changing the differentiated system of compulsory and voluntary insurances. Although the desirability of national health insurance is not really disputed, there is political controversy over the type and number of services to be funded in an elementary insurance system, for it is obvious that the new basic package will not cover all presently insured services. The controversy essentially concerns the inadequacy of the principle of equal access in times of scarcity, since the principle provides little or no guidance on which rationing policies should be applied.

Changes in the pattern of demand and supply in healthcare also necessitate the reconsideration of healthcare policy. The population is ageing: the proportion of those over 65 will increase by 20%, that over 80 by a third by the year 2005 (Government Committee on Choices in Healthcare 1992). As a result, there will be an increasing disease load and more chronic and degenerative disorders. Demand for healthcare facilities (and particularly for chronic care facilities) is bound to increase. At the same time, scientific and technological change in medicine will continue to attract public attention, and fund the demand and expectation for new diagnostic and treatment interventions.

Three options are available to reduce pressure on the healthcare system:

1. Allocate more money for healthcare;
2. become more efficient;
3. make explicit choices about care.

The first option has been ruled out by government. Higher taxation or insurance rates are politically unrealistic and other social goals such as education and good environment also compete for collective resources. Therefore, according to the Cabinet, the volume of care in 1990 (Wachter, 1988) may increase by a maximum of 1% per year.

116

The second option, to increase efficiency, has received much attention over the past decade. It was not considered ethical to make choices in healthcare and deny some patients care so long as money was being wasted by inefficient care. Many projects have started to deliver care efficiently, and to make more efficient use of diagnostic tests and treatment schedules; and much more yet can be done to reduce wastage of resources. However, it is estimated that even maximum efficiency will not lead to more than 15% reduction of the cost of important healthcare services (Van de Ven *et al*, 1988). This implies that increasing efficiency can delay the need to make choices but it cannot prevent the necessity for choice in the long run. Therefore, the third option – making choices in healthcare – is the most realistic one. But then the question is: How should such choices be made?

BASIC HEALTHCARE NEEDS AND CONCEPT OF HEALTH

In August 1990, the State Secretary for Welfare, Health and Cultural Affairs installed a Committee for Choices in Healthcare. Its task was to develop strategies for making choices between existing and new possibilities in healthcare, particularly with regard to the package of necessary services to be included in the new mandatory insurance system. Three main questions appeared on the committee's agenda:

1. Why make choices?
2. Between what do we have to choose?
3. How should we make choices?

The Committee was also explicitly invited to initiate and stimulate a public discussion (as in Oregon, for example), about the relative necessity of services available in the current healthcare system.

The Committee published its report in November 1991. It strongly argued that choices in healthcare are unavoidable and desirable. Even if more resources were to be available for healthcare, explicit choices would still be necessary. Most important, the Committee proposed a set of guidelines for making fair choices.

The starting-point for the Committee's argument is the proposition that everyone who needs healthcare must be able to obtain it. However, equal access to healthcare should not be determined by demand but need. In order to have a just distribution of services, it is not important that all services are equally accessible. Not every healthcare service is equally relevant for maintaining or restoring health. Thus it is important to identify 'basic care', 'essential services' or 'core health services' focused on basic healthcare needs rather than individual preferences, demands or wants. ' Relevant needs' can come from demand or want. In his theory of healthcare needs, Daniels argues that needs are distinct from their object, namely health (Daniels, 1985). The concept of health is therefore the most appropriate standard for characterising healthcare needs, since it is argued that health enables persons to maintain a normal range of opportunities to realise their life plans in a given society. Since health and not healthcare services as such is 'basic' or 'essential', the Committee prefers the expression 'necessary' because it implies a relationship between the particular kind of care or service with a particular goal ('necessary for what?').

STRATEGIES FOR MAKING CHOICES

The Committee defines health in general terms as the ability to function normally. However, 'normal function' can be approached from three different perspectives:

The individual approach

Here, health is related to autonomy and self determination. It is the 'balance between what a person wants and what a person can achieve'.(Government Committee on Choices in Healthcare, 1992). Defined as such, health can vary according to individual preferences. But in this case no distinction is possible between basic needs and preferences; what is a basic need for one will not be for another. This approach therefore is not helpful in determining on a societal level what the 'necessary care'; is that should be accessible to all. Even if through a democratic decision-making process (such as in Oregon) the largest common denominator or the smallest common multiplier of individual demands could be determined, we would lack criteria to identify necessary care (Government Committee on Choices in Healthcare, 1992).

The medical professional approach

Typically the medical profession defines health as 'the absence of disease'. This approach is defended by Daniels. He interprets health as 'normal species-typical function' disease is defined as 'deviation from the natural functional organisation of a typical member of a species' (Daniels, 1985), and the basic functions of the human species being survival and reproduction. Healthcare is most necessary where it presents or removes dangers to life and enhances normal biological function. On this approach, 'necessary care' may be distinguished according to the severity of illness and this was proposed as a criterion by a Norwegian Committee in 1987 (Royal Norwegian Ministry of Health and Social Affairs, 1990). Nevertheless, this approach has a tendency to neglect the psychosocial functioning of individuals. It is also questionable whether normal species-typical functioning can be defined regardless of the social circumstances.

The community-orientated approach

In this approach, preferred by the Committee, health is regarded as the ability of every member of society to participate in social life. Healthcare is necessary 'when it enables an individual to share, maintain and if possible to improve his/her life together with other members of the community' (Government Committee on Choices in Healthcare, 1992) 'Crucial' care is what the community thinks is necessary from the point of view of the patient. This approach is not utilitarian because what is considered to be in the interest of the community is dependent on its social values and norms. Every community exists by presupposing a normative, deontological framework defining the meaning of its interests. In Dutch society at least three normative presuppositions define the communal perspective:

1. the fundamental equality of persons (established in the Constitution),
2. the fundamental need for protection of human life (endorsed in international conventions), and
3. the principles of solidarity (expressed in the organisation and structure of social systems, particularly the healthcare system).

Within the normative framework the Committee has distinguished three categories of necessary care:

1. facilities which guarantee care for those members of society who cannot care for themselves (e.g. nursing home care, psychogeriatrics, care for the mentally handicapped);
2. facilities aimed at maintaining or restoring the ability to participate in social activities when such ability is acutely endangered (eg, emergency medical care, care for premature babies, prevention of infectious diseases, centres for acute psychiatric patients);
3. care depending on the extent and seriousness of the disease. From a community-orientated perspective, the first category is more important than the second or the third, and the second more than the third.

FOLLOW UP

The proposals of the Committee are intended to start a broad public debate on healthcare services. The Ministry of Health has allocated a substantial budget (several million guilders) to increase the number of participants in the discussion. Indeed, especially among organisations of women, patients, handicapped and the elderly many initiatives and activities have been started. However, the political debate so far has been disappointing. The Cabinet response (in June 1992) focused primarily on promoting appropriate care, giving a major role to healthcare professionals in defining standards of care and treatment protocols (Tweede Kamer der Staten-Generaal, 1992).

It seems therefore that in the political arena explicit choices in healthcare are not yet made, notwithstanding the intentions that led to setting up the Committee. This is an unfortunate situation since the medical profession has been given the task to decide how to cope with scarce resources, but the most the profession can do is ameliorate the consequences, it cannot really solve the problems.

Without explicit decision-making at the macro level, the basic principle of solidarity will further erode. Solidarity implies that the autonomous individual learns to recognise that his own interests are best served by promoting the common good. Introducing a uniform package of core health services, without making distinctions between 'needs' provided for by the state, and 'wants' provided for by people themselves, and without clarifying criteria to make such distinctions through broad communal debates, is a recipe for losing control over increasing healthcare costs.

What is needed is a policy which guarantees equal access to services which provide for communally agreed necessary care as well as special protection of vulnerable groups within the community in order to maintain equality of result and opportunity. The Committee report provides a strategy for linking the idea of a basic package of healthcare with the concept of necessary care available to all. Now, or in the near future, healthcare politicians must take up the challenge.

REFERENCES

Boot JM (1990) Health policy in the Netherlands. *BioLaw* 2(35), 1619–1622.

Daniels N (1985) Just Healthcare. Cambridge, Mass, Cambridge University Press.

Government Committee on Choices in Healthcare (1992) Choices in Healthcare. Zoetermeer.

ten Have HAMJ (1990) Health and responsibility as policy tools *BioLaw* 2(35), 1623–1630.

ten Have HAMJ (1988) Ethics and economics in healthcare: a medical philosopher's view. In Mooney G and McGuire A (eds) Medical Ethics and Economics in Healthcare. Oxford, Oxford University Press, 23–39.

ten Have HAMJ and Keasberry HJ (1992) Equity and solidarity: the context of healthcare in the Netherlands. *Journal Medicine and Philosophy* 17, 463–477.

Royal Norwegian Ministry of Health and Social Affairs (1990) Health Plan 2000, Oslo.

Tweede Kamer der Staten-Generaal (1992) 22393, nr 20, Modernising Zorgsector Weloverwogen Verder. Sdu Uitgeverij, Den Haag.

Van de Ven WPMM *et al* (1988) Doelmatigheid in degezondheidszorg: een miljardenkwestie. Nederlands. *Tijdschrift voor Geneeskunde* **132**, 1623.

Verkerk M (1990) Solidarity and health policy *BioLaw* 2(35), 1631–1636.

Wachter MAM De (1988) *Ethics and health policy in the Netherlands.* In Sass HM and Massey RU (eds) Healthcare Systems. Dordrecht, Kluwer. 97–116.

This article was previously published in the Journal of Health Care Analysis *1*(1) 1993. *Reproduced with permission. Copyright John Wiley and Sons Ltd.*

Appendix V

Healthcare System in the Czech Republic

Jan Holcik

THE DEVELOPMENT OF THE SYSTEM

The Czechoslovak state, which emerged in 1918 following the collapse of the Austro-Hungarian Empire, pursued policies underpinned by progressive liberal principles and successfully pressed for ambitious social welfare programmes. From the 1920s until the take-over by a Communist regime, healthcare services were organised around private practices for outpatient services, public hospitals and institutes and private hospitals. Efforts were made in the 1920s to extend sickness insurance coverage to broad segments of the population. This system remained in force until 1948.

In 1948, a centralisation process under the Communist regime was initiated. All private hospitals and medical institutes, as well as segments of the medical service industry and drug distribution were nationalised. Responsibility for financing the system was taken over by the state budget.

A basic element of the healthcare system was the medical territory centre, which provided curative and preventive care for adults and children, and gynaecological and stomatological services. Outpatient care was unified into regional and district public health centres. In addition, there was a system of hygienic and epidemiological services. A hierarchical structure of medical services was established based on a rigorous three-tier system (regional, district, and community levels), with the regional and district centres controlled administratively and financially by National Committees.

Following the "Velvet Revolution" in 1989, a set of proposals on healthcare reform put forward by a multidisciplinary team was formally adopted by the Parliament in 1990. Entitled "The New System of Healthcare in the Czech Republic", the document embraced the following principles:

- healthcare reform is a part of wider strategies for health regeneration;
- healthcare must be based on the full decisions of well-informed citizens and the entire community;
- the state will guarantee healthcare for all;
- the state monopoly in policy and provision will be abolished, and pluralism in financing and provision will be introduced;

- health insurance will be obligatory;
- service development will foster better integration between different elements of provision and primary care.

The reform process has progressed in a number of other areas, including:

- privatisation of healthcare institutions and practices;
- changes in remuneration methods for healthcare personnel;
- organisational and administrative changes including the break-up of District and Regional Health Centres into smaller, independent entities, and elimination of National Committees;
- changes in the system of higher education for medical personnel;
- pharmaceutical policy.

Proposals to divide benefits into "standard" care financed through the compulsory insurance and guaranteed by the state and "above standard" care provided by the private sector is similar to healthcare provision provided in many Western countries. However, the package of "standard" care has yet to be defined in the CR. There is a strong suspicion, that for the time being, the services that individual doctors and facilities offer greatly depend on the financial incentives that are built into the new arrangements for health sector financing. Despite the fact that the existing financial incentives for the healthcare providers in fact might drive them towards over-providing high cost services (some of which will represent very poor value for money in terms of healthy life gained from a particular level of expenditure), there is virtually no information on how the services provided correspond to the real needs of the population.

Increased patient choice is another key element of the proposed reforms. Increased choice in itself, however, will not be without risk in terms of future utilisation of health services. Some checks and balances will always be necessary to prevent over-utilisation and abuse or to encourage utilisation of beneficial services.

The proposal for health sector reform envisages an important future management role for local communities and voluntary organisations. There is a strong desire to have local communities play a leading role in both the financing and provision of healthcare. Much work needs to be done before this objective is achieved. None of the reforms proposed will be possible without considerable investment in research work and training, and all available scientific expertise to design and implement a range of techniques to influence the process of the health sector reform should be mobilised.

EQUITY IN HEALTHCARE

Efficiency, effectiveness and quality of treatment are still vague terms that need to be defined in the CR. Efficiency is often translated as effectiveness which is incorrect and conveys a completely different notion: an efficient use of resources might still be wasteful if the modality of treatment is ineffective (Feachem and Preker, 1991).

Quality of treatment is an even less well defined notion in the CR.

In Western European countries, local concerns about health and access to healthcare, particularly primary healthcare, have led to many initiatives to assess the health, determinants of health, and healthcare needs of residents in the respective area (e.g. Hunter and McKee, 1993; Whincup et al, 1993). The experience of Western countries is useful, but has its limits with respect to generalising of the findings because of the culturally specific conditions in the CR, especially the possible differences in people's preferences and the way in which healthcare providers and consumers may behave.

As a starting point, a clear priority for improving efficiency, effectiveness and quality of the Czech health sector in the future is to have readily available information to examine various complex aspects of these concepts. This means good information systems, readily available methods for evaluation and people who know how to use them. Informed decisions cannot be made without some of this basic knowledge.

Changes in the scale of values associated with society entering plural democracy caused many ethical doubts and objections in terms of the conceptual problems of healthcare. The most important ones are:

- problems of the essence of health and mission of health policy;
- responsibility for healthcare;
- nature of health services under conditions of market economy;
- problems of the interpretation of the right to health;
- health requirements;
- the importance of equity;
- and the role of citizens in the healthcare system.

STRUCTURE AND ADMINISTRATION OF HEALTH SERVICES

The reforms have given rise to a highly decentralised system of organisation and administration. The Ministry of Health controls only national programmes, certain public health services, and university and regional teaching hospitals. All the other healthcare services, facilities (hospitals, ambulances, physicians, etc.) come under District authorities who are responsible to the Ministry of Interior. The Ministry of Finance has the responsibility of financing a portion of the premium income of the general Health Insurance Office and the branch insurance companies.

HEALTHCARE DELIVERY SYSTEM

At the community level, Type I hospitals, polyclinics, diagnostic services, rehabilitation, community health centres and rural health centres provide primary care (formerly for catchment populations of roughly 50,000). Specialised secondary care is provided by type II hospitals, polyclinics, Hygiene Stations, and health education centres (formerly catchment populations were 150,000). The same institutions (formerly under the administration of District Institutes of National Health) additionally provide primary care for populations of 50,000 – 70,000 which are in their immediate territory. Type III hospitals, which are often university affiliated, polyclinics, Hygiene Stations and health education centres (formerly under the administration of Regional Institutes of National Health) provide highly specialised tertiary care to a catchment population of about one million.

Drugs and medical supplies are obtained from hospitals and pharmacies. In major cities, ambulance services are centralised; elsewhere they are available through hospitals. Social services include accommodation for the elderly and orphans, chronic care institutions for the disabled and mentally ill, as well as personal services.

Primary care doctors at the community level formerly acted as gatekeepers to the system, in most cases referring patients to higher tiers. The gatekeeper function has recently been eliminated from the new system where the patients are free to select their specialists as well as a GP physician or a hospital.

THE HEALTH SITUATION

The health status of the population is still extremely unsatisfactory. Czechoslovakia lags behind advanced European countries by 6-7 years, the mortality rate of men in productive age is double that of other countries; as regards the mortality rate from cardiovascular diseases and malignant tumours, we hold one of the worst positions in Europe. There is an extremely high incidence of serious chronic disease, acute myocardial infraction, neuroses, gastric and duodenal ulceration and diabetes. At the same time the severity of mental diseases is rising; thus in 1988 psychiatric invalidity held the third place in the total invalidity and accounted for 10%. These characteristics and developmental trends apply to Czechoslovakia as a whole; in the Czech Republic they are, however, generally worse than in Slovakia.

These facts and trends persist and the gap as regards the health status of our population, as compared with the European countries, is increasing. The state of national health is alarming. The idea that improvement will result spontaneously with the development of democracy and market economy is erroneous. Experience of the advanced Western countries indicates that success in this sphere can be achieved only by systematic and targeted nationwide provisions.

Environmental factors (including working environment), i.e. contamination of the atmosphere, water, soil and foods, pollution of the environment by chemicals, harmful physical factors (noise, radiation, etc.) are responsible roughly (maximally) for the state of about 20% of the country's ill health. The environment is also deteriorating systematically over recent decades.

Healthcare influences national health roughly by 20%. On a long-term basis, healthcare suffered in particular from inadequate preventive policies and an unsatisfactory character regarding early and effective diagnosis and therapy.

The contemporary national health status and its determinants are still unfavourable. The two-year period after November 1989 opened opportunities for a substantial improvement of national health but so far it has not improved.

Lifestyle, environment and healthcare still suffer from the old shortcomings, the public is still indifferent to health, politics are absorbed by social and economic tasks of transformation and in professional circles nothing substantial has changed in relation to improvement of national health. Changes to a more favourable position will not occur automatically. Only a more favourable democratic climate has been created and it must be used to improve national health by a purposeful and systematic effort. This is the sense of the national health programme.

THE HEALTH REFORM PROCESS

There are many persistent problems. The Czech government is currently planning further changes in the healthcare system. Measures under consideration include the following:

- to improve the cost-efficiency of the health insurance scheme; to introduce more effective cost-containment strategies;
- to improve the quality of healthcare;
- to increase co-responsibility in healthcare through the development of acceptable criteria for out-of-pocket payments.

Strategies for the achievement of the above include:

- introducing mechanisms to control the behaviour of providers and health insurance agencies to improve cost containment;
- merging the social sickness insurance fund (providing sickness benefits from the social sector) with the health insurance fund to make the health sector more responsive to the total cost of disease;
- rationalising health insurance management to create a central fund for health insurance (for the distribution of resources, establishing standards, determining price lists, etc.).

CURRENT ISSUES IN HEALTH POLICY

Objectives of recent healthcare reform in the countries of the European Union	Alternative policies for healthcare reform
Achieving equity of access	Introduction of market competition
Efficiency at micro and macro level	More efficiency
Improved health outcomes	Control of income
Patient satisfaction and consumer choice	Managed care
Provider autonomy	Output oriented budget

Table 1: Main problems of healthcare service in CCEE:		
Type of healthcare service	**Problems**	**Targets/strategies**
Primary healthcare	Inefficiency, low quality Separation by age, occupation and social status Unnecessary referrals to specialists and hospitals	Primary care based on GP GP is the first point of contact Referral system Broadening "mix" of primary healthcare benefits Equity in access and availability Free choice of physicians
Hospitals	Unnecessary hospitalisations Underfinancing Separation by age, occupation and social status Low standards "Second economy"	Improve primary healthcare and specialist outpatient services Improve funding Free choice of physician "Privatisation of physicians" Licensing and accreditation

Table 2: Dissatisfaction of citizens and health professionals in CCEE.		
Citizens		
Dissatisfactions	**Reasons**	**Targets/strategies**
Unmet expectations	Differences between entitlements for health services free of charge and actual delivery	Adjust entitlements to available resources
Inequity in access to health services	Inequity in financing Closed healthcare subsystems "Second economy"	Equity at least in financing basic healthcare Free access to healthcare providers "Privatisation" of health professionals
Discontinuity of care	Segmentation of healthcare Absence of General Practitioner	Primary healthcare based on General Practitioners
Low quality of health services	Underfinancing of healthcare Poor salaries, poor motivation Absence of standards and quality control Deficient education and training	Adequate financing Competition between physicians, freedom of choice Standards of contents and quality Accreditation of facilities and of professionals Quality control, indemnity
Deteriorating health status	Lack of programmes for health promotion Inefficient prevention Lack of performance-related financing	Develop and finance targets and strategies for health promotion and illness/prevention Strengthen public and primary healthcare performance- related financing
Ignored "patient rights"	Inadequate standards and control Inadequate education Insufficient information and protection of patients	Standards of patients rights Codes of ethics of health personnel Consumer protection

Objectives of healthcare reform in the countries of the Central and Eastern Europe (CCEE)

financing healthcare system

introduction health insurance
privatisation
availability of necessary health service

availability of affordable drugs
health information system
professional training
primary care

Table 3:Dissatisfaction of citizens and health professionals in CCEE.		
Health professionals		
Dissatisfactions	**Reasons**	**Targets/strategies**
Low level of income	Government monopoly in financing and operation of health services	Eliminate government monopoly in decision making Strengthen power and organization of physicians
	Poorly developed economy	Economic growth
Low social prestige	Pauperisation of physicians Weak position in decision-making	"Privatisation" of physicians Introduce professional organization
	"Second economy" unethical behaviour	Change codes of ethics
		Raise average physicians' incomes; introduce competition for available funds
Inequality in access to public medical facilities and services	Closed healthcare subsystems	"Privatisation" of physicians/providers of personal health services
	Separated primary healthcare	
	Separation of polyclinics from hospitals	Free access to health establishment under equal conditions for all physicians
	Monopoly of employees on the utilisation of equipment	Self-financing of institutions between physicians instead of "command and control"
	Status of physicians as civil servants Authoritarian management	
Inadequate education and training	Too many medical students per medical school Inadequate financing, staffing and equipment of medical schools Guaranteed employment	Reduce number of students per medical school Introduce accreditation of schools and of diplomas Increase standards of examination
	"Specialisation" during undergraduate studies	Eliminate early specialisation
		Eliminate guaranteed employment

REFERENCES

Feachem R and Preker A (1991) The Czech and Slovak Federal Republic, the Health Sector: Issues and Priorities. World Bank, Human Resources Operation Division, Central and Eastern European Department, 53.

Hunter DJW and McKee M (1993) Assessing the need for prostatectomy: prevalence of appropriate indications and patient choice for treatment. Society for Social Medicine 37th Annual Scientific Meeting, Cambridge.

Whincup P, Zahir K and Towe P (1993) Survey of health needs on the Broadwater Farm Estate. Society for Social Medicine 37th Annual Scientific Meeting, Cambridge.

Appendix VI

The Establishment of Priorities in Public Health as an Instrument of Health Policy in Slovenia

M Cesan and Vlasta Mocnic Drnovsek

SUMMARY

The paper deals with the efforts of the Slovenian government to reduce spending in public financing. In Slovenia this is particularly high because of the contributing factor of the high level of social security which is financed exclusively by the public financial sector.

In 1993, expenditures for public and private health insurance amounted to 8.0 % of gross domestic product (93 % of which were public expenditures). The economic burden of public financing is becoming unbearable because the public finance sector, in addition to expenditures for healthcare, also makes considerable payments to the pensioners (23 % of the population are pensioners) and the unemployed (15 % of the working-age population unemployed). In the near future the government will be obliged to come to grips with numerous rights of people, originating in public health insurance, and to transfer a part of the economic burden to private responsibility (the explicit rationalisation of healthcare delivery).

When we weigh and judge the economic and health-related benefits connected with the delivery of various services we discover a discrepancy between the public and the private health-related interests. On this basis we can establish a system of priorities of public health interests in which the public interest (eg preventive medical care delivery, emergency medical care) comes first, while the private interest (eg, plastic surgery) comes last.

If a society establishes the political consensus concerning the limitations of entitlements in the public health insurance area, the portion of healthcare delivery and of non-medical services, ranking last in the system of priorities, will be eliminated first, then that ranked next, etc. The costs of the eliminated services will be either paid directly by the patients or through the system of private health insurance.

INTRODUCTION

Europe is undergoing major political, social and technological changes, which call old solutions into question and raise new challenges for the future. Fundamental reforms of healthcare are taking place in many countries, in an attempt to contain rising costs, through more cost-effective patterns of services provision in response to healthcare needs and expectations as well as increasing demands for a better quality of life of the general population and of different target groups. The question is how reforms should respond to the specific needs by providing adequate services of optimal quality and at the same time ensuring equitable access to healthcare. The challenge is how to develop healthcare systems based on values enshrined in the European Convention on Human Rights and European Social Charter, since the range of potentially beneficial healthcare activities far exceeds what any country can afford. This is the reason why the issue of developing a proper prioritising strategy has become so pertinent in all EU and CEE countries, while different approaches are used to solve these problems.

The growing inadequacy of public financing in the modern world, which is caused primarily by the increase in public expenditures for social security[1], is also forcing the health policy in Slovenia to review the relationship between public and private health-related interests involved in the solving of health problems. The health policy is faced with the difficult task of emphasising public health-related interests and obtaining a relationship between socialised and individualised healthcare that is justified by the altered economic circumstances. This work is difficult and demands considerable responsibility because of the inertia connected with social privileges once they are acquired. An acceptable solution is feasible only if there exists a public agreement as to the necessity of reducing the level of social security (Rupnik, 1992). Only in this case can we hope, in the area of the public health insurance, to be able to control the conflict between medical ethics and economic logic, which is permanently associated with the provision of healthcare.

In Slovenia the adjustment of public health insurance[2] for economic conditions will be exceptionally difficult. The scope of our public health insurance coverage is very considerable. In the past, entitlements to it have steadily increased without regard to economic circumstances and usually without an adequate base in public financing. Public health insurance was especially growing when the country was

---

[1] Social security in Slovenia is composed of public health insurance, old age and disability insurance, unemployment insurance, and social protection.

[2] Public health insurance in Slovenia is regulated by the law of 1992; it stipulates entitlements to three groups of healthcare, namely:
   1. The entitlements based on the public health domain benefiting the entire population (health education, epidemiological, hygienic and health-related ecological activities). They are financed out of the state budget.
   2. The entitlements of employees to employment and workplace-related preventive activities. They are financed by the employer.
   3. The entitlements arising out of public health insurance with compulsory membership covering the curative and preventive health problems of individual people. It comprises about 90% of the entire public health insurance system. It is financed out of employer and employee contributions.

already in economic recession and when it reached its maximum expansion; however, we were not willing to recognise it. These entitlements are co-ordinated with personnel and service capacities of the public health service. At the present time the economic difficulties are accompanied by an extremely high level of public consumption. The relatively excessive scope of public health insurance in comparison with economically more developed countries and the exceedingly high level of total public consumption are forcing us, for the first time in many decades, to tackle the problem of limiting public health insurance entitlements. They can be limited only to the extent that the health status of the population is not endangered. Healthcare policy therefore has to be finely tuned to estimate and compare the public and private health-related interests and the proper balance between the two. It also has to have sufficient authority and skill to affirm the priorities of social health interests that have been established with public consensus.

In addition to public health insurance, private health insurance has also existed in the past few years.

CONCEPT AND APPROACH

Two basic motives underlie the concept of public health insurance, namely:

1. **The economic motive.** An organised society has to ensure and maintain the optimal health status of the present and future productive part of the population in order to protect the process of production (the productivity effect). Here the employer and government interests predominate; the former receives increased profits from a healthy workforce, the latter fulfils its obligation for the support of the entire national economy. This is the production aspect of public health insurance.
2. **The social motive.** It is necessary to provide all people with health insurance appropriate to the stage of the economic development and to the cultural and technical standard of contemporary societies. Every individual strives to maximise his quality of life and his own welfare. Here we are dealing with the physical and mental welfare experienced by every healthy person individually (the welfare effect). The state as well as the individual person are interested in it because it is responsible for the social development of the entire society. The end goals of community development are social rather than economic. This is the non-production aspect of public health insurance.

From these entitlements originating in public health insurance all three interested parties – the state, the employers and the employees – have health-related and economic expectations; these, however, are not identical and are unequal in strength. They are also of unequal value from the viewpoint of a hierarchical ordering of interests. The most important is the (common) public health-related interest on the part of the state. This interest is the highest one and has precedence over the individual health-related interests of employers and the personal interests of individual persons (Letica, 1989). The government has to strive to ensure for all its citizens equal access to medical care provided by the state through the public health insurance system (Cesen, 1988). It is not possible to delineate clearly these three sets of health-related interests from each other. However, for the requirements of health policy it is imperative to distinguish between the public and the private one in order to make decisions on the scope, quality, access and cost of healthcare benefits for all people. In this manner the adjustment to the economic and social development of the nation can be maintained.

In order to be able to distinguish between public and private health-related interests we must establish at least basic parameters for their differentiation. Everyone is expecting the greatest possible health-related and economic benefits. The difference between the expectations of the state and those of the individual develops in the perception of benefits (**Table 1**).

Table 1: Public and personal health interests involved in the entitlements in public health insurance.

Parameters of entitlement	Public health expectations	private health expectations
Scope	Minimum acceptable	Maximum possible
Quality	Appropriate[1]	Optimum[2]
Accessibility	All insured persons	"For myself"
Affordability	All insured persons on the basis of available public funds	"My health is priceless"

Notes:
[1] Minimum technically acceptable medical standard (minimum professional standards)
[2] Technical medical standard incorporating state-of-the-art medical knowledge and the most advanced medical technology (maximum professional standards).

The state views the entitlements to public health insurance from the standpoint of social health protection. The principle of equity requires the state to enable all people to have physical access to the benefits of insurance as well as to be able to afford it. In particular, it must protect those groups of citizens who are disadvantaged in competition with others because of physical or psychological defects or for other objective reasons (groups at health-related risks and marginal groups).

The public health insurance system is interested in health risks, diseases and injuries that most endanger and paralyse national health. Foremost among them are those with known aetiology and effective treatment. They lend themselves to effective prevention, are readily treatable and do not permanently impair the ability to work (either in its entirety or in part) of the sick or injured. The expected results should be achieved with the minimum expenditure of public health services (the direct economic benefits of healthcare delivery), and the results of treatment should enable the sick and the injured to return to work as soon as possible (indirect economic benefits of healthcare delivery). All this can be accomplished only if the healthcare providers employ the minimal, marginally acceptable medical doctrine that is affordable to the public financing system (the "appropriate" professional standard prevailing in a given society).

For an individual person the case is different. As a rule he always behaves rationally and selfishly. If the state provides entitlements he will claim them. He is interested in his own health and in his personal health standard. In the management of his own health problems he insists that the providers of healthcare apply the most modern medical techniques (the optimum professional standards). The cost of treatment is not a major concern to him; he regards it as being free. For the same reason he is not concerned about the fact that public health resources are limited *per se*. As the recipient of considerable compensatory payments in lieu of his salary he is often not even interested in a rapid return to work.

Various societies are not completely indifferent to private health interests. The modern state is, after all, responsible for to the welfare of its subjects, and so it is difficult to speak about pure health interests. Perhaps it can be found in the case of a person desiring plastic surgery correction of a medical problem that is subjectively annoying, but it does not preclude normal physical and psychological functioning, nor does it affect the normal everyday interaction with the social environment. There is probably no public health interest vested in this type of surgery and there are no reasons for it to be paid out of public funds.

We determine the priority of insurance against health risks by estimating the relationship between the public and private health-related interest. In this manner we reach a ranking of public health-related interests, with the completely public one first and the completely private one last. In-between there are health risks where both interests mesh in varying proportions.

The exact point in the priority sequence of public health interests that the state will establish as the cut-off and hereby determine the scope of public health insurance is in the domain of policy-making on the part of the political party in power. The narrower this scope of health insurance, the easier the state with its objectively limited resources (particularly financial ones) will be able to guarantee to all people entitlements to public health insurance. A narrow scope of public health insurance excludes some important health risks from public health insurance. Individual persons are forced to obtain voluntary insurance in various private insurance companies in order to have complete medical coverage.

We have to emphasise another point that is poorly understood in everyday life. In principle it is true that the share of public financing in the provision of individual entitlement is commensurate with its priority. This, however, is not an unconditional rule. There exists no complete interdependence between the ranking in the priority sequence of public health insurance of a certain entitlement and the financial requirements for its consummation. Private persons can participate in the financing of entitlements placed at the very top of the priority sequence. For instance, it is advisable that parents participate in the compulsory vaccination programmes of their children. Their contribution need not necessarily be large. The important point is that the idea is reinforced that their children's health is also their concern, not merely the state's.

PRIORITIES OF PUBLIC HEALTH INTEREST

In the continuation of this paper we are going to present a feasible ordering of medical and non-medical entitlements and monetary benefits from public health insurance according to the priority sequence of public health-related interest.

First Priority

Here the public health interest is dominant. We are dealing with the expectations of medical and economic benefits which contribute most to the attainment of common societal goals: a productive economy and a just society (Rus, 1990).

Health-related prevention

- The promotion and maintenance of health (common medical risks): the creation of suitable living and working conditions for a healthy physical and psychological existence (peace, social justice, lodgings, food, education, employment and income, personal hygiene and healthy recreation, healthy natural and social environment, public health conditions, and similar). The efforts spent in attaining good health greatly transcend the responsibilities and activities of the system of public health protection. They encompass only the public health education and epidemiological, hygienic and health-related ecological activities. The majority of the other tasks belongs to everyday activities of individuals and members of other economic and extra-economic areas.
- The prevention of diseases and injuries (concrete medical risks): surveillance and prevention of infectious diseases, non-infectious diseases and habits detrimental to health, injuries obtained at home, at work and traffic-related, and similar. Included are activities pertaining to additional preventive and educational programmes recommended by various professional associations or movements, such as: CINDI – for chronic non-infectious diseases, MONICA – for cardiovascular diseases, Europe Against Cancer, Slovenia 2000 and Cancer, AIDS and Healthy Sexuality, Healthy Cities, Healthy Schools, Europe Without Smoking, and other programmes dealing with specific health risks (injuries, suicides, occupational diseases, alcoholism, drug addiction, traffic accidents, and similar).
- Compulsive immunisation of pre-school children and youths according to annual programmes and immunisation in connection with exposure to certain risks (e.g., tetanus, hepatitis, influenza).
- Periodic examinations and preventive medicine services in particular, medically endangered subgroups of the population (pre-school children, school children and regular students, pre-menopausal women, other groups medically at risk or otherwise marginal).

- Preventive medical examinations in connection with work and occupational environment.

Emergency medical care
- Emergency medical care is associated with emergency medical transport and emergency medications. Every person is entitled to it regardless of whether he is able to pay for it or not (individually or through health insurance).

Treatment of serious and grave diseases and unusually expensive treatment
- Diseases and "major" injuries, which because of their wide prevalence and severity most seriously paralyse national health (societal medical and economic problems), or those in which treatment is so expensive that the individual cannot afford to pay for it directly without risking financial disaster (individual medical and economic problems). Both are also designated as "catastrophic" medical risks. Example: infectious diseases, occupational diseases, "grave" injuries, exceptionally difficult and expensive medical services, and similar.
- Medical care for selected population groups at medical risk (special social concerns due to demographic, medical, economic or social reasons): children, students, pre-menopausal women, military and civilian invalids, people with retarded physical or mental development, those marginally or completely displaced, members of military and security organisations, and similar.
- Out-patient treatment and domiciliary treatment or substitute for inpatient treatment.
- Required ("emergency") medical transport.
- Essential standardised orthopaedic and other medical implements.

Second Priority
Here we are dealing with the combination of public and private health-related interests in varying proportions, and with expectations of medical and economic benefits that affect the welfare of individuals.

"Ordinary" medical care
- Common, for the patient and his contacts less serious diseases (although still possibly serious), and minor injuries; e.g., treatment in general out-patient clinics, out-patient treatment of dental and oral cavity diseases.
- Medical treatment foreseen by the individual for which he can save ahead of time; e.g., elective surgery, dental prosthetic treatment, treatment of alcoholism and drug addiction (except emergency medical care in acute poisoning), eye glasses and other eye implements, orthopaedic and other implements that are not essential for treatment or are not excessively expensive.
- Medical services and care where there exist fewer reasons for public health

insurance. In this case, the personal health-related interest is strong or dominant, the outcome of treatment is modest and does not justify the high costs of treatment and/or equipment, also some elective medical treatment, e.g. plastic surgery unassociated with causative treatment of serious diseases or major injuries, supportive treatment in sanatoria, non-compulsory immunisations.

Third Priority

Dominant here is the personal health-related interest. Included are non-medical activities and monetary payments benefiting the individual. There are no medical services in this priority class; however, it covers entitlements to cash payments as part of the social security coverage in case of illness and injury.

Non-medical activities associated with the consummation of entitlements in the first and second priority class; e.g. admission to and hospitalisation or sanatorium (the so-called "residence" part of a hospital stay), other personal services.

Cash payments connected with medical treatment and inability to work during recuperation.

- Replacement of salary/wages during temporary absence from work because of illness or injury, or due to other legitimate reasons.
- Funeral costs and posthumous payments in case of death of the insured person and members of his immediate family.
- Reimbursement of travel expenses (cost of transportation, daily payments during travel and stay in alternative location).

Application and expectations

The application of the priority sequence of public health-related interests is the method best suited for the solution of pressing developmental problems in the field of health protection. On the basis of correct decisions we can expect to gradually reach that scope of public health insurance that corresponds to the objective limitations of public financing dedicated by the society to health. At the same time we will reinforce every individual's concern for his own health. The following expectations can be maintained after the establishment of priorities in public health interest:

- The prioritisation of public health interest helps health policy makers to shift the emphasis in public health insurance from curative medicine (particularly hospitalisation) to the promotion of health, disease prevention and so-called primary healthcare (organised medical self-protection, general practice medicine, school medicine, occupational medicine, environmental medicine).

- We will be able to develop a public health insurance system (a realistic health standard) appropriate to the level of economic, social and political development of the Slovene society and within the capabilities of public financing.
- The medical programmes within the public health insurance system (particularly within the compulsory health insurance part) will be flexible and adaptable to the GDP fluctuations. We attain flexibility by the direct inclusion of insured persons into the financing of health programmes participation. With participation we reduce financing malfunctions due to unforeseen cash-flow problems in the area of public financing. Participation therefore exerts a certain stabilising role in the quality assurance and accessibility of insured persons to medical and non-medical services. Direct complementary payments are comparatively small. When a considerable degree of participation is required due to financial constraints in the availability of public financing it is preferable to revise the scope of public health related interests. With any decrease of public health insurance and shifting of economic burdens onto individuals, ethical aspects of such state decisions should be taken into consideration.

With a rational setting of limits of public health insurance associatedwith public health interests, conditions can be established for the affirmation and development of a (true) complementary voluntary health insurance which, in conjunction with the already existing one, will provide complete coverage for the population. Voluntary health insurance based on private funds will establish the concern for personal health as a priority in the disposition and consumption of personal income. The motivation (readiness) of individual persons to participate in voluntary health insurance is an additional indicator of the individual economic value of health.

With a gradual distribution of all financial burdens between the public and private sources of financing, the desired relationship of approximately 80 to 20 will be achieved (at the present time this relationship is 93 to 7).

CONCLUSIONS

In their efforts to reduce public spending the responsible government officials in Slovenia are also under pressure to limit (decrease) the spending of public funds for health-related activities. The dilemma is how to accomplish this without endangering the established level of health standards that at the present time is available almost entirely through public financing. As the instrument for this limitation (decrease) of entitlements we propose here the application of the priority sequence in public health-related interests.

The limitation of acquired social entitlements is not only a very difficult undertaking, but it makes every government extremely unpopular as well. A well informed public is beginning to realise that a gradual explicit rationing of public health activities is unavoidable; even the most developed countries with readily available public sources of funds cannot provide all services to all people (Vienonen et al, 1993) . Nevertheless, we must expect passionate debate about the threat to social morale, ethics and social values, about social justice, danger to national health, and similar. Yet, we consider it worthwhile.

REFERENCES

Rupnik L (1992) Public Finance. Part I: Public finance worldwide. Ljubljana, Ekonomska fakulteta, 213.

Letica S (1989) Health policy in time of crisis. Zagreb, Naprijed, 326.

Cesen M (1988) Health and Money. Ljubljana, Agencija demokratinega inozemskega tiska, 125.

Rus V (1990) The Social State and Social Welfare. Ljubljana, Domus. 434.

Vienonen M Beske F and Affeld D (1993) Management of change. 2nd Meeting of the Working Party on Healthcare Reforms in Europe. Essen, WHO.

Mocnik Drnovsek V (1997) Chronic Illness in Youth and Prioritising in Healthcare. *Allergy Suppl* **37**, 141.

Bibliography

Aaronson NK *et al* (1986) Quality of life assessment in bladder cancer clinical trials: conceptual, methodological and practical issues. *Prog Clin Biol Res* 221, 149–170.

Abel-Smith B *et al* (1994) Report on the Greek Health Services. Athens, Greek Ministry of Social Welfare, Pharmetrica.

Agich GJ and Begley CE (eds) (1986) The Price of Health. Lancaster, D Reidel Publishing Company.

Agt HME van *et al* (1994) Test-retest reliability of health state valuations collected with the Euroqol questionnaire. *Soc Sci Med* **39**(11), 1537–1544.

Aiken W (1982) The quality of life. *Applied Philosophy* **1**, 26–36.

Akehurst R *et al* (1991) The Health of the Nation An Economic Perspective on Target Setting. Discussion Paper 92. York, Centre of Health Economics.

Alexander JL and Williams EP (1981) Quality of life: some measurement required. *Arch Phys Med Rehab* **62**, 261–265.

Alheit P (1994) Everyday time and life time. On the problems of healing contradictory experiences of time. *Time Soc* **3**(3) 305–319.

Anderson JP *et al* (1989) Interday reliability of function assessment for a health status measure. The quality of well-being scale. *Med Care* **27**(11), 1076–1083.

Anderson P (1993) Can doctors punish their patients for risky choice of lifestyle? *Daily Express* 18th August, 19.

Anderson RT Aaronson NK and Wilkin D (1993) Critical review of the international assessments of health-related quality of life. *Qual Life Res* **2**(6), 369–395.

Annual Review of Public Health (1994) Section on Health services. **15**, 413–580.

Anstotz C (1992) Continuing the dialogue on measuring the quality of life in philosophy and psychology: some comments on Boddington and Podpadec. *Bioethics* **6**(4), 356–360.

Appleby J (1994) Evaluating the reforms. *Health Serv J* 10 Mar, 32–33.

Appleby J (1994) Waiting lists. *Health Serv J* 10 Nov, 36–37.

Appleby J and Boyle S (1994) Finding the facts. *Health Serv J* 3 Feb, 24–25.

Aristotle (1995) Politics. Book III Chapter 9. Barker E (trans) Oxford, Oxford University Press.

Aristotle (1990) The Nicomachean Ethics. Book V Chapter 3. Ross D (trans) Oxford, Oxford University Press.

Ashmore M Mulkay M and Pinch T (1989) Health and Efficiency. A Sociology of Health Economics. Milton Keynes, Oxford University Press.

Attfield R (1990) The global distribution of health care resources. *J Med Ethics* **16**, 153–156.

Aylward G Larkin D and Cooling R (1993) Audit of cost and clinical outcome of cataract surgery. *Health Trends* **25**(4), 126–129.

Baddia X *et al* (1994) Reliability of the Spanish version of the Nottingham health profile in patients with stable end-stage renal disease. *Soc Sci Med* **38**(1), 153–158.

Baggott R (1994) Reforming the British health care system: a permanent revolution? *Policy Studies* **15**(3), 35–47.

Baldwin S Godfrey C and Propper C (eds) (1990) The Quality of Life: Perspectives and Policies. Routledge, London.

Baltussen R Leidl R and Ament A (1996) The impact of age on cost-effectiveness ratios and its control in decision making. *Health Econ* **5**, 227–239.

Baker R (1994) BNHS age rationing: a riposte to Bates. *Health Care Anal* **2**(1), 39–42.

Baker R (1993) Visibility and the just allocation of health care: a study of age rationing in the British National Health Service. *Health Care Anal* **1**(2), 139–150.

Bakker C and Vanderlinden S (1995) Health-related utility measurement – an introduction. *J Rheumatol* **22**(6), 1197–1199.

Banner M and Mitchell B (eds) (1988) Ian Ramsey Centre Report Number 2.

Barendregt JJ Bonneux L and Van der Maas PJ (1996) DALYs: the age-weights on balance. *Bull World Health Org* **74**(4), 439–443.

Bates D (1993) Rationing by age: a short philosophical comment. *Health Care Anal* **1**(2), 153–154.

Battin M (1992) Dying in 559 beds: efficiency, best buys, and the ethics of standardisation in national health care. *J Med Phil* **17**, 59–77.

Baum F (1995) Research in public health: behind the qualitative-quantitative methodological debate. *Soc Sci Med* **40**(4), 459–468.

Beecham L (1992) Health authorities are reluctant to ration. *BMJ* **305**, 1049.

Bell JM and Mendus S (eds) (1988) Philosophy and Medical Welfare. Oxford, Oxford University Press.

Bennett L and Duke J (1995) Research note: Decision-making processes, ethical dilemmas and models of care in HIV/AIDS health care provision. *Sociology of Health and Illness* **17**(1), 109–119.

Bennett P Weinman J and Spurgeon P (eds) (1990) Current Developments in Health Psychology. London, Harwood Academic Publishers.

Bensing J (1991) Doctor-patient communication and the quality of care. *Soc Sci Med* **32**(11), 1301–1310.

Benzeval M and Judge K (1994) The determinants of hospital utilisation: implications for resource allocation in England. *Health Econ* **3**(2), 105–116.

Berg R L Hallauer D S and Berk S N (1976) Neglected aspects of the quality of life. *Health Serv Res* **11**(4), 391–395.

Bergner M *et al* (1976) The Sickness Impact Profile: conceptual formulation and methodology for the development of a health status measure. *Int J Health Serv* **6**(12), 393–415.

Bergner M *et al* (1981) The Sickness Impact Profile: development and final revision of a health status measure. *Med Care* **19**, 787–805.

Bernard C (1927) Introduction to the Study of Experimental Medicine. trans Greene HC London, Macmillan.

Berwick BM (1994) Eleven worthy aims for clinical leadership of health system reform. *JAMA* **272**(10), 797–802.

Berzon R Hays RD and Shumaker SA (1993) International use, application and performance of health-related quality of life instruments. *Qual Life Res* **2**(6), 367–368.

Best G Knowles D and Mathew D (1994) Breathing life into the NHS reforms. *BMJ* **308**, 842–845.

Beveridge W (Chairman) (1942) Report on Social Insurance and Allied Services. London, HMSO. Cmd 6404.

Bird AW (1994) Enhancing patient well-being: advocacy or negotiation? *J Med Ethics* **20**, 152–156.

Black D (1991) Paying for health. *J Med Ethics* **17**, 117–123.

Black N (1992) Research, audit, and education. *BMJ* **304**, 698–700.

Blackman T (1995) Recent developments in British national health policy: an emerging role for local government? *Policy Politics* **23**(1), 31–48.

Bleichrodt H and Johannesson M (1997) The validity of QALYs: an experimental test of constant proportional trade-off and utility independence. *Med Dec Mak* **17**(1), 21–32.

Bloor K and Maynard A (1994) An outsider's view of the NHS reforms. *BMJ* **309**, 352–353.

Bochner F *et al* (1994) How can hospitals ration drugs? Drug rationing in a teaching hospital: a method to assign priorities. *BMJ* **308**, 901–908.

Boddington P and Podpadec T (1992) Measuring quality of life in theory and in practice: a dialogue between philosophical and psychological approaches. *Bioethics* **6**(3), 201–217.

Bodenheimer T and Grumbach K (1994) Paying for health care. *JAMA* **272**(8), 634–639.

Bombardier C *et al* (1986) Auranofin therapy and quality of life in patients with rheumatoid arthritis. *Am J Med* **81**, 565–578.

Boorse C (1977) Health as a theoretical concept. *Phil Sci* **44**, 542–573.

Boorse C (1976) What a theory of mental health should be. *J Theory Soc Beh* **6**, 61–84.

Boorse C (1975) On the distinction between disease and illness. *Phil Pub Affairs* **5**, 49–68.

Boughton BJ (1984) Compulsory health and safety in a free society *J Med Ethics* **10**, 186–190.

Bowling A (1996) Health care rationing: the public's debate. *BMJ* **312**, 670–674.

Bowling A (1992) Measuring Health. A Review of Quality of Life Measurement Scales. Milton Keynes, Oxford University Press.

Bowling A *et al* (1991) General practitioners views on quality specifications for "outpatient referrals and care contracts" *BMJ* **303**, 292–3.

Bowling A Jacobson B and Southgate L (1993) Explorations in consultation of the public and health professionals on priority setting in an inner London health district. *Soc Sci Med* **37**(7), 851–857.

Boyle IR *et al* (1976) Emotional adjustment of adolescents and young adults with cystic fibrosis. *J Paed* **88**, 318–326.

Braybrooke D (1968) Let needs diminish that preferences may prosper. in N Rescher (ed) Studies in Moral Philosophy. (American Philosophical Quarterly: Monograph no 1) Oxford, Blackwell.

Brazier J and Dixon S (1995) The use of condition specific outcome measures in economic appraisal. *Health Econ* **4**(4), 255–264.

Brazier JE *et al* (1992) Validating the SF–36 health survey questionnaire: new outcome measure for primary care. *BMJ* **305**, 160–164.

Brazier J Jones N and Kind P (1993) Testing the validity of the Euroqol and comparing it with the SF–36 health survey questionnaire. *Qual Life Res* **2**(3), 169–180.

Brearly S (1992) Manpower. *BMJ* 304, 832–834.

Briggs AH Wonderling DE and Mooney CZ (1997) Pulling cost-effectiveness up by its bootstraps: a non-parametric approach to confidence interval estimation. *Health Econ* **6**, 327–340.

Briggs A Sculpher M and Buxton M (1994) Uncertainty in the economic evaluation of health care technologies: the role of sensitivity analysis. *Health Econ* **3**(2), 95–104.

British National Formulary (1993) Number 26 September 1993. London. British Medical Association and Royal Pharmaceutical Society of Great Britain.

Brock D (1993) Quality of life measures in health care and medical ethics. In: The Quality of Life. Nussbaum M and Sen A (eds) Oxford, Clarendon Press.

Brock DW (1991) Decision making competence and risk. *Bioethics* **5**(2), 105–117.

Brock G (1994) Braybrooke on needs. *Ethics* **104**, 811–823.

Brooks R G (1991) Health Status and Quality of Life Measurement. Issues and Developments. The Swedish Institute for Health Economics, Lund, IHE.

Broome J (1994) Meeting the challenges of justice and rationing: fairness versus doing the most good. *Hastings Center Rep* July–Aug, 36–42.

Brorsson B Ifver J and Hays R D (1993) The Swedish health-related quality of life survey (SWED–QUAL). *Qual Life Res* **2**, 33–45.

Brown WM (1985) On defining disease. *J Med Phil* **10**, 311–328.

Bruin A F de *et al* (1992) Sickness Impact Profile: the state of the art of a generic functional status measure. *Soc Sci Med* **35**(8), 1003–1014.

Bubolz MM *et al* (1980) A human ecological approach to quality of life: conceptual framework and results of a preliminary study. *Soc Indicat Res* **7**, 103–136.

Bucquet D Condon S and Ritchie K (1990) The French version of the Nottingham Health Profile. A comparison of items weights with those of the source version. *Soc Sci Med* **30**(7), 829–835.

Bullinger M Anderson R and Revicki D (1993) Psychometric considerations in evaluating health-related quality of life. *Qual Life Res* **2**(6), 441–450.

Bunker JP Barnes BA and Mosteller F (1977) Costs, Risks, and Benefits of Surgery. New York, Oxford University Press.

Burn J (1993) Screening for cystic fibrosis in primary care. *BMJ* **306**, 1558–1559.

Burrows C and Brown K (1993) QALYs for resource allocation: probably not and certainly not now. *Aust J Pub Health* **17**(3), 278–286.

Bush NE *et al* (1995) Quality of life of 125 adults surviving 6–18 years after bone marrow transplantation. *Soc Sci Med* **40**(4), 479–490.

Busschbach JJV Hessing DJ and De Charro FTh (1993) The utility of health at different stages in life: a quantitative approach. *Soc Sci Med*. **37**(2), 153–158.

Buxton MJ and Drummond MF (1990) Quality of life measurement in the development of medicines. *Pharm J* March 3, 260–262.

Buxton MJ *et al* (1985) Costs and Benefits of the Heart Transplant Programme at Harefield and Papworth Hospitals. London, HMSO.

Buxton MJ and Drummond MF (1990) Quality of life measurement in the development of medicines. *Pharm J* Mar 3, 260–262.

Cairns JA (1994) Valuing future benefits. *Health Econ* **3**(4) 221–229.

Callahan D (1990) Rationing medical progress. The way to affordable health care. *New Eng J Med* **322**(25), 1810–1813.

Callahan D (1988) Allocating Health Resources. *Hastings Center Rep* **18**, 14–20.

Calman KC (1994) The *ethics* of allocation of scarce health care resources: a view from the centre. *J Med Ethics* **20**, 71–74.

Calman KC (1994) The profession of medicine. *BMJ* **309**, 1140–1143.

Calman KC (1984) Quality of life in cancer patients – a hypothesis. *J Med Ethics* **10**, 124–127.

Campbell AV (1995) Defining Core Health Services: The New Zealand Experience. *Bioethics* **9**(3/4), 252–258.

Cambell A (facilitator) (1994) Public Participation in Discussing Ethical Issues in Defining Core Services: A Report to the National Advisory Committee on Core Health and Disability Support Services. University of Otago.

Canguilhem G (1978) On the Normal and the Pathological. Dordrecht, D. Reidel.

Caplan AL Englehart HT and McCartney JJ (1981) Concepts of Health and Disease: Interdisciplinary Perspectives. Addison Wesley.

Caplan RD (1979) Social support, person-environment fit and coping. In: Ferman LA and Gordus JP (eds) Mental Health and the Economy. Michigan WE, Upjohn Institute for Employment Research.

Carlson RJ (1981) Alternative Legislative Strategies for Licensure and Health. Quoted in Childress JF Priorities in Biomedical Ethics. Philadelphia, Westminster Press.

Carr-Hill RA (1994) Efficiency and equity implications of the health care reforms. *Soc Sci Med* **39**(9), 1189–1201.

Carr-Hill RA (1994) Equity for the poor. *World Health 47th year* (**5**), 22–23.

Carr-Hill RA (1991) Allocating resources to health care: is the QALY (Quality Adjusted Life Year) a technical solution to a political problem? *Int J Health Serv* **21**(2), 251–272.

Carr-Hill RA (1989) Assumptions of the QALY procedure. *Soc Sci and Med* **29**(3), 469–477.

Carr-Hill RA and Morris J (1991) Current practice in obtaining the "Q" in QALYs: a cautionary note. *BMJ* **303**, 699–701.

Carr-Hill RA and Sheldon T (1992) Rationality and the use of formulae in the allocation of resources to health care. *J Public Health Med* **14**(2), 117–126.

Carter WB (1976) Validation of an internal scaling: The Sickness Impact Profile. *Health Serv Res* **11**(4), 516–528.

Cella DF *et al* (1993) Integrating health-related quality of life into cross-national clinical trials. *Qual Life Res* **2**(6), 433–440.

Central Statistical Office (1995) Annual Abstract of Statistics 1995. London, HMSO.

Chadwick R (1994) Fairness is at issue. *BMJ* **308**, 907.

Chambers LW *et al* (1982) The McMaster Health Index Questionnaire as a measure of quality of life for patients with rheumatoid disease. *J Rheumatol* **9**, 780–784.

Chant ADB (1989) Practising doctors, resource allocation and ethics. *J Applied Phil* **6**(1), 71–75.

Chantler C (1992) Management and information. *BMJ* **304**, 632–635.

Charlton JR Patrick DL and Peach M (1983) Use of multivariate measures of disability in health surveys. *J Epid Comm Health* **37**, 296–305.

Charny MC Lewis PA and Farrow SC (1989) Choosing who shall not be treated in the NHS. *Soc Sci Med* **28**(12), 1331–1338.

Chibnall JT and Tait RC (1990) The quality of life scale: a preliminary study with chronic pain patients. *Psychol Health* **4**, 283–292.

Childress JF (1981) Priorities in Biomedical Ethics. Philadelphia, Westminster Press.

Chisholm D Healey A and Knapp M (1997) QALYs and mental health. *Soc Psych Psychiat Epidemiol* 32(2), 68–75.

Chisholm R (1994) How go the NHS reforms doctor? *BMJ* **309**, 797–798.

Choo V (1993) Measuring quality of life. *Lancet* **342**, 362

Coast J (1993) Developing the QALY concept. Exploring the problems of data acquisition. *PharmacoEcon* **4**(4), 240–246.

Coast J (1992) Reprocessing data to form QALYs. *BMJ* **305**, 87–90.

Cochrane M *et al* (1991) Rationing: at the cutting edge. *BMJ* **303**, 1039–1042.

Cohen C (1982) On the quality of life: some philosophical reflections. *Circulation* **66**(5), 29–33.

Cohen D (1994) Marginal analysis in practice: an alternative to needs assessment for contracting health care. *BMJ* **309**, 781–784.

Cohen D and Henderson J (1988) Health, Prevention and Economics. Oxford, Oxford University Press.

Cohen J (1996) Preferences, needs and QALYs. *J Med Ethics* **22**(5), 267–272.

Collins SD (1951) Sickness surveys. In: Administrative Medicine. Emerson A (ed) New York, Nelson. 511.

Collis DK and Ponseti IV (1969) Long term follow-up of patients with idiopathic scoliosis not treated surgically. *J Bone Joint Surg* **51**-A, 425–445.

Cook D (1993) Patient's Choice. London, Hodder and Stoughton Publishers.

Cook J Richardson J and Street A (1994) A cost utility analysis of treatment options for gallstone disease: methodological issues and results. *Health Econ* 3(3), 157–168.

Coyle D (1993) Increasing the Impact of Economic Evaluations on Health-Care Decision-Making. Discussion Paper 108. York, Centre for Health Economics.

Crail M (1994) Rationing is better than dying. *Health Serv J* 29 Sept, 12–13.

Crawshaw R (1991) Oregon sets priorities in health care. *Bull Med Ethics* June, 32–35.

Cribb A (1985) Quality of life – a response to K C Calman. *J Med Ethics* **11**, 142–145.

Cribb A (1993) The borders of health promotion – a response to Nordenfelt. *Health Care Anal* 1(2), 131–137.

Cribb A and Haycox A (1989) Economic analysis in the evaluation of health promotion. *Comm Med* 11(4), 299–305.

Crisp R (1994) Quality of life and health care, in Medicine and Moral Reasoning (ed) RWM Fulford GR Gillett and JM Soskice Cambridge, Cambridge University Press.

Crisp R (1991) QALYs and the mentally handicapped. *Bull Med Ethics* April, 13–16.

Crisp R (1989) Deciding who will die: QALYs and political theory. *Politics* 9, 31–5.

Critical Public Health (1993) Rationing health care. Careless talk costs lives. 4(1)

Croog SH *et al* (1986) The effects of antihypertensive therapy on the quality of life. *New Eng J Med* 317(26), 1657–1664.

Cubbon J (1991) The principle of QALY maximisation as the basis for allocating health care resources. *J Med Ethics* 17, 181–184.

Culyer AJ (1995) Editorial: Need: the idea won't do – but we still need it. *Soc Sci Med* 40(6), 727–730.

Culyer AJ (1991) Health, Health Expenditures and Equity. Discussion Paper 83. York, Centre for Health Economics.

Culyer AJ (1976) Need and the National Health Service. Martin Robinson, London.

Culyer AJ and Wagstaff A (1992) QALYs versus HYEs A Theoretical Exposition. Discussion Paper No. 99. York, Centre for Health Economics.

Culyer AJ and Wagstaff A (1992) Need, Equity and Equality in Health and Health Care. Discussion Paper 95. York, Centre for Health Economics.

Culyer AJ and Wagstaff A (1991) Need, Equality and Social Justice. Discussion Paper 90. York, Centre for Health Economics.

Culyer AJ Lavers RJ and Williams A (1971) Social indicators: health. Social Trends 2. London, HMSO.

Currer C and Stacey M (eds) (1986) Concepts of Health, Illness and Disease. A Comparative Perspective. Leamington Spa, Berg Publishers Ltd.

Curtis S Petukhova N and Taket A (1995) Health care reforms in Russia: the example of St Petersburg. *Soc Sci Med* 40(6), 755–765.

Daly J McDonald I and Willis E (eds) (1992) Researching Health Care, Designs, Dilemmas, Disciplines. London, Tavistock/Routledge.

Dang Ha Doan B (1994) How many doctors in 20 years time? *World Health 47th year* (5), 6–7.

Daniels N (1994) Meeting the challenges of justice and rationing: four unsolved rationing problems. *Hastings Center Rep* July–Aug, 27–29.

Daniels N (1994) The articulation of values and principles involved in health care reform. *J Med Phil* 19, 425–433.

Daniels N (1993) Rationing fairly: programmatic considerations. *Bioethics* 7(2/3), 224–233.

Daniels N (1991) Is the Oregon rationing plan fair? *JAMA* 265(17), 2232–2235.

Daniels N (1980) Health-care needs and distributive justice. *Phil Public Affairs* 10(1), 147–176.

Davidge M *et al* (1987) The anatomy of large inpatient waiting lists. *Lancet*. April 4th, 794–796.

Davis DP (1993) Cultural blindspots, wastebasket diagnosis and clinical reality. *Bull Eur Soc Phil Med Healthcare* **1**(1).

Davies B and Knapp M (1994) Survey article: Improving equity and efficiency in British community care. *Soc Policy Admin* **28**(3), 263–285.

Davies K (1994) The tensions between process time and clock time in care-work. *Time Society* **3**(3), 277–303.

Dawson J (1994) Health and lifestyle surveys: beyond health status indicators. *Health Ed J* **58**, 300–308.

Dearlove O (1993) Priority setting in practice. *Bull Med Ethics* Oct, 25–27.

Decker D (1995) Market testing – does it bring home the bacon? *Health Serv J* 9 Jan, 26–28.

Delamothe T (1992) Getting rational over rationing, *BMJ* **305**, 1240–1241.

Department of Health (1990) Improving Prescribing – The Implementation of The GP Indicative Prescribing Scheme. London, Department of Health.

Dixon J and Welsh HG (1991) Priority setting: Lessons from Oregon. *Lancet* **337**, 891–894.

Dobson R (1994) Bones of contention. *Health Serv J* 24 Mar, 11.

Dolan P (1997) The nature of individual preferences: a prologue to Johannesson, Jonsson and Karlsson. *Health Econ* **6**, 91–93.

Dolan P and Gudex C (1995) Time preference, duration and health state valuations. *Health Econ* **4**, 289–299.

Dolan P *et al* (1996) The time trade-off method: results from a general population study. *Health Econ* **5**, 141–154.

Doll HA *et al* (1993) Criterion validation of the Nottingham Health Profile: patient views of surgery for benign prostatic hypertrophy. *Soc Sci Med* **37**(1), 115–122.

Donahue JM and McGuire MB (1995) The political economy of responsibility in health and illness. *Soc Sci Med* **40**(1), 47–53.

Donaldson C *et al* (1988) Should QALYs be programme specific? *J Health Econ* **7**(3), 239–257.

Donaldson C and Mooney G (1991) Needs assessment, priority setting, and contracts for health care: an economic view. *BMJ* **303**, 1529–1530.

Donaldson C (1994) Commentary: possible road to efficiency in the health service. *BMJ* **309**, 784–785

Donaldson C (1994) Formulate, don't formularise. *BMJ* **308**, 905–906.

Donaldson C (1992) Agenda for health: an economic view. *BMJ* **304**, 770–771.

Donovan J and Coast J (1994) Public preferences in priority setting – unresolved issues. In Malek M (ed) Setting Priorities in Health Care. Chichester, John Wiley and Sons.

Dougherty CJ (1995) Quality-adjusted life years and the ethical values of health care. *Am J Phys Med and Rehab* **74**(1SS), S29–S33.

Dougherty CJ (1994) Quality-adjusted life years and the ethical values of health care. *Am J Phys Med and Rehab* **73**(1), 61–65.

Dougherty CJ (1991) Setting health care priorities. Oregon's next steps. *Hastings Center Rep* 1–10.

Dougherty LJ (1994) Quality Adjusted Life Years and the ethical values of health care. *Am J Phys Med Rehab* **73**(1), 61–65.

146

Downie R and Calman K (1987) Healthy Respect. Ethics in Health Care. London, Faber.

Doyal L (1995) Needs, rights and equity: moral quality in healthcare rationing. *Qual Health Care.* **4**. 273–283.

Doyal L and I Gough (1984) A theory of human needs. *Crit Soc Policy* **4**, 6–38.

Drummond M (1992) The role and importance of quality of life measurements in economic evaluations. *Br J Med Econ* **4**, 9–16.

Drummond M (1990) Assessing Efficiency in the New National Health Service. Discussion Paper 75. York, Centre for Health Economics.

Drummond MF (1980) Principles of Economic Appraisal in Health Care. Oxford, Oxford University Press.

Drummond M Stoddard G and Torrance G (1992) Methods for the Economic Evaluation of Health Care Programmes. Oxford, Oxford University Press.

Drummond MF Stoddard GL and Torrance GW (1992) Cost utility analysis. In: Methods for the Economic Evaluation of Health Care Programmes. Oxford, Oxford University Press. 112–148.

Drummond M Torrance G and Mason J (1993) Cost-effectiveness league tables: more harm than good? *Soc Sci Med* **37**(1), 33–40.

Dubos R (1959) The Mirage of Health. New York, Harper and Row.

Dunn PM (1994) Medical ethics: an annotated bibliography. *Ann Int Med* **121**, 627–632.

Eddy DM (1994) Rationing resources while improving quality. How to get more from less. *JAMA* **272**(10), 817–824.

Eddy DM (1991) Oregon's plan: should it be approved? *JAMA* **266**(17), 2439–45.

Eddy DM (1991) Oregon's methods: did cost effectiveness fail? *JAMA* **266**(15), 2135–2141.

Eddy DM (1991) The individual *vs* society: resolving the conflict. *JAMA.* **265**(8), 2399–2406.

Edgar A (1997) Discourse Ethics and the Quality Adjusted Life Year. *Journal d'Economie Médicale* **15**(1), 55–64.

Edgar A (1995) Weighting health states and strong evaluation. *Bioethics* **9**(3/4), 240–251.

Editorial (1993) Rationing infertility services. *Lancet* **342**, 251–252.

Edlund M and Tancredi LR (1985) Quality of life an ideological critique. *Persp Biol Med* **28**(4), 591–607.

Edwards RT and Barlow J (1994) Rationing Health Care by Waiting List: an Extra-welfarist Perspective. Discussion Paper 114. York, Centre for Health Economics.

Elkowitz A (1987) Health care: discrimination against the rich? *Bioethics* **1**(3), 272–274.

Elster T (1992) Local Justice: How Institutions Allocate Scarce Goods and Necessary Burdens. Cambridge, Cambridge University Press.

Engelhardt HTjr and Spicker SF (1975) Evaluation and Explanation in the Biomedical Sciences. Dordrecht, Ð, Reidel Publishing Company.

English DC (1994) Bioethics: A Clinical Guide for Medical Students. London, W. W. Norton & Company.

Erdman RAM *et al* (1993) The Dutch version of the Nottingham Health Profile: investigations of psychometric aspects. *Psych Rep* **72**, 1027–1035.

Essink-Bot ML Bonsel GJ and Van Der Maas PJ (1990) Valuation of health states by the general public: feasibility of a standardised measurement procedure. *Soc Sci Med* **31**(11), 1201–1206.

EuroQol Group (1990) EuroQol – a new facility for the measurement of health related quality of life. *Health Policy* **16**, 199–208.

Evans R *et al* (1994) Health care reform. *Health Econ* **3**(6), 359.

Evans RW *et al* (1985) Quality of life of patients with end-stage renal disease. *New Eng J Med* **312**, 553–559.

Evans RG and Stoddart GL (1990) Producing health, consuming health care. *Soc Sci Med* **31**(12), 1347–1363.

Ewles L and Simnett I (1992) Promoting Health: A Practical Guide. London, Scutari Press.

Faden R and Leplége A (1992) Assessing quality of life: moral implications for clinical practice. *Med Care* **30**(5). 166–175.

Fagot-Largeault A (1991) Reflexions sur la notion de quantité de la vie. *Archives de Philosophie du Droit* **36**, 135–153.

Feder G (1994) Clinical guidelines in 1994. *BMJ* **309**, 1457–1458.

Feldman RR (1994) The cost of rationing medical care by insurance coverage and by waiting. *Health Econ* **3**(6), 361–372.

Feldstein M (1994) Health plans financing gap. *Soc Sci Mod Soc* **2**(1), 64–66.

Ferguson JM Dubinsky M and Kirsch PJ (1994) Court-ordered reimbursement for unproven medical technology. Circumventing technology assessment. *JAMA* **369**(16), 2116–2121.

Fisher ES Welch HG and Wennberg JE (1992) Prioritizing Oregon's hospital resources. *JAMA* **267**(14), 1925–1931.

Fitzpatrick R *et al* (1992) Quality of life in health care. I: Applications and issues in assessment. *BMJ* **305**, 1074–1077.

Flanagan JC (1982) Measurement of quality of life: current state of the art. *Arch Phys Med Reh* **63** 56–59.

Fleck LM (1994) Just caring: Oregon, health care rationing, and informed democratic deliberation. *J Med Phil* **19**, 367–388.

Fleck LM (1994) Just caring: health reform and health care rationing. *J Med Phil* **19**, 435–443.

Fleck LM (1990) Justice, HMOs and the invisible rationing of health care resources. *Bioethics* **4**(2), 97–120.

Fletcher A *et al* (1992) Quality of life measures in health care. II: Design, analysis, and interpretation. *BMJ* **305**, 1145–1148.

Fletcher AE Hunt BM and Bulpitt CJ (1987) Evaluation of quality of life in clinical trials of cardiovascular disease. *J Chron Dis* **40**, 557–566.

Flew A (1967) End and Means. In: Edwards P (ed) The Encyclopedia of Philosophy (Vol 2). New York, MacMillan and Free Press.

Forsberg RP (1995) Rationality and allocating scarce medical resources. *J Med Phil* **20**, 20–42.

Frank RG Sullivan MJ and DeLeon PH (1994) Health care reform in the States. *Am Psychol* **49**(10) 855–867.

Frank RG and VandenBos GR (1994) Health care reform. *Am Psychol* **49**(10), 851–854.

Frankel S (1991) Health needs, health care requirements, and the myth of infinite demand. *Lancet* **337**, 1588–1590.

Frankel S (1989) The natural history of waiting lists – some wider explanations for an unnecessary problem. *Health Trends* **21**, 56–58.

Frankenberg R (ed) (1992) Time, Health and Medicine. London, Sage Publications.

Freeman R (1994) Prevention in health policy in the Federal Republic of Germany. *Policy and Politics* **22**(1), 3–16.

Freemantle N and Maynard A (1994) Something rotten in the state of clinical and economic evaluations? *Health Econ* **3**, 63–67.

Fryback DG and Lawrence WF (1997) Dollars may not buy as many QALYs as we think: a problem with defining quality-of-life adjustments. *Med Dec Mak* **17**(3), 276–284.

Fulford KWM Gillett GR and Soskice JM (1994) Medicine and Moral Reasoning. Cambridge, Cambridge University Press.

Funck-Brentano JL (1994) Medical practice and data-processing. *World Health 47th year* (5), 17.

Furnham A (1994) Explaining health and illness: lay perceptions on current and future health, the causes of illness, and the nature of recovery. *Soc Sci Med* **39**(5), 715–725.

Gabbott M and Hogg G (1994) Slim pickings. *Health Serv J* 20 Jan, 31.

Gafni A (1997) Alternatives to the QALY measure for economic evaluations. *Supportive Care Cancer* **5**(2), 105–111.

Gafni (1996) HYE's: do we need them and can they fulfil the promise? *Med Dec Mak* **16**(3), 215–216.

Gafni A and Birch B (1995) Preferences for outcomes in economic evaluation; an economic approach to addressing economic problems. *Soc Sci Med* **40**(6) 767–776.

Garratt AM *et al* (1993) The SF–36 health survey questionnaire: an outcome measure suitable for routine use within the NHS? *BMJ* **306**, 1440–1444.

Gill DG Ingman SR and Campbell J (1991) Health care provision and distributive justice: end stage renal disease and the elderly in Britain and America. *Soc Sci Med* **32**(5), 565–577.

Gill TM and Feinstein AR (1994) A critical appraisal of the quality of quality-of-life measurements. *JAMA* **272**(8), 619–626.

Gillon R (1986) Philosophical Medical Ethics. Chichester, John Wiley and Sons.

Gillon R (1994) Principles of Health Care Ethics. Chichester, John Wiley and Sons.

Gilson BS *et al* (1975) The Sickness Impact Profile: development of an outcome measure of health care. *Am J Pub Health* **65**, 1304–1310.

Glasman D (1994) Mum's the word. *Health Serv J* 10 Mar, 15.

Glennerster H and Matsaganis M (1994) The English and Swedish health care reforms. *Int J Health Serv* **24**(2), 231–251.

Glover J (1977) Causing Death and Saving Lives. London, Penguin.

Goldacre MJ Lee A and Don B (1987) Waiting list statistics. I: relation between admissions from waiting list and length of waiting list. *BMJ* **295**,1105–1108.

Goodman NW (1991) Resource allocation: idealism, realism, pragmatism, openness. *J Med Ethics* **17**, 179–180.

Goold SD (1996) Allocating health care: cost-utility analysis, informed democratic decision making, or the veil of ignorance? *J Health Politics Pol Law* **21**(1), 69–98.

Goosens WK (1980) Values, health and medicine. *Phil Sci* **47**, 100–115.

Gore A (1990) Oregon's bold mistake. *Academic Med* **65**(11), 634–635.

Gormally L (1994) Against voluntary euthanasia. In Principles of Health Care Ethics. Gillon R (ed) London, John Wiley.

Grant KAM (1992) Which model for delivering care? *BMJ* **304**, 566–568.

Gray D *et al* (1990) Audit of coronary angiography and bypass surgery. *Lancet* **335**, 1317–1320.

Greaves D (1979) What is medicine?: towards a philosophical approach. *J Med Ethics* **5**, 29–32.

Greek Ministry of Health, Welfare and Social Insurance (1992) Report of a Working Group. The Health of the Greek Population. Athens.

Griffin J (1986) Well-Being: Its Meaning, Measurement, and Moral Importance. Oxford, Clarendon Press.

Griffin J (1977) Are there incommensurable values? *Phil Public Affairs* **7**(1), 39–59.

Grimes DS (1987) Rationing health care. *Lancet* Mar 14, 615–616.

Groves T (1993) Public disagrees with professionals over NHS rationing. *BMJ* **306**, 673.

Gudex C (1986) QALYs and Their Use by the Health Service. Discussion Paper No 20. York, Centre for Health Economics.

Gudex C *et al* (1990) Prioritising waiting lists. *Health Trends* **22**(3), 103–108.

Gudex C and Kind P (1988) The QALY Toolkit. Discussion Paper No 28. Centre for Health Economics. University of York.

Guyatt GH (1993) The philosophy of health-related quality of life translation. *Qual Life Res* **2**(6), 461–465.

Guyatt GH *et al* (1987) Quality of life in patients with chronic airflow limitation. *Br J Dis Chest* **8**, 45–54.

Guyatt GH and Cook DJ (1994) Health status, quality of life, and the individual. *JAMA* **272**(8) 630–631.

Guyatt GH Feeny DH and Patrick DL (1993) Measuring health-related quality of life. *Ann Int Med* **118**, 622– 629.

Hack TS Degner LF and Dyck DG (1994) Relationship between preferences for decisional control and illness information among women with breast cancer: a quantitative and qualitative analysis. *Soc Sci Med* **39**(2), 279–289.

Hadorn DC (1991) The Oregon priority-setting exercise: quality of life and public policy. *Hastings Center Rep* Su 11–16.

Hadorn DC (1991) Setting health care priorities in Oregon: cost-effectiveness meets the rule of rescue. *JAMA* **265**, 2218–2225.

Hadorn DC (1991) The role of public values in setting health care priorities. *Soc Sci Med* **32**(7), 773–781.

Haes JCJM de and van Knippenberg FCE (1985) The quality of life of cancer patients: a review of the literature. *Soc Sci Med* **20**(8), 809–817.

Hall MA (1994) The problems with rule-based rationing. *J Med Phil* **19**, 315–332.

Hall W (1987) Disease costs and the allocation of health resources. *Bioethics* **1**(3), 211–225.

Ham C (1994) An alternative for the NHS. *BMJ* **308**, 485–486.

Ham C (1994) Managing the market; anarchy rules. *Health Serv J* 1 Sept, 18–20.

Ham C (1994) Where now for the NHS reforms? *BMJ* **309**, 351–352.

Ham C (1993) Priority setting in the NHS: reports from six districts. *BMJ* **307**, 435–438.

Ham C (1993) Rashly rationed? *BMJ* **307**, 73.

Ham C and Maynard A (1994) Managing the NHS market. *BMJ* **308**, 845–847.

Ham C Robinson R and Benzeval M (1990) Health Check. Health Care Reforms in an International Context. London, Kings Fund Institute.

Hancock C (1993) Getting a quart out of a pint pot, Rationing in Action. London, BMJ Publishing Group.

Hansson LF Norheim OF and Ruyter KW (1994) Equality, explicitness, severity, and rigidity: the Oregon plan evaluated from a Scandinavian perspective. *J Med Phil* **19**, 343–366.

Hardy G and West M (1994) Happy talk. *Health Serv J* 7 July, 24–26.

Harris J (1996) Would Aristotle have played Russian roulette? *J Med Ethics* **22**(4), 209–215.

Harris J (1995) Double jeopardy and the veil of ignorance – a reply. *J Med Ethics* **21**(3), 151–157.

Harris J (1994) Does justice require that we be ageist? *Bioethics* **8**(1), 74–83.

Harris J (1991) Unprincipled QALYs: a response to Cubbon. *J Med Ethics* **17**, 185–188.

Harries J (1989) The Value of Life. London, Routledge & Kegan Paul.

Harris J (1988) The survival lottery. In: Singer P (ed) Applied Ethics. Oxford, Oxford University Press.

Harris J (1987) QALYfying the value of life. *J Med Ethics* **13**, 117–123.

Harries U and Hill S (1994) Two sides of the coin. *Health Serv J* 22 Sept, 25.

Harrison S and Hunter DJ (1994) Rationing Health Care. London, The Institute for Public Policy Research.

Harwood A (1981) Ethnicity and Medical Care. Cambridge, Harvard University Press.

Haug MR and Folmar SJ (1986) Longevity, gender and life quality. *J Health Soc Beh* **27**, 332–345.

ten Have H (1990) Health and responsibility as policy tools. *Biolaw* **2**, 1623–1630.

ten Have H and Keasberry H (1992) Equity and solidarity: the context of the Netherlands. *J Med Phil* **17**, 463–477.

ten Have H Kimsa GK and Spicker SF (eds) (1990) The Growth of Medical Knowledge. Holland, Kluwer Academic Publishers.

Hävry H and Hävry M (1990) Euthanasia, ethics and economics. *Bioethics* **4**(2), 154–161.

Hävry M and Hävry H (1990) Health care as a right, fairness and medical resources. *Bioethics* **4**(1), 1–21.

Haydock A (1992) QALYs – a threat to our life? *J Applied Phil* **9**(2), 183–188.

Hayes MV (1992) On the language of risk: language, logic and social science. *Soc Sci Med* **35**(4), 401–407.

Hays RD Anderson R and Revicki D (1993) Psychometric considerations in evaluating health-related quality of life measures. *Qual Life Res* **2**(6), 441–449.

Hayes RD *et al* (1993) The states versus weights dilemma in quality of life measurement. *Qual Life Res* **2**(3), 167–168.

Heginbotham C (1993) Health care priority setting: a survey of doctors, managers, and the general public. Rationing in Action. London, *BMJ* Publishing Group.

Heginbotham C (1992) Rationing. BMJ **304**, 496–499.

Hicks NR (1994) Some observations on attempts to measure appropriateness of care. *BMJ* **309**, 730–733.

Hicks NR and Baker IA (1991) General practitioners' opinions of health services available to their patients. *BMJ* **302**, 991–993.

Higgs R (1993) Human frailty should not be penalised. *BMJ* **306**, 1049–1050.

Hochman HM (1994) Economics and distributive *ethics. Soc Sci Mod Soc* **32**(1), 35–42.

Hollwey G (1994) Island remedies. *Health Serv J* 28 July, 28–29.

Holm M and Husted J (1991) General practitioners' attitudes to prescription of psychotropic drugs. Autonomy versus paternalism, education and understanding of disease. *J Danish Med Assoc* **153**(27), 1929–1933.

Holmes AM (1995) A QALY-based societal health statistic for Canada, 1985. *Soc Sci Med* **41**(10), 1417–1427.

Holmes J (1994) Psychotherapy – a luxury the NHS cannot afford? More expensive not to treat. *BMJ* **309**, 1070–1071.

Honigsbaum F (1991) Who Shall Live? Who Shall Die? Kings College Fund, London.

Hope T Sprigings D and Crisp R (1993) "Not clinically indicated": patients' interests or resource allocation? *BMJ* **306**, 379–381.

Hopkins A (ed) (1992) Measures of the Quality of Life and the Use to Which Such Measures May be Put. London, Royal College of Physicians of London.

Hopkins A (1990) Measuring the Quality of Medical care. London, Royal College of Physicians of London.

Hopkins A and Costain C (1990) Measuring the Outcomes of Medical Care. London, Royal College of Physicians of London.

Howell JBL (1992) Re-examining the fundamental principles of the NHS. *BMJ* **304**, 297–299.

Hunt SJ et al (1981) The Nottingham Health Profile: subjective health status and medical consultations. *Soc Sci Med* **15A**, 221–229.

Hunt, SJ and McEwen J (1990) The development of a subjective health indicator. *Soc Health Illness* **2**(3), 231–246.

Hunt SM (1993) Cross-cultural comparability of quality of life measures. *Drug Info J* **27**, 395–400.

Hunt SM et al (1980) Quantitative approach to perceived health status: a validation study. *J Epidemiol Comm Health* **34**, 281–286.

Hunt SM McEwen J and McKenna SP (1986) Measuring Health Status. London, Croom Helm.

Hunt SM and Wiklund I (1987) Cross-cultural variation in the weighting of health statements: a comparison of English and Swedish valuations. *Health Policy* **8**, 227–235.

Hunter DJ (1992) Accountability and the NHS. *BMJ* **304**, 436–438.

Hyland M (1997) Health and values: the values underlying health measurement and health resource. *Psych Health.* **12**, 389–403.

Iatridis SG (1987) Health care systems in Greece. *Lancet* 4th April, 792–794.

Jecker NS and Pearlman RA (1992) An ethical framework for rationing health care. *J Med Phil* **17**, 79–96.

Jefferson T Mugford M and Demicheli V (1994) QALY league tables. *Health Econ* 3(3), 205–206.

Jenkins CD (1992) Assessment of outcomes of health intervention. *Soc Sci Med* **35**(4), 367–375.

Jenkinson C (1991) Why are we weighting? A critical examination of the use of item weights in a health status measure. *Soc Sci Med* **32**(12), 1413–1416.

Jenkinson C Coulter A and Wright L (1993) Short form 36 (SF 36) health survey questionnaire: normative data for adults of working age. *BMJ* **306**, 1437–1440.

Jennett B (1987) Waiting lists: a surgeon's response. *Lancet* 4th April, 796–794.

Jensen UJ and Mooney G (1990) Changing Values in Medical and Health Care Decision Making. John Wiley and Sons, Chichester.

Johannesson M (1995) QALYs – a comment. *J Pub Econ* **56**(2), 327–328.

Johannesson M (1994) QALYs, HYEs and individual preferences – a graphic illustration. *Soc Sci Med* **39**(12), 1623–1632.

Johannesson M and Gerdtham UG (1996) A note on the estimation of the equity-efficiency trade-off QALYs. *J Health Econ* **15**(3), 359–368.

Johannesson M and Johansson P-O (1996) The discounting of lives saved in future generations – some empirical results. *Health Econ* **5**, 329–332.

Johannesson M Jönsson and B Karlsson G (1996) Outcome measurement in economic evaluation. *Health Econ* **5**, 279–296.

Johannessson M Pliskin JS and Weinstein MC (1994) A note on QALYs, time trade-off, and discounting. *Med Dec Mak* **14**(2), 188–193.

Johnson KE (1994) Striving towards health care for all. *World Health 47th year.* (5), 120–13.

Joint Working Party of the Welsh Council of the Royal College of General Practitioners and the Welsh General Medical Services Committee (1994) Patient care and the general practitioner. *BMJ* **309**, 1144–1147.

Jones J (1993) Heart surgery ban for smokers defended. *Independent* 18th August, 1.

Jones L Leneman L and Maclean U (1987) Consumer Feedback for the NHS: A Literature Review. London, King Edward's Hospital Fund for London.

Jones MA and Morris AE (1992) Blackstone's Statutes on Medical Law. London, Blackstone Press Limited.

Jones MB (1977) Health status indexes: the trade-off between quantity and quality of life. *Socio Econ Plan Sci* **11**, 301–305.

Kagawa-Singer M (1993) Redefining health: living with cancer. *Soc Sci Med* **37**(3) 295–304.

Kalimo E *et al* (1968) In the Utilisation of the Medical Services and its Relationship to Morbidity, Health Resources and Social Factors. Helsinki, Research Institute for Social Security. National Pensions Institute of Finland, Series A3.

Kamm FM (1994) Meeting the problems of justice and rationing: to whom? *Hastings Center Rep* July-August, 29–33.

Kamm FM (1987) The choice between people: common sense morality and doctors. *Bioethics* **1**(3), 255–271.

Kaplan RM (1994) Value judgement in the Oregon Medicaid experiment. *Med Care* **32**(10), 975–988.

Kaplan RM (1994) Using quality-of-life information to set priorities in health policy. *Soc Ind Res* **33**(1–3), 121–163.

Kaplan RM and Bush JW (1982) Health-related quality of life measurement for evaluation research and policy analysis. *Health Psychol* **1**(1), 61–80.

Kaplan RM Bush JW and Berry CC (1976) Health status: types of validity and the Index of Well-being. *Health Serv Res* **11**, 478–505.

Kaplan RM Feeny D and Revicki DA (1993) Methods for assessing relative importance in preference outcome measures. *Qual Life Res* **2**(6), 467–475.

Kappel K and Sandøe P (1994) Saving the young before the old – a reply to John Harries. *Bioethics* **8**(1), 84–92.

Kappel K and Sandøe P (1992) QALYs, age and fairness. *Bioethics* **6**(4), 297–316.

Kaptein A (ed) (1994) *Psychology and Health.* Special issue: Quality of life and HIV: a symposium on quality of life methodology. **9**(1–2).

Katz DA and Welch HG (1993) Discounting in cost-effectiveness analysis of healthcare programmes. *PharmacoEcon* **3**(4), 277–285.

Katz S (1983) Assessing self-maintenance: activities of daily living, mobility and instrumental activities of daily living. *J Am Ger Soc* **31**, 721–727.

Katz S *et al* (1963) Studies of illness in the aged: the index of ADL: a standardised measure of biological and psychosocial function. *JAMA* **185**, 914–919.

Kellett J (1993) Long term care on the NHS: a vanishing prospect. *BMJ* **306**, 846–848.

Kennedy I and Stone J (1990) Making public policy on medical-moral issues. In: Byrne P (ed) *Ethics* and Law in Health Care and Research. Chichester, John Wiley and Sons. 81–103.

Key P Dearden B and Lund B (1994) Perspectives on purchasing. Fearless quest. *Health Serv J* 3 Feb, 28–29.

Kind P (1990) Measuring Valuations for Health States: A Survey of Patients in General Practice. Discussion Paper 76. York, Centre for Health Economics.

Kind P and Carr-Hill R (1987) The Nottingham Health Profile: a useful tool for epidemiologists? *Soc Sci Med* **25**(8), 905–910.

Kind P and Gudex C (1991) The HMQ: Measuring Health Status in the Community. Discussion Paper 93. York, Centre for Health Economics.

Kind P Rosser R and Williams A (1992) Valuation of quality of life: Some psychometric evidence. In: Jones-Lee MW (ed) The Value of Life and Safety. Amsterdam, Elsevier.

Kingwell M (1994) Mad people and ideologues: an issue for dialogic justice theory. *Int Phil Quart* **34**(1), 59–73.

Kitzhaber JA (1993) Prioritising health services in an era of limits: the Oregon experience. *BMJ* **307**, 373–377.

Kitzhaber J (1989) The Oregon health initiative. *Lancet* **2**, 106.

Klein R (1993) Dimensions of rationing: who should do what? *BMJ* **307**, 309–311.

Klein R (1991) On the Oregon trail: rationing health care. *BMJ* **301**, 1–2.

Klein R (1989) The role of Health Economics: Rozencrantz to medicine's Hamlet. *BMJ* **299**, 275–276.

Klein R and Redmayne S (1992) Patterns of Priorities (Research Paper 7). Birmingham, NAHAT.

Kollemorten I *et al* (1981) Ethical aspects of clinical decision-making. *J Med Ethics* **7**, 67–69.

Koopmanschap MA *et al* (1992) Costs of home care for advanced breast and cervical cancer in relation to cost-effectiveness of screening. *Soc Sci Med* **35**(8), 979–985.

Koopmanschap MA and Rutten FFH (1994) The impact of indirect costs on outcomes of health care programmes. *Health Econ* **3**(6), 385–394.

Kotlikoff LJ (1994) Passing the generational buck? *Soc Sci Mod Soc* **32**(1), 70–71.

Kottke FJ (1982) Philosophical consideration of quality of life for the disabled. *Arch Phys Med Rehab* **63**, 60–62

Krupinski J (1980) Health and quality of life. *Soc Sci Med* **14A**, 203–211.

Kuhse H and Singer P (1988) Age and the allocation of medical resources. *J Med Phil* **13**, 101–116.

Kunze ZM Lumley CE and Walker SR (1993) Socioeconomic Evaluation of Medicines. Centre for Medicines Research, Report of a Survey.

Kyriopoulos JE and Levett J (eds) (1992) Financing and Delivering Health Care in the Balkan Region. Athens, Athens School of Public Health.

Kyriopoulos JE and Niakas D (1994) Topics of Health Economics and Policies. Athens, Centre for Health and Social Sciences.

La Puma J and Lawlor EF (1990) Quality-adjusted life-years. Ethical implications for physicians and policymakers. *JAMA* **263**(21), 2917–2921.

Lamb D (1990) A plea for a touch of idealism. *J Med Ethics* **16**, 134–135.

Lamb D (1989) Priorities in Health care: reply to Lewis and Charney. *J Med Ethics* **15**, 33–34.

Lamm RD (1994) Rationing and the Clinton health plan. *J Med Phil* **19**, 445–454.

Langford MJ (1992) Who should get the kidney machine? *J Med Ethics* **18**, 12–17.

Lawton MP (1972) Assessing the competence of older people. In: Kent *et al* (eds) Research, Planning and Action for the Elderly. New York, Behavioural Publications. 122–143.

Lawton MP *et al* (1982) A research service orientated multilevel assessment instrument. *J Gerontol* **37**, 91–99.

Le Grande J (1993) For better or worse? *New States Soc* 19th Nov, 22–23.

Leder D (1988) The hermeneutic role of the consultation-liaison psychiatrist. *J Med Phil* **13**, 367–378.

Ledley FD (1994) Distinguishing genetics and eugenics on the basis of fairness. *J Med Ethics* **20**, 157–164.

Leff J (1981) Psychiatry Around the Globe; a Transcultural Review. New York, Dekker.

Levine S and Croog SH (1984) What constitutes quality of life? A conceptualisation of the dimensions of life quality in healthy populations and patients with cardiovascular disease. in Wenger NK *et al* (eds) Assessment of Quality of Life in Clinical Trials of Cardiovascular Therapies. New York, Le. Jacq. 46–56.

Levinsky NG (1990) Age as a criterion for rationing health care. *New Eng J Med* **322**(25), 1813–1815

Lewis JR (1994) Patient views on quality care in general practice: literature review. *Soc Sci Med* **39**(5), 655–670.

Lewis PA (1990) Resource allocation: whose realism? *J Med Ethics* **16**, 132–133.

Lewis PA and Charney M (1989) Which of two individuals do you treat when only their ages are different and you can't treat both? *J Med Ethics* **15**, 28–32.

Light DW (1992) Equity and efficiency in health care. *Soc Sci Med* **35**(4), 465–469.

Limb M (1994) BMA appeals for further debate on Government's healthcare rationing. *Health Serv J* 23rd June, 6.

Lindström B and Eriksson B (1993) Quality of life among children in the Nordic countries. *Qual Life Res* **2**, 23–32.

Liss P-E (1993) Health Care Need. Meaning and Measurement. Aldershot, Avebury.

Llewellyn-Thomas H *et al* (1984) Describing health states. Methodologic issues in obtaining values for health states. *Med Care* **22**(6), 543–552.

Lomasky LE (1980) Medical progress and national health care. *Phil Public Affairs* **10**(1), 65–88.

Loomes G and McKenzie L (1989) The use of QALYs in health care decision making. *Soc Sci Med* **28**(4), 299–308.

Lowry S (1992) Incontinence services. *BMJ* **304**, 464–465.

Lumley C (1997) New report from CMR International on the nature of automated databases in Health Economics. *CMR International News* **15**(3), 12–13.

Lumley P (ed) (1993) Rationing Medicine. Agenda for Health 1993. London, ABPI.

Lustig BA (1993) The common good in a secular society: the relevance of a Roman Catholic notion to the healthcare allocation debate. *J Med Phil* **18**, 569–587.

Lydick E and Epstein RS (1993) Interpretation of quality of life changes. *Qual Life Res* **2**, 221–226.

Lyttkens CH (1994) QALY league tables. *Health Econ* **3**(2). 57–58.

Macara AW (1994) Reforming the NHS reforms. *BMJ* **308**, 848–849.

Macer DRJ (1994) Perception of risks and benefits of *in vitro* fertilisation, genetic engineering and biotechnology. *Soc Sci Med* **38**(1), 23–33.

MacKeigan LD *et al* (1993) Time preference for health gains versus health losses. *PharmacoEcon* **3**(5), 374–386.

Mägi M and Allander E (1981) Towards a theory of perceived and medically defined need. *Soc Health Illness* **3**(1), 49–71.

Malcolm L (1994) Replacing the hospital. *World Health, 47th year.* (5), 14.

Mariner WK (1994) Outcomes assessment in health care reform: promise and limitations. *Am J Law Med* **20**(1&2), 37–57.

Marks I (1994) Unevaluated or inefficient approaches are hard to justify. *BMJ* **309**, 1071–1072.

Mason JM (1994) Cost-per-QALY league tables – their role in pharmacoeconomic analysis. *PharmacoEcon* **5**(6), 472–481.

Mason J Drummond M and Torrance G (1993) Some guidelines on the use of cost-effectiveness league tables. *BMJ* **306**, 570–572.

Mavreas VG (1989) Psychiatric Morbidity Among Greek Cypriot Immigrants in London: a Community Survey. PhD Thesis. London.

May A (1994) Hearing voices. *Health Serv J.* 21st July, 9.

May A (1990) Equity in the balance. *Health Serv J* 29th Sept, 14.

May A and Millar B (1994) Fasten your seatbelts.... *Health Serv J* 19th May, 14–15.

Maynard A (1994) Can competition enhance efficiency in health care? Lessons from the reform of the UK National Health Service. *Soc Sci Med* **39**(10), 1433–1445.

Maynard A (1991) Developing a health care market. *Econ J* **101**, 1777–1786.

Maynard A (1989) Whither the National Health Service? NHS White Paper Occasional Series. York, University of York Centre for Health Economics.

McBride G (1992) US listens to its citizens on health. *BMJ* **304**, 1131–1132.

McCullough LB (1984) Concept of the quality of life: a philosophical analysis. In: Wenger NK *et al* Assessment of Quality of Life in Clinical Trials of Cardiovascular Therapies. New York, Le Jacq. 25–36.

McDonnell S (1994) In defence of QALYs. *J Applied Phil* **11**(1), 89–97.

McDowell I and Newell C (1987) Measuring Health: a Guide to Rating Scales and Questionnaires. New York, Oxford University Press.

McGuire A Henderson J and Mooney G (1988) The Economics of Health Care. London, Routledge.

McGuire A (1986) Ethics and resource allocation: an economist's view. *Soc Sci Med* **22**(11), 1167–1174.

McHarney-Brown C and Kaufman A (1994) More than just a pill.... *World Health 47th year.* 5, 8–9.

McKie J *et al.* (1996) Another peep behind the veil. *J Med Ethics* **22**(4), 216–221.

McKie J *et al.* (1996) Double jeopardy, the equal value of lives and the veil of ignorance – a rejoinder. *J Med Ethics* **22**(4), 204–208.

McKie *et al* (1996) Allocating healthcare by QALYs: the relevance of age. *Camb Quart Health Ethics* **5**(4), 534–545.

McTurk L (1994) Using QALYs to allocate resources: a critique of some objections. *Monash Bioethics Rev* **13**(1), 22–33.

Mechanic D *et al* (1994) Effects of illness attribution and depression on the quality of life among persons with serious mental illness. *Soc Sci Med* **39**(2), 155–164.

Mechanic D (1992) Professional judgement and the rationing of health care. *Uni Pennsylvania Law Rev* **140**, 1713–1754.

Mechanic D (1986) The concept of illness behaviour: culture, situation and personal predisposition. *Psych Med* **16**, 1–7.

Mechanic D (1980) Rationality of medical care and the preservation of clinical judgement. *J Family Prac* **11**, 431–433.

Meenan RF (1985) New approaches to outcome assessment: the AIMS questionnaire for arthritis. *Adv Int Med* **81**, 167–185.

Mehrez A and Gafni A (1992) Preference based outcome measures for economic evaluation of drug interventions: Quality Adjusted Life Years (QALYs) versus Healthy Years Equivalents (HYEs). *PharmacoEcon* **1**(5), 338–345.

Mehrez A and Gafni A (1990) Evaluating health related quality of life: an indifference curve interpretation for the time trade-off technique. *Soc Sci Med* **31**(11), 1281–1283.

Mehrez A and Gafni A (1989) QALY, utility theory and healthy years equivalents. *Med Dec Mak* **9**(2), 142–149.

Menzel PT (1992) Equality, autonomy, and efficiency: what health care system should we have? *J Med Phil* **17**, 33–57.

Menzel PT (1990) Strong Medicine: The Ethical Rationing of Health Care. (Esp Ch 5) New York and London, Oxford University Press.

Menzel PT (1986) Medical Costs, Moral Choices. New Haven and London, Yale University Press.

Merrison A (Chairman) (1979) Report of the Royal Commission on the National Health Service. London,. HMSO.

Meulen R ter Topinková E and Callahan D (1994) What do we owe the elderly? Allocating scarce medical resources. *Hastings Centre Rep* Special Supplement March–April.

Moatti JP *et al* (1995) QALYs or not QALYs: that is the question? *Rev Epidemiol Sante Pub* **43**(6), 573–583.

Moffit RM (1994) Personal freedom and responsibility: the ethical foundations of a market-based health care reform. *J Med Phil* **19**, 471–481.

Mooney G (1994) What else do we want from our health services? *Soc Sci Med* **39**(2), 151–154.

Mooney G (1992) Economics, Medicine and Health Care. 2nd Edn. London, Harvester Wheatsheaf.

Mooney G (1989) QALYs: an economist's view. *J Med Ethics* **15**, 148–152.

Mooney G (1986) Economics, Medicine and Health Care. London, Harvester Wheatsheaf.

Mooney G (1984) Medical ethics: an excuse for inefficiency? *J Med Ethics* **10**, 183–185.

Mooney G and Lange M (1993) Ante-natal screening: what constitutes benefit? *Soc Sci Med* **37**(7), 873–878.

Mooney G and McGuire A (eds) (1988) Medical Ethics and Economics in Health Care. Oxford, Oxford University Press.

Mordue A and Kirkup B (1989) An appraisal of waiting list problems. *Health Trends* **1**, 110–113.

Morreim EH (1994) Of rescue and responsibility: learning to live with limits. *J Med Phil* **19**, 454–470

Morreim EH (1992) The impossibility and the necessity of quality of life research. *Bioethics* **6**(3), 218–232.

Mossialos E (1997) Citizens' views on health care systems in the 15 member states of the European Union. *Health Econ* **6**, 109–116.

Mulkay M *et al* (1987) Measuring the quality of life: a sociological invention concerning the application of economics to health care. *Sociology* **21**(4), 541–564.

Muris TJ (1994) Overstating savings/underestimating costs. *Soc Sci Mod Soc* **32**(1), 67–68.

Murray CJ (1994) Quantifying the burden of disease: the technical basis for Disability-Adjusted Life Years. *Bull World Health Org* **72**(3), 429–445.

Murray CJ Lopez AD and Jamison DT (1994) The global burden of disease in 1990 – summary results, sensitivity analysis and future directions. *Bull World Health Org* **72**(3), 495–509.

Murray JR (1995) Do you CEA the need for CMAs or have a CUA about extra QALY ratios. *J Dermatol Treat* **6**(1), 3–4.

Myers G and Jones L (1994) Culture shock. *Health Serv J* 17th November, 30.

Najman JM and Levine S (1981) Evaluating the impact of medical care and technologies on the quality of life. *Soc Sci Med* **15**, 107–115.

National Association of Health Authorities and Trusts (1990) Healthcare Economic Review 1990. Birmingham, NAHAT.

National Center for Health Statistics (NCHS), 1963, Origin, program and operation of the U.S. National Health Survey. In: Vital and Health Statistics. Rockville MD, DHEW PHS Pub No 1000 Series 1(1).

Naughton NJ and Wikland I (1993) A critical review of dimension-specific measures of health-related quality of life in cross-cultural research. *Qual Life Res* **2**(6), 397–432.

Nelson JL (1994) Publicity and pricelessness: grassroots decision making. *J Med Phil* **19**, 333–342.

Nelson RM and Drought TD (1992) Justice and the moral acceptability of rationing medical care: the Oregon experiment. *J Med Phil* **17**, 97–117.

Newdick C (1993) Rights to NHS resources after the 1990 Act. *Med Law Rev* **1**, 53–82.

NHS Management Executive (1992) Local Voices: The Views of People in Purchasing for Health. London, NHSME.

Niakas DA (1993) Health and Regional Development; Regional Health Policy in Greece. Athens, Centre for Health and Social Sciences. 120–129.

Nicholl JP Beeby NR and Williams BT (1989) Role of the private sector in elective surgery in England and Wales, 1986. *BMJ* **298**, 243–247.

Nord E (1996) Health status index models for use in resource allocation decisions. *Int J Tech Assess Health Care* **12**(1), 31–44.

Nord E (1994) The QALY– a measure of social value rather than individual utility? *Health Econ* **3**(2), 89–93.

Nord E (1993) The relevance of health state after treatment in prioritising between different patients. *J Med Ethics* **19**, 37–42.

Nord E (1993) Towards quality assurance in QALY calculations. *Int J Tech Ass Health Care* **9**(1), 37–45.

Nord E (1992) An alternative to QALYs: the saved young life equivalent (SAVE). *BMJ* **305**, 875–877.

Nord E (1992) Methods for quality adjustment of life years. *Soc Sci Med* **34**(5), 559–569.

Nord E (1992) The use of EuroQol values in QALY calculations. In: Bjork S (ed) EuroQol Conference Proceedings. Lund, Swedish Institute of Health Economics. IHE Working Paper No 2. 87–97.

Nord E (1991) The validity of a visual analogue scale in determining social utility weights for health states. *Int J Health Plan Man* **6**, 234–242.

Nord E (1989) The significance of contextual factors in valuing health states. *Health Policy* **13**, 189–198.

Nord E *et al* (1995) Who cares about cost – does economic-analysis impose on social values. *Health Policy* **34**(2), 79–94.

Nord E (1995) Maximising health benefits *vs* egalitarianism – an Australian survey of health issues. *Soc Sci Med* **41**(10), 1429–1437.

Nord E *et al* (1993) Social evaluation of health care versus personal evaluation of health states. *Int J Tech Ass Health Care* **9**(4), 463–478.

Nordenfelt L (1994) A constructed dilemma about health promotion: a reply to Alan Cribb. *Health Care Anal* **2**(1), 37–38.

Nordenfelt L (1993) Quality of Life, Health and Happiness. Aldershot, Avebury.

Nordenfelt L (1993) On the nature of ethics of health promotion. An attempt at a systematic analysis. *Health Care Anal* **1**(2), 121–130.

Nordenfelt L (1987) On the Nature of Health. An Action-Theoretic Approach. Holland, D. Reidel Publishing Company.

Normand C (1992) Funding health care in the United Kingdom. *BMJ* **304**, 768–770.

Nussbaum M and Sen A (eds) (1993) The Quality of Life. Oxford, Clarendon Press.

O'Brien J *et al* (1991) Urinary incontinence: prevalence, need for treatment, and effectiveness of intervention by nurse. *BMJ* **303**, 1308–1312.

O'Connell LJ (1994) Ethicists and health care reform: an indecent proposal? *J Med Phil* **19**, 419–424.

O'Donnel M (1986) One man's burden. *BMJ* **293**, 59.

O'Neill S (1993) International justice and health care. *Bull Med Ethics* December, 17–22.

Oakley J (1994) Sketch of a virtue ethics approach to health care resource allocation. *Monash Bioethics Rev* **13**(4), 27–33.

OECD (1997) OECD Health Data 1997: A Software for the Comparative Analysis of 29 Health Systems. Paris, OECD.

OECD (1993) OECD Health Systems: Facts and Trends 1960–1991. (Volume 1) Health Policy Studies No 3. Paris, OECD.

Office of Health Economics (1995) Compendium of Health Statistics. London, Office of Health Statistics.

Office of Population Censuses and Surveys (OPCS) (1995) General Household Survey 1993. Series GHS No 24. London, HMSO.

Olsen JA (1994) Persons *vs* years: two ways of eliciting implicit weights. *Health Econ* **3**(1), 39–46.

Olweny C (1994) Bioethics in developing countries: ethics of scarcity and sacrifice. *J Med Ethics* **20**, 169–174.

Orley J and Kuyken W (eds) (1994) Quality of Life Assessment: International Perspectives. Berlin Heidelberg, Springer-Verlag.

Os J van and Neeleman J (1994) Caring for mentally ill people. *BMJ* **309**, 1218–1221.

Packwood B (1990) Oregon's bold idea. *Academic Med* **65**(11), 632–633.

Parfit D (1975) Personal Identity in Personal Identity. Perry J (ed) Berkeley and Los Angeles, University of California Press.

Parkerson GR Broadhead WE and Tse CJ (1990) The Duke Health Profile. A 17–item measure of health and dysfunction. *Med Care* **28**(11), 1056–1072.

Parsonage M and Neuburger H (1992) Discounting and health benefits. *Health Benefits* **1**, 71–76.

Parston G (1994) Power with responsibility. *Health Serv J* 27 October, 25.

Patrick DL (1992) Health-related quality of life in pharmaceutical evaluation – forging progress and avoiding pitfalls. *PharmacoEcon* **1**, 76–78.

Patrick DL *et al* (1985) A cross-cultural comparison of health status values. *Am J Pub Health* **75**(12), 1402–1407.

Patrick DL Bush JW and Chen MM (1973) Methods for measuring levels of well-being for a health status index. *Health Serv Res* **8**, 229–244.

Patrick DL Bush JW and Chen MM (1973) Toward an operational definition of health. *J Health Soc Beh* **14**, 6–23.

Patrick DL and Deyo RA (1989) Generic and disease-specific measures in assessing health status and quality of life. *Med Care* **27**, S217–S232.

Paul EF Miller FDJr and Paul J (1985) Ethics and Economics. Oxford, Basil Blackwell.

Pearson V and Parkinson M (1994) Breast screening, health promotion and empowerment: the districts' dilemma. *Health Ed J* **53**, 282–290.

Pereira J (1993) What does equality in health mean? *J Soc Policy* **22**(1), 19–48.

Perret RW (1992) Valuing lives. *Bioethics* **6**(3), 185–200.

Petrie JC (1994) First consider the overall process of care. *BMJ* **308**, 906.

Petrou S Malek M and Davey PG (1993) The reliability of cost-utility estimates in cost-per-QALY league tables. *PharmacoEcon* **3**(5), 344–353.

Phin N (1990) Can Economics be applied to Prenatal Screening? Discussion Paper 74. York, Centre for Health Economics.

Platt S *et al* (eds) (1993) Locating Health. Avebury, Aldershot.

Pliskin JS *et al* (1980) Utility functions for life years and health status. *Operations Research* **28**, 206–224.

Pochin Sir E (1982) Risk and medical ethics. *J Med Ethics* **8**, 185–188.

Pollock AM Brannigan M Liss P-E (1995) Rationing health care: from needs to markets? *Health Care Anal* **3**(4), 299–314.

Porren P and Maynard A (1993) Searching for the Holy Grail in the Antipodes. The Market Reform of the New Zealand Health Care System. Discussion Paper 103. York, Centre for Health Economics.

Prades J-LP (1997) Is the person trade-off a valid method for allocating health care resources? *Health Econ* **6**, 71–81.

Rakowski E (1994) Meeting the problems of justice and rationing: the aggregation problem. *Hastings Center Rep* July–August, 33–36.

Ramsey M (1992) Human Needs and the Market. Aldershot, Avebury.

Ranade W (1994) A Future for the NHS? Health Care in the 1990s. London, Longman.

Rawles J (1989) Castigating QALYs. *J Med Ethics* **15**, 143–147.

Redmayne S and Klein R (1993) Rationing in practice: the case of *in vitro* fertilisation. *BMJ* **306**, 1521–1523.

Redmayne S Klein R and Day P (1993) Sharing Out Resources. Birmingham, NAHAT.

Reinhardt UE (1989) Economists in health care: saviours, or elephants in a porcelain shop? *Am Econ Rev* **79**(2), 337–342.

Reischauer RD (1994) Costs of health care reform. *Soc Sci Mod Soc* **32**(1), 66–67.

Relman AS (1990) Is rationing inevitable? *New Eng J Med* **322**(25), 1809–1810.

Rennie D (1994) Let us focus your worries! Health care policy: a clinical approach. *JAMA* **272**(8), 631–632.

Revicki DA and Kaplan RM (1993) Relationship between psychometric and utility-based approaches to the measurement of health-related quality of life. *Qual Life Res* **2**(6) 477–487.

Rich G and Purdy S (1994) On your marks. *Health Serv J* 17th Nov, 27.

Richardson AJ and Charny MC (1992) Public survey of resource allocation preferences (letter). *Lancet* **339**, 185.

Richardson A Charny M and Hanmer-Lloyd S (1992) Public opinion and purchasing. *BMJ* **304**, 680–682.

Richardson J (1987) The accountant as triage master: an economist's perspective on voluntary euthanasia and the value of life debate. *Bioethics* 1(3), 226–240.

Richardson J and Nord E (1997) The importance of perspective in the measurement of quality adjusted life years. *Med Dec Mak* **17**(1), 33–41.

Rittenhouse BE (1997) Healthy years equivalents versus time trade-off. *Int J Tech Assess Health Care* **13**(1), 35–48.

Roberts C *et al* (1995) Rationing is a desperate measure. *Health Serv J* 12 Jan, 15.

Robinson R (1994) Small change. *Health Serv J* 24 Feb, 31.

Robinson R (1993) Cost-benefit analysis. *BMJ* **307**, 924–926.

Robinson R (1993) Cost-effectiveness analysis. *BMJ* **307**, 793–795.

Robinson R (1993) Cost-utility analysis. *BMJ* **307**, 859–862.

Robinson R (1993) Costs and cost-minimisation analysis. *BMJ* **307**, 726–728.

Robinson R (1993) The policy context. *BMJ* **307**, 994–996.

Robinson R (1993) What does it mean? *BMJ* **307**, 670–673.

Robinson R and Le Grand J (eds) (1994) Evaluating the NHS Reforms. London, Kings Fund.

Rodgers J (1994) Power to the people. *Health Serv J* 24 Mar, 28–29.

Rosenthal MM (1994) Whatever happened to the reform of American health policy? *BMJ* **309**, 1383–1384.

Rosser R (1993) The history of health related quality of life in 10 1/2 paragraphs. *J Royal Soc Med* **86**, 315–318.

Rosser RM (1990) From health indicators to quality adjusted life years: technical and ethical issues. In: Hopkins A and Costain D (eds) Measuring the Outcomes of Medical Care. London, Royal College of Physicians of London.

Rosser R and Kind P (1978) A scale of valuations of states of illness: Is there a social consensus? *Int J Epidemiol* **7**, 347–358.

Rosser RM and Watts VC (1972) The measurement of hospital output. *Int J Epidemiol* **1**, 361–368.

Ruane S and Robins L (1994) The politics and administration of the NHS. *Talking Politics* 6(3), 130–136.

Rutten F and Drummond M (1994) Making Decisions about Health Technologies: A Cost-Effectiveness Perspective. York, Centre for Health Economics.

Rutten-Van Mölken MPMH *et al* (1992) Economic appraisal of asthma and COPD care: a literature review 1980–1991. *Soc Sci Med* 35(2), 161–175.

Ryan M (1994) Health in a cold climate. *Health Serv J* 1st Dec, 28–29.

Saari-Kemppainen A *et al* (1990) Ultrasound screening and perinatal mortality: controlled trial of systematic one-stage screening in pregnancy. *Lancet* **336**, 387–391.

Sackett DL and Torrance GW (1978) The utility of different health states as perceived by the general public. *J Chron Dis* **31**, 697–704.

Salek MS (1993), Health-related quality of life measurement. A new challenge for pharmacy practitioners. *J Pharm Pharmacol* **45**(Suppl 1), 387–392.

Salek MS (1990) Development, Validation and Clinical Evaluation of a Health- Related Quality of Life Instrument. Thesis presented to the University of Wales, Welsh School of Pharmacy.

Salek MS *et al* (1993) Cyclosporin greatly improves the quality of life of adults with severe atopic dermatitis – randomised double-blind, placebo controlled trial. *Brit J Dermatol* **129**, 422–430.

Salek MS and Luscombe DK (1992) Health-related quality of life assessment: a review. *J Drug Dev* **5**, 137–153.

Salek MS and VandenBurg MJ (1988) Measuring the quality of life in angina pectoris. *J Drug Ther Res* **13**(5), 186–191.

Salter B (1995) The private sector and the NHS: redefining the welfare state. *Policy Politics* **23**(1) 17–30.

Saltman RB (1994) Patient choice and patient empowerment in Northern European health systems: a conceptual framework. *Int J Health Serv* **24**(2), 201–229.

Sarna L (1993) Women with lung cancer: impact on quality of life. *Qual Life Res* **2**, 13–22.

Savage W (1993) Will the NHS survive the operation? *New States Soc* 19th Nov, 20–21.

Scally G (1994) Perspectives on purchasing. Public ally no 1? *Health Serv J* 6th Jan, 23–24.

Scanlon TM (1982) Contractualism and utilitarianism. In: Utilitarianism and Beyond. Sen A and Williams B (eds) Cambridge, Cambridge University Press.

Schiff GD *et al* (1994) A better-quality alternative. Single payer national health system reform. *JAMA* **272**(10), 803–808.

Schramm CJ (1992) Oregon: a better method to reallocate resources. *JAMA* **267**(14), 1967.

Schipper H (1983) Why measure quality of life? *Can Med Assoc J* **128**, 1367–1370.

Schipper H and Levitt M (1985) Measuring quality of life: risks and benefits. *Can Treat Rep* **69**, 1115–1125.

Schwuebel V (1994) The DALY: an indicator for measuring disease burden. *Rev Epidemiol Sante Pub* **42**(2), 183–184.

Scott S *et al* (eds) (1992) Private Risks and Public Dangers. Aldershot, Avebury.

Scrambler G (ed) (1987) Sociological Theory and Medical Sociology. London, Tavistock Publications.

Seedhouse D (1992) Does the National Health Service have a purpose? In: Grubb A (ed) Challenges in Medical Care. Chichester, John Wiley and Sons. 141–154.

Seedhouse D (1986) Health: The Foundation for Achievement. Chichester, John Wiley & Sons.

Selai CE and Rosser RM (1993) Good quality quality? Some methodological issues. *J Royal Soc Med* **86**, 440–443.

Selby P (1993) Measurement of quality of life in cancer patients. *J Pharm Pharmacol* **45**(Suppl 1), 384–386.

Sen A (1987) On Ethics and Economics. Oxford, Basil Blackwell.

Shaw A (1988) QL revisited. *Hastings Center Rep* **18**, 10–12.

Sheldon T (1994) A continental shift. *Health Serv J* 6th Jan, 11.

163

Sheldon TA (1992) Discounting in health care decision-making: time for a change? *J Public Health Med* **14**(3), 250–256.

Sheppard B (1994) Homeward bound. *Health Serv J* 20th Oct, 28–29.

Shiu M (1993) Refusing to treat smokers is unethical and a dangerous precedent. *BMJ* **306**, 1048–1049.

Siegrist HE (1977) The special position of the sick. In: Landy D (ed) Culture, Disease and Healing: Studies in Medical Anthropology. New York, MacMillan. 388–394.

Siegrist J (1987) Impaired quality of life as a risk factor in cardiovascular disease. *J Chron Dis* **40**, 571–578.

Siegrist J and Junge A (1989) Conceptual and methodological problems in research on the quality of life in clinical medicine. *Soc Sci Med* **29**(3), 463–468.

Singer P *et al* (1995) Double jeopardy and the use of QALYs in health-care allocation. *J Med Ethics* **21**(3), 144–150.

Singer P (1987) A report from Australia: which babies are too expensive to treat? *Bioethics* **1**(3), 275–283.

Sintonen H (1981) An approach to measuring and valuing health states. *Soc Sci Med* **15**, 55–65.

Sipes-Metzler PR (1994) Oregon health plan: ration or reason. *J Med Phil* **19**, 305–314.

Slevin ML (1992), Quality of life: philosophical question or clinical reality. *BMJ* **305**, 466–469.

Smart B (1994) Fault and the allocation of spare organs. *J Med Ethics* **20**, 26–30.

Smith A (1992) Setting a strategy for health. *BMJ* **304**, 376–378.

Smith A (1987) Qualms about QALYs. *Lancet*, 1134–1136.

Smith R (1991) Rationing: the search for sunlight. *BMJ* **303**, 1561–1562.

Sobel D (1994) Full information accounts of well-being. *Ethics* **104**, 784–810.

Sommerville MA (1989) Justice across the generations. *Soc Sci Med* **29**(3), 385–394.

Spiegelhalter DJ *et al* (1992) Quality of life measures in health care. III: resource allocation. *BMJ* **305**, 1205–1209.

Spilker B *et al* (1990) Quality of life bibliography and indexes. *Med Care* **28**(12), supplement.

Spilker B (ed) (1990) Quality of Life Assessments in Clinical Trials. New York, Raven Press.

Spitzer WO (1987) State of science 1986: quality of life and functional status as target variables for research. *J Chron Dis* **40**, 465–471.

Spitzer WO *et al* (1981) Measuring the quality of life of cancer patients: a concise QL– index for use by physicians. *J Chron Dis* **34**, 585–597.

Starr P (1976) The politics of therapeutic nihilism. *Hastings Center Rep* **6**, 24–30.

Starfield B *et al* (1994) Costs vs quality in different types of primary care settings. *JAMA* **272**(24), 1903–1908.

Stason WB (1991) Oregon's bold Medicaid initiative. *JAMA* **265**(17), 2237–2238.

Steuerle CE (1994) Financing and administering health care. *Soc Sci Mod Soc* **32**(1), 69–70.

Stevens L (1995) What the patients said. *Health Serv J* 19th Jan, 29.

Stevenson R and Hegarty M (1994) In the picture. *Health Serv J* 24th Nov, 22–24.

Stewart A (1994) Compound interests. *Health Serv J* 1st Dec, 30–31.

Stewart AL and Ware JEJr (eds) (1992) Measuring Functioning and Well-Being. The Medical Outcomes Approach. Durham and London, Duke University Press.

Strosberg MA *et al* (1992) Rationing America's Medical Care: The Oregon Plan and Beyond. Washington, DC, The Brookings Institute.

Strosberg MA Fein IA and Carroll JD (1989) Rationing of Medical Care for the Critically Ill. Washington, The Brookings Institution.

Sturm R and Wells KB (1995) How can care for depression become more cost-effective? *JAMA* **273**(1), 51–58.

Sutherland HJ and Till JE (1993) Quality of life assessments and levels of decision making: differentiating objectives. *Qual Life Res* **2**(4), 297–303.

Szasz T (1994) Psychiatric diagnosis, psychiatric power and psychiatric abuse. *J Med Ethics* **20**, 135–138.

Szczepura A (1994) Finding a way through the cost benefit maze. *BMJ* **309**, 1314–1315.

Taylor C (1993) Engaged agency and background in Heidegger. In: The Cambridge Companion to Heidegger. Guignon CB (ed) Cambridge, Cambridge University Press.

Teeling-Smith G (1985) The Measurement of Health. London, Office of Health Economics.

Tengs TO (1996) An evaluation of Oregon's Medicaid rationing algorithms. *Health Econ* **5**, 171–181.

The Association of the British Pharmaceutical Industry (1992–3) The Cost of Health, the Price of Medicines. Annual Review. London, ABPI.

The *Hastings Center Repo*rt (1994) Symposium. Caring for an ageing world: allocating scarce medical resources. **24**(5), 3–41.

The Medical Outcomes Trust (1993) How to Score the SF–36 Health Survey. Boston, The Medical Outcomes Trust.

The National Advisory Committee on Core Health and Disability Support Services (1993) Ethical Issues in Defining Core Services. New Zealand, National Advisory Committee on Core Health and Disability Support Services.

Thorsen H McKenna SP and Gottschalck L (1993) The Danish version of the Nottingham Health Profile: its adaptation and reliability. *J Primary Health Care* **11**, 124–129.

Till JE Sutherland HJ and Meslin EM (1992) Is there a role for preference assessments in research on quality of life in oncology? *Qual Life Res* **1**, 31–40.

Times Law Report (1995) Court judges lawfulness of decision. *Times* 15th March, 23.

Torrance GW (1987) Utility approach to measuring health-related quality of life. *J Chron Dis* **40**, 593–600.

Torrance GW (1986) Measurement of health state utilities for economic appraisal. *J Health Econ* **5**, 1–30.

Torrance GW Boyle MH and Horwood SP (1982) Application of multiattribute utility theory to measure social preferences for health states. *Op Res* **30**(6), 1043–1069.

Tunbridge M (ed) (1993) Rationing of Health Care in Medicine. London, Royal College of Physicians of London.

Turner BS (1987) Medical Power and Social Knowledge. London, Sage.

Uhde A (1983) The need for health indicators. In: Culyer AJ Health Indicators: An International Study for the European Science Foundation. Martin Robinson, Oxford.

Underwood MJ and Bailey JS (1993) Coronary bypass surgery should not be offered to smokers. *BMJ* **306**, 1047–1048.

Uniacke S (1987) *In vitro* fertilisation and the right to reproduce. *Bioethics* **1**(3), 241–254.

Vagerö D (1994) Equity and efficiency in health reform. A European view. *Soc Sci Med* **39**(9), 1203–1210.

Van der Wilt GJ (1994) Health care and the principle of fair equality of opportunity. *Bioethics* **8**(4), 329–349.

Various (1993) Rationing in Action. London, BMJ Publishing Group.

Ville I *et al* (1994) Self-representations and physical impairment: a social constructivist approach. *Soc Health Illness* **16**(3), 301–321.

Vuori H (1994) The many faces of quality. *World Health, 47th year.* (5), 10–11.

Wagner EH (1994) The cost-quality relationship. Do we always get what we pay for? *JAMA* **272**(24), 1951–1952.

Wagstaff A (1991) QALYs and the equity – efficiency trade-off. *J Health Econ* **10**(1), 21–41.

Wainwright D (1994) On the waterfront. *Health Serv J* 7th July, 28–29.

Wakker P (1996) A criticism of Healthy-Years Equivalents. *Med Dec Mak* **16**(3), 207–214.

Walker SR and Rosser RM (eds) (1993) Quality of Life: Assessment and Application. 2nd Edition. London, Kluwer Academic Publishers.

Ward S (1994) Too many beds on the block. *Health Serv J* 19th May, 21.

Ware JE (1993) Measuring patient's views: the optimum outcome measure. *BMJ* **306**, 1429–1430.

Ware JE *et al* (1981) Choosing measures of health status for individuals in general populations. *Am J Public Health* **72**, 620–625.

Ware JE Davies-Avery A and Donald CA (1978) Conceptualisation and Measurement of Health for Adults in the Health Insurance Study: General Health Perceptions. Santa Monica CA, The Rand Corporation. **5**.

Ware JE Johnston SA and Davies-Avey A (1979) Conceptualisation and Measurement of Health for Adults in the Health Insurance Study: Mental Health. Santa Monica CA, The Rand Corporation. **3**.

Ware JE and Sherbourne CD (1992) The MOS 36–item short-form health survey (SF–36): 1. Conceptual framework and item selection, *Med Care* **30**, 473–483.

Watkins SJ (1994) Public health 2020. *BMJ* **309**, 1147–1149.

Wedderburn Tate C (1995) What do patients really think? *Health Serv J* 12th Jan, 18–20.

Weinstein MC (1986) Risky choices in medical decision making: a survey. *Geneva Papers on Risk and Insurance* **11**(4), 197–216.

Weinstein MC (1988) A QALY is a QALY is a QALY – or is it? *J Health Econ* 289–290.

Wells N (1992a) Economic evaluation of drugs – a UK pharmaceutical industry perspective. *PharmacoEcon* **1**(1), 14–19.

Wells N (1992b) Health Economics and the UK pharmaceutical industry. *Br J Med Econ* **3**, 17–24.

Welsh Office (1991) Health: A Charter for Patients in Wales. Cardiff, Welsh Office.

Welsh JA Buchsbaum DG and Kaplan CB (1993) Quality of life of alcoholics and non-alcoholics: does excessive drinking make a difference in the urban setting. *Qual Life Res* **2**, 335–340.

Wenger NK *et al* (1984) Assessment of quality of life in clinical trials of cardiovascular therapies. *Am J Cardiol* **54**, 908–913.

Whitaker P (1989) Resource allocation: a plea for a touch of realism. *J Med Ethics* **15**, 129–131.

WHOQOL Group (1993) Study protocol for the World Health Organisation project to develop a Quality of Life assessment instrument (WHOQOL). *Qual Life Res* **2**(2), 153–159.

Wicclair M (1991) A response to Brock and Skene. *Bioethics* **5**(2), 118–122.

Wicclair M (1991) Patient decision-making capacity and risk. *Bioethics* **5**(2), 91–103.

Wiggins D (1991) Needs, Values, Truth. Second edition. Oxford, Blackwell.

Wilensky GR (1994) Inside the black box. *Soc Sci Mod Soc* **32**(1), 68–69.

Wilkin D Hallam L and Doggett MA (1992) Measures of need and Outcome for Primary Health Care. Oxford, Oxford University Press.

Wilkund I Tibbin G and Dimenäs E (eds) (1990) Quality of life and hypertension. Where do we stand? New methods, new possibilities. Definition and measurement of quality of life from a medical perspective. *Scand J Primary Health Care.* **Suppl 1**.

Williams A (1997) Intergenerational equity: an exploration of the 'fair innings' argument. *Health Econ* **6**, 117–132.

Williams A (1996) QALYs and ethics – a health economist's perspective. *Soc Sci Med* **43**(12), 1795–1804.

Williams A (1994) Economics, QALYs and Medical Ethics. A Health Economist's Perspective. Discussion Paper 121. York, Centre for Health Economics.

Williams A (1993) Natural Selection, Health Economics and Human Welfare. Discussion Paper 111. York, Centre for Health Economics.

Williams A (1992) Cost-effectiveness analysis: is it ethical? *J Med Ethics* **18**, 7–11.

Williams A (1990) Health Economics, Priority Setting and Medical Ethics: Implications for Multiple Sclerosis. Discussion Paper 71. York, Centre for Health Economics.

Williams A (1989) Creating a Health Care Market: Ideology, Efficiency, Ethics and Clinical Freedom. NHS White Paper. Occasional Paper 5. York, Centre for Health Economics.

Williams A (1987) Screening for risk of CHD: is it a wise use of resources. In: Oliver M Ashley-Miller M and Wood D (eds) Strategy for Screening for Risks of Coronary Heart Disease. London, John Wiley.

Williams A (1985) Economics of coronary bypass grafting. *BMJ*, 291.

Williams A (1985) The value of QALYs. *Health Soc Serv J* Centre 8 Suppl 18th July.

Williams A (1985) Keep Politics Out of Health! Discussion Paper 8. York, Centre for Health Economics.

Williams A *et al* (1995) Health Economics and health care priorities. *Health Care Anal* **3**(3), 221–234.

Williams B (1972) Morality: An Introduction to Ethics. Cambridge, Cambridge University Press.

Williams R (1983) Concepts of health: an analysis of lay logic. *Sociol* **17**(2), 185–205.

Wilson IB and Cleary PD (1995) Linking clinical variables with health-related quality of life. *JAMA* **273**(1), 59–65.

Wimo A *et al* (1994) Cost effectiveness analysis of day care for patients with dementia disorders. *Health Econ* **3**(6), 395–404.

167

Wing AJ (1993) Ageism in British renal units: a view from the inside. *Health Care Anal* **1**(2), 151–152.

Winslow GR (1982) Triage and Justice. Berkeley and Los Angeles, University of California Press.

World Health Organisation (1947) The constitution of the World Health Organisation. *Chorn* **1**(29).

World Health Organisation (1957) Measurement of Level of Health: Report of a Study Group. WHO Technical Report Series, 137.

World Health Organisation Basic Documents (1976) 26th ed Geneva. WHO, 1.

World Health Organisation (1984) Uses of Epidemiology in Ageing: Report of a Scientific Group 1983. Geneva, WHO Technical Report Series. 706.

Wu AW and Rubin HR (1992) Measuring health status and quality of life in HIV and AIDS. *Psychol Health* **6**, 251–264.

Young R (1975) Some criteria for making decisions concerning the distribution of scarce medical resources. *Theory* Dec 6, 439–455.

Zaner RM (1993) Voices and time: the venture of clinical ethics. *J Med Phil* **18**(1), 9–31.

Ziebland S Fitzpatrick R and Jenkinson C (1993) Tacit models of disability underlying health status instruments. *Soc Sci Med* **37**(1), 69–75.